RUNNING WITH PHEIDIPPIDES

Sports and Entertainment

Steven A. Riess, *Series Editor*

Weary from his bid to catch defending champion Johnny Kelley, Kyriakides still managed to glance at this watch as he crossed the finish line
the victor, setting a personal best and the best time in the world for
1946. Courtesy of the *Boston Globe*.

Running with PHEIDIPPIDES

STYLIANOS KYRIAKIDES
The Miracle Marathoner

NICK TSIOTOS & ANDY DABILIS

With a Foreword by Johnny Kelley

SYRACUSE UNIVERSITY PRESS

The paper used in this publication meets the minimum
requirements of American National Standard for Information
Sciences—Permanence of Paper for Printed Library
Materials, ANSI Z39.48–1984.∞™

Library of Congress Cataloging-in-Publication Data
Tsiotos, Nick.
Running with Pheidippides : Stylianos Kyriakides, the miracle marathoner / Nick
Tsiotos and Andy Dabilis ; with a foreword by Johnny Kelley.
p. cm.—(Sports and entertainment)
Includes bibliographical references (p.   ) and index.
ISBN 0-8156-0703-2 (alk. paper)
1. Kyriakidås, Stylianos. 2. Runners (Sports)—Greece—Biography. I. Dabilis, Andy. II.
Title. III. Series.
GV1061.15.K97 T75 2001
796.42'52'092—dc21
[B]   00-049264

Manufactured in the United States of America

In memory of my beloved grandparents, Christos and Eleni Tsiotos and Nikos and Lefkothea Condakes, who lived through the horrors of occupation and passed on their courageous stories and rich Greek heritage (Nick Tsiotos)

To my grandparents, Andrew Dabilis and Fotini Bouka, from Greece and to John Gibbons of Ireland and Louise Dummett from England, who came from different countries but never forgot from where they came (Andy Dabilis)

To the people of Greece whose bravery and resistance to tyranny—from Marathon to Thermopylae to World War II—helped save Western civilization and preserve the institutions of freedom and democracy and to the people of Cyprus

From now on, we'll say that heroes fight like Greeks.
—Winston Churchill

There's seldom been more drama behind any single human being's athletic effort and none probably felt himself so truly obligated to give better than his best in an attempt to do something for others.
—Bill Cunningham,
Boston Herald, 1946

It was, without doubt, the most significant Boston Marathon of them all. His story, that of a hungry, impoverished Greek who journeyed thousands of miles to run a 26-mile errand of mercy, will be retold a century from now in Greece.
—Jerry Nason,
Sports Editor, *Boston Globe,* 1946

Today they know in the hills of Athens that the human spirit is imperishable.
—Dave Egan,
Boston Advertiser, 1946

How can you beat a man who's running for his country?
—Johnny Kelley, 1946

I knew I had to win or die.

—Stylianos Kyriakides, Boston, 1946

Nick Tsiotos and Andy Dabilis are the authors of *Harry Agganis, "The Golden Greek": An All-American Story*, a biography of one of America's greatest athletes. Mr. Tsiotos is a Boston public school teacher listed in *Who's Who in American Teaching*. He played professional basketball in Greece and lectures on Greek history. Mr. Dabilis is a journalist at the *Boston Globe* and has taught journalism at Boston University, Northeastern University, Emerson College, and the American College of Greece in Athens.

Contents

Illustrations

The Fates

Johnny Kelley

Johnny Kelley in many ways is the most remarkable and recognized marathoner the world has ever known: he ran sixty-one Boston Marathons, won two, in 1935 and 1945; finished second seven times; competed in two Olympics, in 1936 and 1948 (it could have been four but there were no games in 1940 and 1944); and was one of America's premier distance runners, at ranges from ten kilometers to the marathon, for more than two decades. In 1999, Runner's World magazine named him "Marathoner of the Century."

He was almost ninety years old when he sat down in the living room of his modest Cape Cod home on June 10, 1997, to do this foreword and talk about his friendship and rivalry with Stylianos Kyriakides, about the Olympic Games in Berlin in 1936, where he met the famous Finnish long-distance runner Paavo Nurmi, who recognized him to his delight, and where he was amazed to see a man whose exploits he admired, Spiridon Loues, winner of the first Olympic marathon in the modern times in Athens in 1896.

An exuberant Kelley, bounding with energy and acting sprightly, laughed vividly and talked easily at length about his own career. His memory still sharp and accurate, he rolled through the thousands of miles of competition of his life, including the 1946 golden anniversary Boston Marathon duel with Kyriakides: Kelley, the defending champion, and Kyriakides, a man who was running for his country and to save the lives of his starving countrymen. Kelley was fond of calling his friend "Stanley."

Kelley's eyes moistened several times, especially as he looked at a photo-

graph of himself in his 1936 Olympic uniform, a picture he had given to Kyri-
akides and autographed when Kyriakides came to Boston to run in the 1938
race. Surrounded by some of his many trophies and artwork he loved, Kelley
could look out the picture window of his home on a warm early spring day,
past the quietude of a pond, the starting point of his daily walk, followed by
forty-five-minute runs. It's what he loves to do best, he said. [NT and AD]

My father took me to see my first Boston Marathon in 1921. Frank Zuna
was coming down the road to win it and a police officer said, "Come on
there, kid, get under the ropes," and my father said, "Look at all the pepper he's got." My parents used to watch the marathon, but my mother
said she never thought she'd have a son who would run in it.

I first met Kyriakides at the Berlin Olympics in 1936. We were rivals,
friendly rivals. I met Kyriakides at the starting line and we wished each
other well. Germany was getting ready for the war and you could feel
the tension. When I walked into the stadium for the Olympic Games
with an American uniform on, I can't describe the feeling of joy and
pride. My eyes were moist; you have to go through it yourself to understand. It was there; with my own eyes, I saw the original marathon winner, Loues, give an olive branch to Hitler. Loues was wearing a little
white skirt and a black vest. I may be the last man alive who saw this.

I have very fond memories of our race in 1946. I read and heard all
about the sacrifices the people in Greece made—that he had hardly
anything to back up his strength and training while we in this country
had everything. I remember (*Boston Globe* sportswriter) Jerry Nason
saying Stanley was coming here and people in Greece were giving him
their food so he could have the strength to compete, which was really
something. I felt I had a chance to win again and I expected to.

When I heard about Stanley's visit to Boston and what he had to go
through, I said, "Oh no, that's awful." I thought, "More power to him." I
felt sorry for him doing this. Here I had plenty of food while this poor
runner had hardly anything, just a few peas, and was running for his
country. When I read what Nason said about the sacrifices people made
so he could run and train, that bothered me. That was the only race that
affected me emotionally, the only one. Most runners had all the facili-

ties and this poor guy was coming over here empty-handed, with no food, nothing, and the people in the country were sacrificing so he could do this.

When I was running with Stanley in 1946, I did something I never should have done. I paced myself improperly. I was running broken pace and you can't do that in a marathon; you should run a long, steady pace. I was going fast and slow and fast and slow and with four miles to go I could hardly do anything. I'm not saying that I would have won, because four miles from the finish I could hardly move. I made a very sad mistake in not pacing myself properly. I've always been a very impatient person and it cost me dearly because I could have had two more Boston Marathons. Jerry Nason from the *Globe* pointed to his head and said, "Why don't you use this?" In 1945, I had said, "I'm going to run with my head," and I paced myself and with two miles to go I was all alone. By my standards, I ran a very poor race, which I never would have done now.

During the 1946 race we didn't talk very much, but we handed each other water as a friendly gesture. We didn't carry on much of a conversation. I could feel his determination. I couldn't get away from him. This fellow was pretty darn good. I was awful, awful tired. I could hear the crowd yelling both "Stanley" and "Kelley." It was like a roar. What carried me was determination, my background, and my youth. I was a young man then, but he pulled away from me about three miles from the end, and I thought, "There he goes" and I couldn't hold him. He ran a very nice race.

We owe a great debt to the country of Greece and to Loues, because without them we wouldn't have any Boston Marathon. The race is one of the greatest in the world and they come from all over the world now . . . all because we must thank Loues and Greece for this. The Greeks are the cause of all the happy times we runners are having all over the world because of the foundation and their contribution. I give my thanks to them and their countryman Stelios Kyriakides.

God bless everybody in Greece. I hope someday I can meet his children and family. I want to go to Greece. I want to go to Marathon.

Acknowledgments

The authors want to thank those whose cooperation made this work possible, especially the family of Stylianos Kyriakides for providing documents, photographs, letters, and other information, and Greek hospitality. His wife, Iphigenia, who sat through countless hours of interviews, some of which were emotional to recall; her son, Dimitri; daughters, Eleni Contos and Maria Kalaforia; and son-in-law, John Contos. And in Greece, Taki and Natasha Karamboulis and George and Eleni Meletis for their hospitality.

And Johnny Kelley, the great Boston Marathon champion and friend of Stylianos Kyriakides, along with Payton Jordan, the great American sprinter who never had the chance to succeed Jesse Owens as the world's greatest sprinter because the Olympics were not held in 1940 and 1944, when he was the fastest man on the track. Jordan's friendship with Kyriakides provided critical information and photographs and enriched this work.

Special thanks to our agent, attorney Susan Julian Gates, for her indefatigable work and belief in this project, and also to our attorney, Chris Tsiotos, and to Ourania Nitsa Tsiotos and Yianna Antoniou in Athens. Thanks to Boston Athletic Association director Guy Morse and press officer Jack Fleming; Spiro Frangules and officials of Olympic Airlines. Also, officials of the Greek consulate in Boston, Consul-General George Chatzimichelakis, press officer Dino Siotis, and former consul John Economides, and George Georgacopoulos. Cypriot ambassador Andros Nicolaides, press officer Miltiades Miltiadou; and Sports

Museum of New England curator Dick Johnson and his staff, including Brian Codagnone. And, Dr. John S. Tegeris; Eugene Rossides and Nick Larigakis of the American-Hellenic Institute for their insights into Cyprus; Dimitri Avramopoulos, mayor of Athens; the library staff of the *Boston Globe*, Dr. Constantine Hionidis, and Nancy and Jimmy Earl.

Also Judge Harry Demeter, Adele Foy, Peter Nicholas Stamas, Annick Haller, Georgia Condakes, Peter Sutton, Pan Theodore, Nick Spiliotis, Effie Orgettas, Domenic Mastrototaro, Karen Baroosian, Peter and Helen Laskaris, Nick Mitropoulos, the Greek Amateur Athletic Union SEGAS; Achilles Senopoulos, George Kyriakou and Maria Polydoro of Cyprus, Fred Lewis, marathoner Ted Vogel, Athanasios A. Vulgaropulos, Dr. Charles Robbins, attorney George P. Gonis, Anna Maria DiCamillo, and Nancy Agris Savage, publisher of the *Hellenic Chronicle*. And Constantine and Polixeni Tsiotos.

And Ioanna Savidou, former governor Michael Dukakis, and Fani Constantinou of the Benaki Museum in Athens photo archives. Also, Athan and Maria Anagnostopoulos of the Greek Institute in Cambridge, Massachusetts, and Athens, and Ted Sarandis of WEEI radio in Boston. And Greg Pappas of Chicago, publisher of the *Greek America*, and Takis Simitsek, for his recollections of his father, Otto, who was Stelios Kyriakides' trainer and great friend.

The late Jerry Nason, sports editor of the *Boston Globe*, whose precise memorabilia was a treasure trove of information on the Boston Marathon and who was a great friend to Kyriakides; retired Air Force colonel Peter Andrews, who died during the writing of this book, after providing so much invaluable assistance through his late father, Andrew Cougialis, who was a runner and an official at the finish line of the Boston Marathon for many years, and who kept an archive of photos and information.

And to the people of Athens, who were so hospitable during two trips there to research this story.

RUNNING WITH
PHEIDIPPIDES

A Crown of Wild Olive

Ancient history is as much myth and legend as fact, and even historians today can not always agree on which is which. The Greeks especially cherish the images of gallantry and bravery, some of which, of course, are at odds with human nature and experience. Although the facts may be uncertain, or disputed, the results of battles are not. Whether a Greek named Pheidippides was the runner of marathon lore has not diminished the role of that victory in Greek and Western history. What follows, then, is much of what happened and some historical conjecture.

Marathon, Greece, 490 B.C.

The clash of swords had almost stopped as the Greek general Miltiades surveyed the broad plain of Marathon on the eastern coast of Greece, and he smiled, watching the vast Persian army flee before the hoplites he had led into their ranks, surprising and decimating the invaders, who had vastly outnumbered the Athenians and Greeks standing between them and all of Greece.

There were 192 Greek dead; the fleeing Persians had left behind sixty-four hundred on the field. Miltiades needed to get word to Athens of the victory, twenty-five miles away, as quickly as possible and he summoned a warrior and professional messenger, Pheidippides, who was fleet and would not stop until he reached the city.

Before the battle, Pheidippides had been sent to run from Athens to Sparta, 150 miles, to request aid. When he got there, Pheidippides delivered this message: "Men of Sparta, the Athenians ask you to help them, and not to stand by while the most ancient city of Greece is crushed and enslaved by a foreign invader; for even now Eretria has been enslaved by a foreign invader; and Greece is weaker by the loss of one fine city." He then ran back to rejoin his colleagues, where the signal for attack was given.

But now that the battle had been won, he had a new mission, and turned to it, in his fatigue. Pheidippides ran from the field, where the wounded were still moaning and where the Greeks could see the Persians scrambling into their ships. He ran over a hill onto a dusty road, away from the diminished din of the battle, and was quickly alone with his thoughts, his eyes set on the horizon, his sandaled feet clapping softly into the dirt, kicking up puffs that looked like wings behind his heels.

His breathing settled into a rhythm and he found a pace that would get him to the city quickly, he thought. His uniform chafed against his sweating body and his adrenaline from the fight provided him further impetus.

Then, on the road ahead, he thought he could see another figure, a pale shadow in the wind, a man dressed curiously in almost no clothing, odd-looking soft shoes on his feet, paving the way, running ahead, his step beckoning him to follow, Pheidippides so close now he could almost touch the ghost on the shoulder, the sight making the Greek warrior shiver in his steps. Then, in a moment, it was gone, but as he passed the spot where he thought he saw the strange man, Pheidippides could almost sense the presence of something that had been there.

He aimed his steps and thoughts now at Athens, arriving there breathless, a crowd quickly collecting to find out what he had to say about what had happened at the battlefield. He came into the agora, the marketplace and gathering spot at the center of the city, and was quickly surrounded by his fellow citizens, their eyes anxiously waiting.

He stopped, placed his hands to his knees, picked up his head, smiled painfully, and uttered one word: *nenikikamen*.

We are victorious.

Thermopylae, Greece, 480 B.C.

The Spartans prepared for death. They had braided their hair and groomed themselves, a practice that amazed the Persian king Xerxes when he learned of it. He had already been furious and frustrated that his massive army, estimated at 180,000, had been unable to defeat the small band of three hundred Spartans and a contingent of Thessalians and Thespians who had refused to leave the narrow pass, keeping the Persians from invading the rest of Greece.

It had been ten years since King Darius had been defeated by the Greeks at the Battle of Marathon, and Xerxes was determined he would not suffer the same fate. He had been so confident when he arrived just outside the fifty-foot-wide pass and saw only a small group of defenders that he waited two days for them to leave, before a Greek in his army, Demaratus, told him that he was facing the Spartans, led by King Leonidas, who had given his word to Greece he would not withdraw.

Xerxes sent for Demaratus, who sighed and told him again about the odd behavior of the Spartans. "Once before, when we began our march against Greece, you heard me speak of these men," said Demaratus. "I told you then how I saw this enterprise would turn out and you laughed at me. I strive for nothing, my lord, more earnestly than to observe the truth in your presence, so hear me once more. These men have come to fight us for possession of the pass and for that struggle they are preparing. It is the custom of the Spartans to pay careful attention to their hair when they are about to risk their lives. But I assure you that if you can defeat these men and the rest of the Spartans who are still at home, there is no other people in the world who will dare to stand firm or lift a hand against you. You have now to deal with the finest kingdom in Greece, and with the bravest men." Xerxes was unconvinced and waited four days. He would be the one who would conquer the Hellenes and Leonidas and the Spartans would not stop him.

When Leonidas himself greeted an emissary sent out to meet the Spartans, the Persian sheepishly said he had instructions from Xerxes: πεμψοντασπλα, throw down your weapons and you may go free. Leonidas smiled, barely visible under the sculpted metal helmet that hid most of the warrior's features, and replied laconically: Μολων Λαβε. It meant: "Tell your king to come and take them."

When the Spartans were told not to resist because the Persians had so many archers alone that, when they fired, the number of arrows would blot out the sun, they got another answer, this from Dieneces: "Good, we shall fight in the shade."

An angry Xerxes ordered the Medes to go in and overwhelm the Spartans, who suddenly wheeled and ran away to the amazement of Xerxes' men who chased them. Too late they realized what was happening. The Spartans turned about and formed a tight group and with a ferocious counterattack cut them down.

Xerxes would have no more. He would send in his personal guard, the supposedly invincible Immortals, tall, tough men chosen for their bravery who would not bow before the Spartans, he knew. He set up a chair on the plain just on the other side of the water before Thermopylae, which was halfway down the eastern coast of Greece, guarded by Mount Oeta and the Malian Gulf, the key geographical spot for any army. There he would watch his Immortals defeat the Spartans, of whom he had heard so much, and he told them to take Leonidas alive.

When the Immortals advanced, stolidly and confident, the Spartans again ran away and the enemy suffered the same fate as the Medes when the Spartans turned about again, and, with their superior armament and spears, decimated the best of Xerxes' army. Three times, in fear for his army, being routed by the Spartans, Xerxes leaped to his feet, the words of Demaratus pounding in his head. The pass had now been held for two days and the Persian king was furious.

He retreated to his tent until told there was a frightened Greek who wanted to see him.

"Send him in!" Xerxes said.

The disheveled and wide-eyed man, a poor shepherd named Ephialtes, smelling of goat, and dreaming of a reward, came to Xerxes and told him he knew of a pass in the mountain through which the Persians could get behind the Spartans. The Spartans knew of it as well, and other passes, and had sent a group of Phocians to protect it, after learning of Ephialtes' treachery.

But Leonidas was not confident the Greeks could keep the Persians from getting behind his group and ordered most of the defenders to leave, except for the Thebans, whom he did not trust, and the Thessalians, whose homeland was in danger and who refused to go. So the Spartans set about to prepare themselves for death, and so they cleaned themselves and combed their hair and waited.

When the Persians skirted the Phocian guard and advanced with all their might, even the mighty Leonidas and the Spartans could not stop them. One Spartan, blinded in battle, told his comrades to put a sword in his hand and point him toward the enemy, and Leonidas himself fought in front of his men, where an arrow cut him down and left his body vulnerable. His last order was to march forward and to kill Xerxes, an impossible task, but that had never stopped Spartans before.

The Spartans, who had formed a circle, fought furiously to retrieve his body and tightened their group as their numbers fell. Xerxes ordered a final volley of hundreds of arrows, which fell on the Spartans like a thundering rain and killed them. He had won his victory—for now.

The Persians began a belated march through Greece, meeting fierce resistance everywhere, until they suddenly seemed to have disappeared, bewildering him. "Where are the Greeks?" a puzzled Xerxes asked. He was told they had gone to celebrate a festival known as the Olympics, athletic competitions. Now he was even more befuddled.

"And what do they strive for?" Xerxes asked his emissary.

"A crown of wild olive," he was told.

"Heavens!" he exclaimed. "What manner of men are these I have come to battle with, men who contest not for gain, but for glory?"

The bravery of the Spartans allowed the Athenians to prepare a navy to meet the Persians at Salamis, after they had sacrificed their city, knowing they could not stop the huge army. When Xerxes, watching from his chair outside Athens, saw his proud fleet rammed and sunk by the small, more maneuverable Greek ships, he fled and left behind Mardonius to have his army fight its way back to Persia. A year later, at Platea, the Persians were crushed again and Greek culture—and western civilization—had been saved.

For centuries thereafter, Thermopylae, as much as the Battle of

Marathon, defined for Greeks the watchword of bravery and heroic self-sacrifice and the desire to do their duty for their country. Herodotus would explain why the Spartans stood their ground: "Thus there was no cause for alarm—for, after all, it was not a god who threatened Greece, but a man, and there neither was nor ever would be a man who was not born with a good chance of misfortune. The present enemy was no exception; he too was human, and was sure to be disappointed of his great expectation."

1

They Were Going to Kill Me

Athens, Greece, 1955

It had been a decade since Stylianos Kyriakides, then the champion runner of all the Balkans, had stood in the pass of Thermopylae, drawing inspiration for the greatest challenge of his life: win the modern world's most famous marathon, in Boston. He wanted to do it so the world would know that thousands of his countrymen were starving in the aftermath of World War II and a civil war raging in Greece. He liked to visit the site and imagine the Greek heroes standing defiant, knowing what they had to do.

It was a story he was relating now, to a new and suddenly close friend. It was another perfect Mediterranean night sky over Athens, bright and warm and sparkling with stars. Payton Jordan, a famous American track coach, sat down on a hillside outside the home of his host, Kyriakides, so the two could talk about running and how Jordan could help the Greek team for the 1956 Olympics. Beyond them, the hills rose in a hulking curve that looked like a huddle of men from ancient times, listening.

Jordan, a former champion sprinter from the University of Southern California, who was once one of the world's fastest men, was the track coach at Occidental College in Los Angeles, and had been recruited to come to Greece by Otto Simitsek, the Hungarian-born Greek-speaking coach of Greece's national team. The two had taken an immediate lik-

7

ing to each other at the first international track coaches meeting that Jordan, who was president of the group, had helped organize in California. Simitsek talked him into coming to Greece.

Here Simitsek introduced him to his most famous protégé, Kyriakides, who was now forty-five years old and no longer running competitively. Jordan had heard of Kyriakides, the champion runner of all the Balkan countries and the man whose stirring run in the 1946 Boston Marathon had galvanized world attention to the plight of starving Greeks after World War II, and helped make the event an international competition that would soon draw thousands of runners from throughout the world.

He wasn't prepared for how soft-spoken and humble Kyriakides was, how reluctant he was to talk about his own accomplishments, and for the horror story that would unfold as the two sat in the dark warmth of a Greek night in the Athenian suburb of Filothei, amidst scattered hillside homes in a city with centuries of heroes.

The homes sat along dirt roads in a placid area of olive trees and orange groves, and there was a simple pace to the life that pleased Jordan. He could smell the sweetness of lamb cooking on an outdoor spit, and it made his mouth water, especially when he saw a plate of fresh-picked tomatoes, black and brown olives, crisp, cool cucumbers, covered with tart olive oil, sprinkled with oregano and the slight bite of the Greek feta cheese, made from goat's milk and cured in brine. It was irresistible. Like many Greek homes, Kyriakides had a garden in the backyard, providing the vegetables for their dinner. A fine Greek wine was served.

The two men talked of their business of running—the differences between the sprints Jordan preferred and the longer distances that Kyriakides loved. They had taken to each other, although Kyriakides was almost eight years older. Jordan was an acclaimed athlete in the United States before he began coaching, but he had continued to run too. A lean, muscled Jordan was on the cover of *Life* magazine in 1939 after helping the University of Southern California win the national collegiate track championship. His upright running form looked a lot like Jesse Owens, the great sprinter who had won four gold medals at the 1936 Olympics in Berlin, where Kyriakides had competed.

As a boy of fourteen, in 1931, Jordan had won his first race, a hundred-yard dash, and was then approached by a man who told him, "Young man, I think someday you're going to be a real champion, keep at it." The man was Charlie Paddock, a 1924 Olympic gold medalist who was called "The World's Fastest Human."

Then Jordan talked about his disappointment in 1940, when, as America's best sprinter, he was dreaming of the Olympics, scheduled for Tokyo. The games were canceled with the onset of World War II. He talked about Jesse Owens, whom Kyriakides had met in Berlin, and their missed opportunities at the canceled Tokyo Olympics in 1940 and the canceled games scheduled for London in 1944. It seemed so distant now, as they sat and reminisced softly in the warm, enveloping night; the only other sound, between the exchanged order of their words, was the chirps of cicadas.

Jordan and Kyriakides had talked about that and their running, and Kyriakides said he had a special treat for him: he was going to take him out to the plains of Marathon, to the original site of Pheidippides' run, and Jordan kidded Kyriakides about going for one last run there. Kyriakides' son, Dimitri, went with them and Kyriakides couldn't resist putting on his running clothes for another run at the ancient site, under a perfect Greek blue sky on a day that had helped cement the friendship with Jordan even more. Jordan had run a 9.6 100-yard dash and a 21.1 in the 220-yard run in college and played for USC's 1938 Rose Bowl football champions. He was a world-class athlete, but he felt a little in awe of Kyriakides.

Kyriakides was a slight man still, little more than 5'7" and slim, and Jordan had to strain to hear him speak because Kyriakides talked so softly. But his English was good, honed from years before when he worked for British families in Cyprus, where he was born. Kyriakides had accompanied Jordan throughout many villages and places in Greece to talk about training techniques for runners, and Jordan was stunned to see the response whenever Kyriakides walked into a room.

The crowds would converge on the Greek like filings to a magnet, and everyone wanted to talk to him and touch his hand. Some, crying, would say, simply: "Thank you."

Kyriakides had given up competitive running by 1955, but he couldn't resist a last run at Marathon in Greece, where he took U.S. Olympic team coach Payton Jordan, who was a guest in his house. Courtesy of Payton Jordan.

"You see those hills?" Kyriakides said to Jordan, pointing to just outside his neighborhood. "They are called *Tourko Vounia*, that's where I trained for Boston in 1946." His gravelly voice was broken only slightly by a clipped accent, but his black eyes burned like coal showing he had not lost the thoughts of what had driven him. Jordan thought of Pheidippides, another Greek who had almost run himself to death from Marathon to Athens. Now, again, another of Grecian blood had run another historic race for love of people and his country.

In the yard, Kyriakides' wife, Iphigenia, cleaned up after the outdoor meal, and their children, Eleni and Dimitri and Maria, ran and played. That's when Kyriakides talked about how he almost hadn't survived the war at all, how the Nazis had almost executed him on the same kind of night as tonight. The dramatic story made Jordan sit up, astonished, his eyes unblinking. Jordan, a veteran of the U.S. Navy during World War II, winced at what he saw: the strong man's eyes getting wet as he told of the constant dread of living in an occupied country. "They were going to kill me," Kyriakides said, his voice falling, but the piercing bravery in his eyes never wavering as he looked directly at his new American friend. "They were going to kill me . . . they were going to kill me."

2

No One Loses Who Has Hope

Statos, Paphos, Cyprus, 1910/Athens, 1934

Cyprus was still a British colony in 1910, although most of the thirty-five-hundred-square-mile island off the coast of Turkey and the western shore of Syria, and not far from the northern end of Africa, had a Greek-speaking populace of people yearning to be reunited with Greece. Its history dating nine thousand years, it was the supposed birthplace of the goddess Aphrodite, who was said to have come from the foam of the sea near Paphos, a seaside port town about seventeen miles from the small village of Statos, where the family of Ioannis and Eleni Kyriakides lived a hard existence, trying to make a living off the land to feed their family. The name of the island came from a derivation of a Greek name for Aphrodite, Kypros, or Cyprus. Most of the country consisted of a wide plain lying between two mountain ranges, the highest point being Mount Olympus at 6403 feet.

Cyprus was the site of early Phoenician and Greek colonies and for centuries it had been ruled by various conquerors, including the Turks, who seized it in 1571 and settled a large Turkish population on the island, not far from its own coast. The island was an important geographic location, being the gateway to the Middle East and Far East and Africa, and was an irresistible target for centuries of conquerors.

Like most of the other villages on the island, Statos was small and poor and barren, with rocks and dusty roads between small houses. With not many residents, the center was the most frequent meeting place for villagers. Ioannis Kyriakides was born in 1869, and was a tall man with an athletic build, what Greeks called a *Levendi*, a strong, strapping man with a warriorlike stance. He had an indomitable air and a gritty spirit of independence that sustained him during hard times in the small village. Eleni, his wife, was a thin woman who dressed in traditional clothing, a long dress that fell to her ankles and a scarf on her hair. She had an outgoing personality and kept the house while her husband and children toiled in the fields, where she would on occasion also help out.

Kyriakides' family began with a son, Hristostomos, born in 1898 and then another, Dimitri. The Kyriakides had another son, Elias, and a daughter, Harithea. Then, on January 15, 1910, with Ioannis Kyriakides already worried about how to feed his family, a fifth child was born. He was named Stylianos Ioannis, and was born two months prematurely, in a difficult birth. He was tiny and underweight. Unlike his father and brothers and sisters, he was short and slim, even in his early years.

Ioannis wore traditional Cypriot garb, wide blooming pants and a loose-fitting shirt, and, like his clothes, he was a traditionalist, used to hard work and a living from the land. Everyone was expected to work. The family lived in a two-room home: one room for the parents, the other for the children. Below the house, a storage area was in the cool dirt, the place to store barrels with a wine made after they stomped their own grapes, and there were corn and potatoes and oil and seeds for planting vegetables. Outside, ovens were imbedded in stone. Goats rustled outside, their neck bells clinking, next to chickens squawking and rabbits in cages and other farm animals, the mixed sounds a symphony in the air. Every morning, a rooster awakened the village of fewer than three hundred people.

Stylianos, called Stelios by his family, was reed-thin even as he grew and his tight body and skinny legs gave him a birdlike appearance, although his face, with high cheekbones and determined eyes that glowed like black coal when he was attempting a task, gave him an air of persistence and strength. He was the only one in his family with a short body, but it never made him feel inferior.

When he was about two, an old woman in the village named Sophia told Kyriakides' mother, "That little boy that you see so thin and scrawny, tell him to open his hand and let me read his palm."

She brought her son before the woman and told him to open his hand. He looked at the woman quizzically but did as his mother said. He did not know of fortune telling and oracles but thought this was a game that was fun.

The woman looked carefully at his hand. The woman held the boy's arm stiff and looked again at the hand, shaking her head, she a little unnerved by what she was seeing.

"What do you see in his hand?" his mother said, her belief in this ancient art unswerving.

"Someday when this boy grows up, he will be a great man and he will go through wide doors," the old woman said, her voice frail but determined, trying to explain she saw him conquering great obstacles. Then, she turned slowly and looked at his mother, pointed her finger, and said strongly, "You remember what I said. I will no longer be of life, but you remember what I said."

The soothsayer's words rattled Kyriakides' mother, but she wondered what could have been meant. This was a tiny village, far from even the next town and where could he, or anyone else from this village, go to become great? She put the thought aside, even though Sophia was known as a wise woman, religious and true.

For the next few years, there was nothing to show that that prophecy would ever come true. Life in the village was as it always has been, hard work and routine, the simple joys of a family life and the small social gathering of the neighbors and friends, broken only by the stories that would be brought back from those who would go to Paphos to work and return.

Even as a child, eight years old, Stelios would awaken early in the morning and help his father tend their sheep, feeding them and working until another family would come to help. The sheep would provide milk and dairy products, and some would be sold to raise money. They also had donkeys and mules, which—except for walking—were the main methods of transportation in the rocky and mountainous and rural areas of the island.

Like everyone else in the village, Stylianos didn't think much about the world outside, because he had not seen it. People expected to live their whole lives where they were born and raised. Many did not have shoes and lived and worked barefoot. But there was a sense of family and communion.

As a boy, he had to concentrate on school and helping his family till the land. He would work side by side with his father on the farm, and the two would often take long walks together, the barefoot strolls over dirt and rocky roads toughening his feet.

Sometimes, he would have to stay overnight in a little shed called a *kaliva*, a place for storing farm equipment for feeding and watering the animals. It was about a mile from the home and it was easier to stay there than walk home late at night. His father would be there often and the two would share a campfire, talk, and sing traditional Cypriot songs, their voices joined, the words soaring into the empty night sky around them, the bond unspoken. It was there the boy learned to love song.

Kyriakides had to go to school in the nearby town of Paphos, where there was only one room and six grades. During breaks from classes, the students would be taken outside and allowed to play, and sometimes were taken for runs around the building for physical exercise. Stelios took to the running with zeal, but never thought about athletics because in his family there was only work. Often, he would run around the church in the village for fun and then between villages, carrying food. He began to rely on his legs and his desire to run.

Paphos gave Kyriakides exposure to a community bigger than his tiny village, and people from other areas came off the ships of the seaport. Many priests were in the town because of the several monasteries there, and although the young boy saw a more commercial and cosmopolitan atmosphere, he remained shy. Many people from Statos made the daily trek to Paphos to work in small shops or factories, but Kyriakides' father stayed home to care for the land and the few farm animals they had.

During World War I, when Kyriakides was a boy, there was a change of government on Cyprus, where Greeks lived under an uneasy relationship with the ruling Turks. There had always been tension between Greeks and Turks, and in the early twentieth century there was still a remembrance of the bitter war of independence Greeks had won only a century before from the ruling Ottoman Empire, which had occupied Greece for generations.

In World War I, though, Great Britain annexed the island during hostilities with Turkey and it became a crown colony in 1925, bringing in many British officials and a government to oversee the third largest island in the Mediterranean. There was an influx of British businesses and education systems because the island was ripe with prosperous economic opportunities, including vine products, citrus, potatoes, and vegetables, and asbestos mining, gypsum, timber, and marble.

The British brought many professionals, people who wanted servants and help from the Cypriots, providing more jobs for the local families and especially young men. Kyriakides, though, was still in elementary school and the war was far away. He was too young to understand what the change in government meant for his island. When Kyriakides was ten in his little village, a Greek-American busboy from New York City, Peter Trivoulidas, entered the Boston Marathon, which would be used as the 1920 Olympic trials for American runners. He weighed 131 pounds and was due to become an American citizen soon. It was the second time he had run and little hope was given that an immigrant could conquer the field, especially with three previous winners running.

They included defending champion Carl Linder of Finland, Bill Kennedy, the bricklayer who had won three years before, and Arthur Roth. Little was known about Trivoulidas, who had finished seventh the year before, but the seventy-five-man field was considered one of the strongest in the young history of the event.

Newspapers still dominated news and coverage, not just about the race, but all news, because radio stations hadn't started yet and television was far off in the future. The United States was in the midst of a post–World War I change into a new decade, and the Boston Athletic Association was starting to change too. Some burgeoning social upheaval was in the country, including in Boston, which had an infamous police strike in 1919.

Trivoulidas worked in the famous Wanamaker's restaurant in New York and was a small, deep-chested man with big round eyes and was still a Greek national but had been living in the United States for a while. He looked funny running, with a high back kick and his socks flopped around his shoes. He was twenty-nine, a Spartan, and had served in the Greek navy. He had run the original course of Marathon in Greece in 1911.

He started the race uneventfully, fitting into a pack near the front runners for the first ten miles, at the town of Natick, where Jimmy Hennigan, a specialist in five- and-ten-mile races, was holding the lead, although he was not a long-distance man. By the halfway checkpoint of the town of Wellesley, Roth had closed into the second spot and was running comfortably, while Trivoulidas, biding his time, was back in fourteenth. Roth caught Hennigan at the seventeen-mile mark, and the other top challengers had started to drop back or out, worn out or caught up in heat and the choking fog and fumes of following cars.

Trivoulidas had not expected to win and was running easily and happily, glad with his pace, which he thought seemed well ahead of the previous year, when he had run 2:38:10. Roth was waning quickly now as the end of the race loomed and he struggled to hold on, rolling side to side with desperate fatigue. Trivoulidas could not believe he was within challenging distance of Roth and the Greek began to close when he saw Roth dying. And with only five-eighths of a mile left, halfway between Kenmore Square and the finish line on Exeter Street, Trivoulidas caught Roth, who suddenly stopped the surging of his arms when he was passed, giving up the ghost of chance. Trivoulidas rolled past him and won in 2:29:31, Roth staggering across the line a minute later followed by Linder, almost three minutes more back.

Trivoulidas was elated and it was reported he said: "Sure, me pretty tired, but my how light I feel when I see only one man ahead of me! Happy too, I can make a gain. I know I win. No tired anymore." And he smiled. He was the most unlikely of champions, but ineligible to represent the United States in the Olympic Games, where he ran for Greece instead.

Trivoulidas came back in 1921 to defend his title and improved his time measurably, running 2:27:41, but this time it was good enough only for third. Frank Zuna, a plumber from Newark, New Jersey, who had finished the 1920 race in his stockings and had been dropped from the Olympic team because the coach, Boston Marathon recordholder Mike Ryan, felt he was not fit enough, set a course record in an astonishing time of 2:18:57. And, of course, he broke the record held by the coach who denied him a chance to run in the Olympics. Watching in the crowd was a young Irish-American boy who said he would one day run the race: Johnny Kelley.

But, in Cyprus, Kyriakides had not even heard about the famous race in Boston or thought much about running, other than what needed to be done outside while conducting chores, or as a way to get between villages. He left school when he was fourteen, after completing elementary school, with little knowledge or need for English. "My father thought I had learned enough letters." His formal education had ended.

Because there was so little food and life was so hard, Kyriakides was going to be sent to a relative who owned a bakery in the city of Limassol, the largest community at the western end of Cyprus, where he could find work and make enough money to send some home to his family. Kyriakides left his village with a friend, Agoustis Alexiou.

"When I finished elementary school, I left my village alone to look for luck," he said. He felt he had to help his struggling family and went to where he could raise money for them. "I was a burden on my family. My father could not afford our family. I had to find work. Statos was poor and life was tough," he said. It was a difficult decision for a boy to make, to leave his family.

In Limassol, Kyriakides lived with an uncle, Socrates Charalambous. It was hard, grueling work and it wore down the young boy. He made little money for a year's work. "I worked like a dog and made very little money," he told his friend Alexiou, who was working in Limassol too, trying to help himself and his family. Kyriakides worked rolling

dough with his hands, night and day, although he was underage, because his family needed all the money he could send.

He worked at the bakery for more than two years, an exhausting experience for the slim boy who started to feel some growing pains in his
legs as he grew even a little, to only 5'7". But he needed more money,
and went to work at a hotel, doing many menial jobs, as a busboy and
dishwasher and waiter.

To relieve the drudgery, Kyriakides took to running alone late at
night where he could be by himself with his thoughts, and feel the
breeze flow through his hair as he streaked along the streets under the
moon. It felt good, and he would run as far and as fast as he could, to test
himself. He wanted to see how much he could endure.

It was an odd sight, the gawky young man running, his servant's
pants flopping, his waiter's vest left by the side of the road for his return.
And it made him the target of gibes from his friends, who thought he
must be crazy. But Kyriakides believed he could be an athlete.

He imagined the city streets as a stadium and pictured the track and
people in the stands cheering for him as a champion runner. He worked
out for a month, at first for fun, to see what his aptitude would be for
running. Many people saw him running alone at midnight and wondered what he was. His childhood friends made fun of him.

"No one in your family is an athlete. How are you going to become
one?" they asked him. He thought the practice would do him good mentally and physically, and was unsure if he could become a good athlete
but felt driven by their skepticism. "You are going to gather the pebbles
of all your opponents. You are going to finish last," they told him, doubt-
ing his ability. He began to doubt himself too, but then he told them,
"You'll see what I'll do in a short time. I want to win the Pan-Cypriot
Games. You will all see. Then you'll be calling me Mr. Kyriakides." A
poor boy from a poor family, who tilled the land, Kyriakides wanted to
succeed, to have respect, to accomplish.

Then he said softly to them, "No one loses who has hope."

But he couldn't keep up the practice up for long, because work was so
demanding and there was not enough time to test his unshakable desire
to want to run.

By day, he served people and washed big pots and pans called *kaza-nia*. The work was even harder than at the bakery and the teenager became covered with oil and sweated with the heat of stoves, making him slick with grime and fatigued. He liked serving customers but was not happy with the rest of the work, which didn't pay much more than what he was earning at the bakery.

Kyriakides left to work for a British family named Brown, but he didn't stay long. He was anxious and ambitious and looking around for some direction in his life. He was doing odd jobs and earning little money, but his English was improving.

It was nearly six years since he had left his family in Statos. A young man, Kyriakides changed jobs again, going to work for the big Kontopoulos grocery store, which was starting to thrive under the British rule. Kyriakides was starting to wonder what his life would hold, if he would ever do more than labor on the island for other people.

> Let him that would move the world, first move himself
>
> —Socrates

One day he felt very tired and his legs hurt. He went to see a British doctor, Reginald Cheverton, a tall athletic man who had been an amateur runner and a trainer for other athletes. He had participated himself in the 1927 Pan-Hellenic Games and loved sports and running.

Kyriakides had been growing more quickly now because he had been eating better. As his legs grew he tried to lengthen his trousers, although he was still very slim. Cheverton saw some athletic potential in the young man. When Cheverton checked Kyriakides, the doctor found the boy had a low heartbeat of forty to fifty beats per minute, ideal for a runner, especially in distances.

"Would you like to become a runner?" he asked. Kyriakides was eager. Cheverton told him about running and offered to help train him—and to give him a job as a servant in his household. Cheverton took him out running, three to four miles in the morning and sometimes at night and saw he had a great aptitude.

Cheverton took a great liking to him. Kyriakides worked "with thankfulness and willingly," staying two years. He sent much of his pay to his father and was pleased to do so. Cheverton was a true sportsman and he talked about athletics all the time, intriguing the young man looking for a direction. Kyriakides asked Cheverton many questions, improving his English, and a bond developed between the two. Cheverton gave him advice and courage.

One day, Cheverton said, "Stelios, I am going to England on business," and Kyriakides was crestfallen that the man, who had become like a second father to him, was leaving Cyprus even for a little while. Cheverton recommended him to a friend, a local official, and a prefect named Green, who owned a store. On September 19, 1931, when Kyriakides was twenty-one, Cheverton gave him a letter of reference, which stated:

> I have great pleasure in giving this testimonial to Stelios Kyriakides who has been my house boy for two years. He is a very reliable and willing worker, honest, punctilious and trustworthy. He is gifted with a thoughtful mind which is not derived of a sense of humor and I have no hesitation in recommending him as a tried servant both as a houseboy or as a government official.

Kyriakides keenly felt the loss of Cheverton, but he had found running was becoming important for him now, giving him another purpose in his life. Working for the Greens was much like the work he did for Cheverton, although there was little time for running. Still, Kyriakides was becoming more driven about the idea, which would not let him rest mentally. He fidgeted and thought about running, but fretted about finding the time.

Then, in January of 1933, at twenty-three years old, he decided he would become a real runner and started working out at 11:00 P.M. running the main road of Limassol back to the river of Germasoyias, retracing his old route, alone in the warm moonlight under a star-filled Cypriot sky. He wore rubber-soled shoes his boss's wife gave him and he was wearing his work clothes. All he took off was his jacket and he ran in his servant's uniform.

One day, reading the newspaper, he saw that the Athletic Club of

Olympia, *Gymnastikos Syllogos Olympus* (GSO), was hosting the twenty-second annual Pan-Cypriot Games and he decided to enter to see how good he was. It took him a while to find the club.

He found the person in charge, Pavlos Agalines.

"Excuse me. Can I run in the games?" Kyriakides asked shyly.

"Are you an athlete?" he was asked.

"No, I am not. But I will become one," he said.

"What's your name and what do you do?" the man asked skeptically of the shy, slender man before him.

"Stelios Kyriakides. I work for Mr. Green and I want to compete in the games," he said.

The director looked at him. "Come and run and we'll take a look at you," he said.

The next day, Kyriakides went to a real athletic facility with a track for the first time. Nobody was there. It was his first time at an official, groomed track and he was impressed. He looked around, shrugged, and ran nine-thousand meters, which was thirty times around.

To keep track, though, he put pebbles in his hand, dropping one at the completion of a lap. Before too long, there was a littered pile of thirty pebbles and Kyriakides knew he would be a runner. Breathing hard and smiling and looking down each time he passed the stones, he knew he had the strength and ability to do this.

When he stopped, he realized he wasn't tired and had the stamina to run further. He felt confident and buoyant. Maybe Cheverton was right, and he had the natural ability to be an athlete and maybe a champion.

The next day, he came back again and met the attendant, Christos Tavvas, who looked at the slender man who didn't look much like an athlete. "Go run sixteen laps," Tavvas said, not knowing Kyriakides had run thirty laps effortlessly the day before. Tavvas watched in amazement.

"You're good," he said, when Kyriakides finished. "Come back tomorrow when Mr. Agalines is here. I want him to see you," Tavvas said.

Kyriakides did. Agalines, alerted by Tavvas, wanted to see the new boy perform. "Go ahead," Agalines said. "Run."

That's all Kyriakides needed. He was more confident than ever because he impressed these officials. But they had something to teach him too, past his natural ability. "You are good," said Agalines. "But you run too much on your feet. You need to run more on your toes. If you can correct that, you should do well in the Pan-Cypriot Games next month. You can win the ten-thousand-meter, but in the five-thousand-meter there is somebody better than you. It will be difficult for you to beat him." Kyriakides listened hard. He trained too with some of the other athletes who were better known and more recognized by him. About two weeks before the games, though, while chopping wood, the ax head slipped and struck him on the left foot, grazing it but causing enough injury to make him worry. He had been an inch or so away from more serious harm. He went to Cheverton, who told him: "Stop working out. Stop being an athlete," but only until he was recovered, Kyriakides was assured.

Before the Pan-Cypriot Games, there would be trial events to select competitors. Because of his injured foot, Kyriakides missed the trials. That meant he could not compete in the Pan-Cypriot Games—unless he could show officials he could beat a trial winner.

He felt good and he wanted to show Agalines he could be a champion. "I will be okay. I want you to let me run against the victor of the trials," he said. He was referring to a runner named Araouzos, a five-thousand-meter specialist.

Agalines smiled, but was delighted in Kyriakides' confidence.

"Let's see if you can run," he said, though.

Kyriakides' foot had healed enough, he thought. Agalines arranged a match race, eight days before the Pan-Cypriot Games. Araouzos was confident he could beat the newcomer from a tiny village.

Early in the race, it appeared Kyriakides' boasting was better than his running. Araouzos took an early lead but Kyriakides never diminished his belief he could win. He started to sprint, feeling deep inside himself he could test himself and excel. Like a racehorse galloping at the end, he caught Araouzos and passed him and won by more than six-hundred meters, an astonishing difference.

He had won his first great victory. He felt happiness swell inside him like a flower bursting from the ground in spring, the buds seeking the sunshine.

Ειμαι αθλητης [I am an athlete].

But he still almost didn't get to run in the Pan-Cypriot Games at all. He went to Mrs. Green, for whom he worked as well, and said, "Madam, may I have a few days leave? I want to go to [the town of] Ammohostos and run in the Pan-Cypriot Games."

She was not pleased. Kyriakides was a valuable worker and needed. "Ammohostos is a long way off. We have a lot of work to do in this house. If you leave, the other servant will not be able to do the work all by himself," she said adamantly.

He was upset with the words, and, for one of the few times in his life, felt real fury and frustration raging inside him. He spun away without talking and went to the other servant. "I'm going to Mr. Green to ask for a leave of absence. If he does not give me my leave, I am going to quit. I hope he gives me the leave of absence," Kyriakides said, trying to explain how important the race was to him.

Kyriakides went to see Green, anxious at what he would say. "I want five days leave of absence so I can go to the Pan-Cypriot Games," Kyriakides said directly.

Green looked at him quizzically. "Is it that necessary?"

Kyriakides' face lit up. He would not back down. "I want to go because I have hope to win," he said, the hope rising in his voice. Green wasn't convinced.

"It's going to be difficult because the other servant is going to be left by himself and he's going to get tired," Green said. He had never had such a request from the mild-mannered Kyriakides before. And he was even more surprised at the strength of Kyriakides' tone.

"I want to go. I insist that I go," Kyriakides said. His face was tight with resolution and Green could see it. He waited a moment and thought.

"Okay, you can go," he said, wondering what would prompt Kyriakides to give up five days pay to go off to run in a foot race.

Two days later, Kyriakides left Limassol with eighteen other athletes from the athletic club for Ammohostos, where the event would be held. His teammates took a liking to the newcomer, even when Kyriakides said, "I am going to win." He said it matter-of-factly, without boast in his voice, and they looked astonished that he seemed so serious.

"You'll see tomorrow with my victory," he said. Then they started laughing and kidding him and called him an egotist, but in a good-natured way because he seemed so humble, even in his confidence.

In Ammohostos, Kyriakides' face lit up when he saw the prizes, silver cups, on a table. "God help me," he said. "I'm going to win that tomorrow," he added, his heart racing with his anxious feet.

When the games came, he was ready. He would run against another five-thousand-meter man named Pappadopoulos, who was not leery of the newcomer. Kyriakides had told his friends, "If I feel strong and have courage, I will lift my hand up."

He didn't have a chance to lift his hand the first lap because Pappadopoulos surged to an early lead. But by only six-hundred meters, little more than one and a half laps into the race, Kyriakides took the lead and lifted his hand and ran away from the field to win in seventeen minutes, twenty-eight seconds. Agalines was delighted. He saw in Kyriakides someone with championship potential for Cyprus and then Kyriakides won the ten-thousand meters too, in 37:26.

Agalines asked him to run in the Pre-Balkan Games in Athens in 1933, where athletes would be selected for the national team to compete against the nations surrounding Greece: Albania, Yugoslavia, Romania, Bulgaria, and Turkey.

That suited Kyriakides, who suddenly found a new passion in his running, devoting himself because he felt happiest when exercising. Something, he said, was pushing him to run. "I don't like to stay put," he told friends, and running was the perfect outlet for that pent-up energy that he worked so hard to confine. Offered cigarettes, he refused, and said he didn't like to smoke or drink, and, when he could, tried to get to sleep early, except for those nights when he would run late. Kyriakides had never been to Greece and was thrilled to be asked. He was awed to arrive in Athens, which seemed so gigantic and cosmopolitan compared with his village, and even Limassol. He was amazed at the bustling pace of the city and finding himself in the company of other athletes from the islands and smaller areas outside Athens.

The team was sent to the mountains to rest, because it was so high it was difficult to run or train there. He tried gamely anyway to keep his

Kyriakides was a distance runner primarily, but here he struck a sprinter's pose before a shorter race on Cyprus, where he honed his skills. Courtesy the Kyriakides family.

running up. Then they were sent back to Athens, and were put up in rooms downstairs in Panathenaic Stadium, the site of many athletic games since being built in 1896 for the first modern Olympic games. He went up against two runners named Vlahos and Nanos. But Nanos got injured running and finished third in the five-thousand-meter race. Kyriakides finished second, surprising Greek and Athenian officials, who didn't know the slender man from Cyprus.

Vlahos won in 34:14 and Kyriakides ran 34:34 but he was not selected for the national team because the Greeks chose another runner from Greece, named Paouris, who they thought was better, despite Kyriakides' strong showing. But the coaches didn't forget how strong he had run, especially Otto Simitsek, a Hungarian-born coach who headed the team and saw in Kyriakides a raw potential and burning drive, but a runner still unseasoned and without, he thought, the experience needed yet for international competition. But Simitsek, who was known to his athletes as "Uncle," made sure he kept close to Kyriakides. Simitsek was a soft-spoken but driven man who expected his runners to be dedicated and disciplined, and he would keep a record of their performances. He dressed elegantly and was a strong presence with his tall, powerful frame and close-cut hair.

He saw in Kyriakides a rare combination of desire and humility and he liked the Cypriot's quiet, unassuming manner, especially his willingness to pay attention to advice and to seek it out. Simitsek saw the raw talent and Kyriakides' drive to excel. Kyriakides didn't know this yet, and he returned to Cyprus disappointed and uncertain why he hadn't been selected for the national team. But the decision fueled a new fire in him and he took to the roads with a mission, running ten to fifteen miles a day, the determination etched on his face. He would make the national team and to help make sure, he wrote to Simitsek on December 16, 1933, to tell him how he was working out.

Simitsek remembered the thin young man who ran with eyes as intense as his desire. But he was so busy with the national team it took until February 5, 1934, before he could reply, just before the Pan-Cypriot Games. The letter came at a crucial time for Kyriakides, who

Kyriakides gave much of the credit for his development as a runner to the great Hungarian track coach, Otto Simitsek (left, in suit), who talked with Kyriakides (right) and a teammate. Courtesy of the Kyriakides family.

had been disappointed in his time in Athens and wondered whether he would be accepted or find a place on the Greek national team and a chance to run in the Olympic Games in Berlin in two years. He didn't know it yet, but Simitsek already was enamored of what he had seen in Kyriakides, the kind of indomitable spirit that can't be coached or taught, but could be channeled to make a champion. It was something Simitsek had sought since coming to Greece, and he was impressed that the shy young man had taken the time to write him and keep him abreast of the workouts. Simitsek had become an important part of the Greek athletic structure, especially since he had become so adept with the language and the Greek mindset, the kind, ornery resistance to authority but simultaneous respect for wisdom and teaching. He wanted to make sure he would keep Kyriakides close. He had plans for the Cypriot too.

Simitsek thought carefully before he wrote, wanting to embody Kyriakides with the enthusiasm to continue.

My Dear Kyriakides,

I received your letter of the 16th of Dec. 1933. I hope you forgive me for not responding to you until now. With a lot of thankfulness, I read your letter and saw you are exercising in the proper manner with good practice exercises. I beg of you though, when you feel a little tired to skip two or three practices. This will help you with your form so you will stay in good physical condition.

Your good physical condition is everything, and you may be able to improve your condition in the following way: every time you work out, weigh yourself immediately after and the weight you come in will show if you are losing too much and then you should stop for a few days. Make sure you check the distance you are running every time, and your time. Hopefully, you are running with a watch. All of these you will put down in a little memo pad. That way you can control your body and your exercise. I would like very much for you to send me, in a half month, your notebook so I can follow along and see how you are exercising and then I can give my analysis.

In the meantime, write if you have any doubts or questions and I will answer you. Give my regards to all the boys. Make sure you exercise hard for the upcoming athletic games.

With Love,
Otto Simitsek

Kyriakides followed the advice, but wanted to give Simitsek and the Greek athletic leaders a new reason why he should be on the team. He trained at the athletic club of Xenon, and then briefly went back to Statos to stay with his family because he had been so disappointed with his reception in Athens. In the Pan-Cypriot Games in March of 1934, he won the fifteen-hundred-meter, in 4:21, the five-kilometer in 16:20, the ten-kilometer in 34:47, and the twenty-kilometer, a half marathon, but he also did that in a two-day period, so dominating the competition that the national team leaders could not ignore him.

Agalines and the Cypriots knew what they saw too. "You are too big for this island," Kyriakides was told. In Athens, Simitsek was waiting.

Kyriakides traveled by boat to Athens and was put up at the Panathenaic Stadium, in rooms downstairs, below the elegant marble of the stadium, where runners and athletes from the islands and outside of Athens were given accommodations. They had little money for food and knew they would have to prove themselves against the best of the mainland. For Kyriakides, from the small village on a small island, the sight of the ancient stadium where the modern Olympic Games began was inspiring. He would sit in the empty stadium, the wind whistling softly through its almost perfect symmetry, the graceful sloping slides of the seating arrangements around a tightly curved track in the middle, and admire the moment, drawing deep breaths and sighing in a quiet happiness. Here, he thought, is where I will run. He felt the harmony, that was the goal of the ancient Greeks in their athletics and lives, and he was happy. He could almost see the ghosts of the games below, the javelin throwers running with their arms outstretched, the sprinters dashing before the crowds, so close to the runners they could almost see the smiles and wide-eyed exhortations. Now, he thought, he would be one of them, running with his ancestors.

In the Pan-Hellenic, or Greek, national games, on May 26, Kyriakides, skinny and anxious, won the five-kilometer race in 16:12. He became a double victor when he also won the ten-kilometer in 34:53, this time overtaking Vlahos in the early part of the race, running away from him handily at the end. In an interview with the daily newspaper *Proini,* he praised Vlahos, but said a lot of the other coaches interfered with Simitsek's advice and were spoiling the runners.

Simitsek knew Kyriakides would listen and he decided to coach him one-on-one, to take him under his wing and groom him not just for the championship of Greece, but for the Balkan countries, the upcoming Olympics in Berlin in 1936, and beyond.

3

The Beautiful and the Good

Cyprus-to-Athens, 1934–1937

Simitsek was the coach of the national team of Greece at the Balkan Games. This time Kyriakides was a member of the team and he was to run the long-distance marathon for Greece, although he had specialized in the shorter five-kilometer and ten-kilometer races, with some experience in the twenty-kilometer, the half marathon.

The games in 1934 were to be held at Zagreb, and the Yugoslavs were fierce rivals of the Greeks. Kyriakides would have to face the two-time defending champion of the marathon, the famed Ludovic Gal of Romania, who had run 3:02:41 the year before, and who would be the overwhelming favorite again. Many of Kyriakides' teammates, especially the hurdler Mandikas, were lighthearted competitors, who liked jokes. But Kyriakides was serious and took that approach to his running too, rarely smiling and concentrating on the task of putting one foot in front of the other as fast as he could. He showed more responsibility and had leadership qualities that made him the team leader.

One morning, before the marathon, which counted heavily in the standings, Simitsek took him and the other Greek runner, Arvanites, aside. "You have to run a smart race so we can get the first two places," Simitsek said. Earlier that day, the two runners went to the Esplanade for a walk and saw the famous park and gardens of Zagreb, which one of the other athletes likened to a famous garden in Athens, Zappeion.

They came back in the afternoon enlightened and fresh, but Kyriakides didn't have an appetite at dinner.

Kyriakides was thinking of his double duty, running the ten-kilometer and marathon, and he was worried about a great Serb runner, Broutsan, whom he would have to race. This was his first international experience and he was representing Cyprus and Greece. The Greeks loosened up each other with jokes and horsing around to make light of the pressure, and Kyriakides became friendly with a woman on the Greek sprinting team, Dominitsa Lanitou, feeling comfortable with her because she was a Cypriot too and they shared talk of their running specialties, the sprints versus the distance running.

The Greeks felt a little dispirited when they saw Serbs everywhere they went. "Hey, Greeks, we are going to beat you," the Serbs said, laughing. It was psychological warfare. The Greeks respected the Serbs' ability, but answered them, "Greece will finish last—but with record-breaking time."

Georgacopoulos, an eight-hundred-meter man, would tell the Serbs to watch out for Kyriakides in the five-thousand meters. "He has a record of one minute fifteen seconds," he laughed, about fifteen minutes faster than anyone could run that distance.

Another Greek runner, the captain, Karabatis, told him to stay close to Gal and shadow him. "Don't let him get ahead of you," he said to Kyriakides, who agreed. But Kyriakides said a runner should have faith in his own pace. "You should keep a close eye only on your watch," and not the other runners, Kyriakides said. He felt if a runner ran within himself and his ability, the leaders would fall and that running a strong pace by his own mark would give him the lead anyway.

"In a marathon, in big races, a runner should not get behind other runners. He should be able to use his own free will as a runner and his own experience. He should not look just at what type of race position the others are in. If they are a few yards ahead, you should look at your watch." Kyriakides had already adopted Simitsek's idea of using a watch and it helped him keep a pace for himself.

Before the first event, Simitsek called his team together. They stood huddled together as the tall man, dressed as usual in a suit with the coat buttoned, fastidious and precise, looked at them carefully. They waited to hear what he would say, knowing his Greek was as good as their own. Studying them, he talked of their ancestors, the ancient athletes who had first competed, against themselves as much as each other, and of the challenge his own team faced. And then he reminded them of why they were athletes, and Greeks: "Καλος και αγαθος," he said [the beautiful and the good]. Then he smiled softly.

In the four by one-hundred meter relay, Mandikas came from fifteen meters behind to catch the Yugoslavs and give Greece a victory, positioning them only seven points behind the home team with the marathon coming up. A win in the marathon would give Greece the team championship, so the pressure was on the newcomer from Cyprus.

The Yugoslavs protested that Kyriakides should not be allowed to run because he was a Cypriot and not a Greek citizen, but it was not upheld after the Greeks asserted that the Yugoslavs had themselves wrongly used citizens from Chile and Germany in previous years events.

The race turned out to be a surprise at twenty-kilometers, two-thirds into the marathon; Kyriakides took the lead, after pacing himself with his watch. He passed Gal and as the Greek came into the stadium and heard his friend yell, "Run Cypriot! That's it, good, bravo!" Kyriakides could see his teammates screaming for him too and he felt further heartened and encouraged. There was not much cheering from the other fans, who were disappointed, their faces blank.

Then he heard words that made him leap forward faster. It was the announcer on the loudspeaker: "That is the Hellene, Kyriakides," he said to the crowd. Kyriakides crossed the finish line, cutting the rope with his body, his teammates grabbed him and hugged him and kissed him and put him up on their shoulders so everyone in the stadium could see him.

He ran his victory lap waving an olive branch and held it aloft while his smiling teammates beamed in their *ELLAS* sweatshirts, the name of their country. He had run 2:49:31 to break the Greek record set by the 1896 Olympic gold medalist Spiridon Loues, who won in 2:55, and on only a forty-kilometer course, which was shorter than the marathon course in Zagreb. Kyriakides' time was also the best in Europe for the year and established him as a world-class runner immediately. It was fourteen minutes faster than Gal's time the year before and three minutes faster than the winning time at the European games in Turin, Italy.

Kyriakides was overcome with joy and was speechless. He felt he was living a dream. A year after running in a waiter's uniform on dirt roads on Cyprus, he was the new champion of all the Balkan countries. And when the Greek flag was raised, he started to cry.

He felt like yelling, "For Greece! For Cyprus!" because he was so emotional and proud to have won for his home and his country. He wanted to grab the blue and white Greek flag and hug it and kiss it. He started to cry more freely now, so much emotion exploding to the surface after a grueling run in which he had become a victor for Greece.

Then he started trembling, from the release and a chill that had come into the stadium. The president of SEGAS, the Greek amateur athletic union that had sent the team, Mr. Rinopoulos, came with his teammates to congratulate him further. There was a big party that night for the team.

When the marathon started, the Greeks needed a victory to repeat their Balkan Games win of 1933, when they had routed Yugoslavia, 169–107. This time, the games were closer, despite a record-setting effort by Mandikas.

Kyriakides' victory was worth twelve points and gave Greece the win over Yugoslavia again, this time by only 164–155. It was another Balkan title, cherished by countries that saw the games as their own version of the Olympics and a symbol of important bragging rights and pride. The Greeks in 1934 set ten Balkan records, finishing far ahead of Romania, Turkey, Bulgaria, and Albania. The only record not broken by a Greek was by the Yugoslavian Stepenovich, in the hammer.

Stylianos Kyriakides, hoisted upon the shoulders of his friends, including the discus thrower Syllas and the hurdler Mandikas, was the champion of all the Balkan countries, only twenty-four, a young, handsome man with a shy heart, big smile, and long stride, with curly, black hair and a growing belief he could be one of the best long-distance runners in the world, with his natural talent and his drive to excel. He held an olive branch in his hand and allowed himself the start of a smile. It was a long way from Cyprus now.

Their jocular prerace optimism notwithstanding, the Serbs were gracious and gave them a wonderful meal and were very friendly. What made it especially sweet was that Greece won the Balkan Games, thanks largely to Kyriakides' high point win in the marathon, his first victory in that race.

This was not a team made up of aristocrats or athletes from affluent families. They came from poor families, united by their backgrounds as workers and as disciplined men who wanted to use athletics to achieve excellence. As one headline read:

ΟΙ ΠΡΟΤΑΘΛΗΤΑΙ ΜΑΣ ΕΙΝΕ ΟΛΟΙ ΦΤΟΧΟΠΑΙΔΑ
ΕΧΟΝΤΑ ΑΝΑΓΚΗΝ ΕΡΓΑΣΙΑΣ ΔΙΑ ΝΑ ΖΟΥΝ

[Our Champion Athletes Are All Poor Boys;
They Need Work So They Can Live]

Besides Kyriakides, son of a poor farmer who had to leave his family's home as a teenager to work as a servant, there was Nanos, a five-thousand-meter runner, who was a waiter; Silas, who worked in a village coffee shop; Arvanites, a gardener; and Mandikas, Georgacopoulos, Petropoulos, Skiathas, and Travlos, sons of working-class families who knew hard work and discipline.

Upon returning to Greece, on September 5, 1934, there was a big celebration and reception for the team, the band playing the national anthem. They were hailed throughout the country and they were cheered wherever they went. At the railroad station in Athens, people were standing on top of train cars, waving and cheering, the happiness washing over the team and the masses. Men raised their right fists in the air in exultation and boys dressed in shorts jockeyed for a precarious position on the railcar tops to see the champions as the train pulled into the station. Greece, a poor country with a glorious past, had triumphed again, not long from devastating wars against other Balkan nations, and from World War I.

Kyriakides cried because he was a sensitive man, and his teammates were similarly affected as people waving flags and bursting with pride

Kyriakides took this photo himself of adoring Greek fans waiting for the Balkan champion Greek team returning to Athens in the mid-1930s. Courtesy of the Kyriakides family.

swamped them. The team was hustled to the mayor's office where the minister of education congratulated them too.

There he made a sacred promise he would one day bring a greater victory to Greece. "I will be in a bigger stadium someday and I will bring back a bigger victory for Greece," he said.

Not long after, he had a chance to be photographed with Greece's other great runner, Spiridon Loues, the marathon champion of the first modern Olympic Games in 1896. Loues, in a white shirt and blue vest and still displaying his wide mustache, had his arm on Kyriakides' shoulder. The young runner looked in awe.

The photograph came after a meeting on a sunny afternoon in the Athenian suburb of Marousi, where Loues was still working, as a goodwill ambassador for the city. Even nearly forty years after his great win

The two great Greek marathon champions, Kyriakides and the winner of the first modern Olympics, Spiridon Loues (left), finally met to share advice about running. Courtesy of the Kyriakides family.

that had galvanized the country, Loues was a mesmerizing figure and one of the most recognized people in Greece, with a wrinkled, handsome face and bright sparkling eyes.

When they met, in a private room, it was dramatic and emotional for both; the young runner was suddenly compared with the greatest athletic hero of Greece. Loues made him feel comfortable, grasping the victor of Zagreb with a tight hug, stepping back to smile and say, "Καλως τη λεβεντια" [Welcome, brave young man].

It was a warm term of endearment and the two took an instant liking to each other, although the wizened veteran, Loues, was so emotional that he tried to hide his tears of joy. "You remind me of what happened years ago," Loues said, taken back to his own great triumph.

Kyriakides looked at him respectfully and suddenly bent his face to kiss Loues' hand in respect, an act that touched the old man whose deeds generations before had brought Greece into a new century. Kyriakides put his hand on Loues' shoulder gently, in thanks.

"Someday, we will come to reach your age, grandfather," said Kyriakides. "And my victory in Zagreb will be nothing more than a memory to me," he added, knowing where Loues stood in Greek history.

Loues paused a moment to accept the congratulations. Then, he said softly, "We Greeks were born to run. We will run and we will always run." The emotion was genuine, and Loues reached up and, with a masculine turn, twisted the corner of his big mustache with his right hand, his lips upturned in a tight, wry irony and remembrance of his own deeds, looking at Kyriakides with approval. It was an important act for the young man, and the photograph touched people.

Kyriakides was offered a job in the office of the mayor of Athens, to be paid without working. He refused at first. "I will only accept if I am a permanent member of the staff and working, because I don't like not working." His terms were accepted, and he went to work there—but not for long, and not before going back to Cyprus, where he was hailed again. This time, his friends called him Mr. Kyriakides.

> Circumstances rule men; men do not rule circumstances
> —Herodotus

Kyriakides did not rest long on his laurels. He started training almost right away for a meet against Hungary, where his coach Simitsek would meet again some of his colleagues from his homeland. Kyriakides was living off the three-thousand drachmas a month from his job as an aide in the mayor's office, and sending five-hundred drachmas a month home to his family in Cyprus. The balance was little enough to live on but he had the room in Panathenaic Stadium and needed little to sustain himself, and he had the camaraderie of teammates and other young men who shared a common experience in track and field.

In Hungary, Kyriakides won the ten-kilometer with a new Balkan record of 33:49:02 and then won a thirty-kilometer race, about twenty miles, in 1:56:35. Kyriakides said he would have preferred to be at a meet in Norway because he wanted a chance to run against the 1932

Olympic champion of the Los Angeles games, an Argentinian named Carlos Zabala.

In November 1934, Kyriakides took part in a meet in the Greek port city of Volos, in the northern Aegean, and won the fifteen-hundred-meter, the equivalent of almost a mile, in 4:30:02, and on November 11 ran an astonishing 29:45 in the ten-kilometer, which the Greeks claimed was a world record. The stopwatches were sent to Athens to be checked because the time would have been twenty seconds faster than that set by the great Finn Paavo Nurmi. No new record was ever documented.

Kyriakides was twenty-four now and the talk of Greece. Simitsek felt he was a potential Olympic champion and European rivals talked about Kyriakides' machinelike style of running, his quiet intensity, and the way he would never relent from the pace he believed should be set. His eyes always seemed set on a distant target they could not see. There were no rewards for the athletes and it was not even always possible to eat right or enough because they had to work for a living while they were training.

He was thinking about the 1936 Olympics that would be held in Berlin, even as talk of a burgeoning anti-Semitism in Germany was surfacing throughout Europe, heightening tension and bringing worry to athletes and politicians alike.

There were greater fears for the Jews, including the scores of thousands of them, many from Romaniot backgrounds, who lived in Greece's second largest city, Thessalonika, one of the most cosmopolitan places in Europe, and a major urban crossroads between Europe, the Balkans, and the Middle East.

Kyriakides was living a Spartan bachelor's life, staying in the stadium room and working out and occasionally going back to Cyprus. By 1935, he had wearied of the work in the mayor's office and wanted something he felt was more productive and would get him outside more to meet with people. He found a job as a bill collector for the Athens-Piraeus Electricity Company. This would take him door-to-door in Athens's neighborhoods, where he quickly became a friendly presence and surprise to clients who knew of his spreading fame as a runner.

Kyriakides had his eyes set first, though, on the 1935 Balkan Games and a chance to repeat as the marathon champion. First, he went back to Cyprus for a visit, before the May games. Kyriakides had to take a boat from Cyprus to Alexandria, Egypt, and then to Athens. He was losing training time to traveling and only had a day in Egypt to take a run to keep himself in race shape.

Alone on the boat, he had no one to talk with about the games and when he arrived in Athens, there was no one to meet him or greet him or thank him. He got on a bus, alone, and went to the SEGAS offices of the Greek amateur athletic federation, walked in, and put down his suitcase.

"Here I am," he said simply.

A surprised official came up and told him, "You will run in the marathon." That was it. No special conditions, no support. Kyriakides was given a poor room in a hotel and thirty-five drachmas a day for food, not even enough for the green bean soup, his *fasolatha*. Shy to being almost withdrawn, Kyriakides nevertheless was angry enough to complain that he and his teammates needed more to be able to compete. His complaints as a team leader were taken seriously and conditions improved for them.

Kyriakides was happiest running and now came his chance again to run against other Balkan champions whom he had gotten to know so well the past few years when he had stepped out of the shadows of track and cross-country running in Cyprus to the track and road and the interest of challenges from other runners, some of whom were nearly as good as he. The running was done over dusty, uneven dirt roads that created obstacles and made smooth running impossible.

But when the games came—and just before the start of the marathon—the Yugoslavians again protested his participation under the flag of Greece, although their protest the year before, in their own homeland, had been denied by the international officials overseeing the games. But this time, to the surprise of Kyriakides and his teammates, the Greeks accepted the protest and it looked as if he would not run at all, a cruel disappointment after his training and the circuitous trip that took him to Greece.

A sudden compromise was reached, allowing him to run officially—

and two minutes behind the other runners, including his old rival, the Romanian Gal. By the time he was allowed to even begin, he was six-hundred to eight-hundred meters behind, an impossible gap against world-class runners in an event in which two minutes could be the difference between winning and finishing back in the pack, even for a runner of his stature.

Kyriakides ran like a man possessed, the anger and disappointment cutting into his heart as he ran in the homeland he considered his, on the soil where he had won and run before, in front of Greeks and in the city and to the stadium where Greeks had run for their country. By the end, he had passed all the other runners except Gal and was closing hard on him when the finish came. He was second, twenty-seven seconds behind, finishing in 3:08:07.

Despite the handicap of running behind Gal, the close loss gave Kyriakides new impetus to do well in the London marathon in July, where he would compete in the Amateur Athletic Association games, one of the most prestigious for European runners and members of the United Kingdom and British Commonwealth.

In London, there was intense heat and a stiff breeze for the race held at the White City stadium, famous for the 1908 Olympic marathon run of Italian Pietro Dorando, who collapsed at the end and was disqualified after race officials helped the staggering man cross the finish line.

On this day, forty prime runners, including the Scotsman who had won three consecutive times, D. McNab Robertson, were competing. But the heat would be too much for many who either had to walk part of the way or who would drop out altogether.

With runners trying to survive the ferocious heat as much as anything, the two leaders after $22\frac{1}{2}$ miles were the English veteran A. J. Norris and the man newspapers described as "Near Eastern champion, Kyriakides, of Cyprus." The heat made both occasionally slow to a near walk and Kyriakides, after falling behind by some distance, managed to close to within two-hundred yards of Norris late in the race, but the Greek was still far behind when Norris came into the last lap of the stadium about a half lap ahead of Kyriakides.

Here the Greek showed his mettle. Sweating and gasping, his body radiating heat, Kyriakides started a furious charge at Norris, who, as the papers said, "could only jog-trot," he was so dead. Kyriakides' long stride and big heart had him closing the gap by yards at a time and it seemed he would impossibly catch Norris in front of twenty-five-thousand spectators in the stadium. The Greek closed half the distance in the stadium alone and Norris was almost fainting from the prospect of being caught as much as fading in the heat of the midday.

Kyriakides was gaining visibly and fast when an excited supporter came running toward him on the track, stopped by race officials, but throwing him off stride just a little, a critical pause when he was in the midst of chasing down Norris like a hunting dog on the scent of a deer just ahead.

Norris managed to wallow across in the astonishingly slow time of 3:02:57, more than a half hour behind the usual time for the world-class runners. Kyriakides' kick brought him in second, only twenty-two seconds behind. Only five men finished, the rest debilitated and beaten by the heat while Kyriakides, almost overcome himself, pushed through. A British publication, *The Sporting Life*, wrote that "only Kyriakides, the Cypriot stayer, had any spirit left at the finish."

He was even invited to try out for the 1936 British Olympic team, a right to which he was entitled as a citizen of Cyprus. He did not accept.

Fortune is not on the side of the faint-hearted

—Sophocles

While Kyriakides was cruising to the championships of the Balkans, a slight, shy Irish-American with a gap-toothed grin named Johnny Kelley was becoming one of the top runners in the United States, with his eye on the Berlin games as well. There would be some startling similarities between the two runners and their lives, and how their running paths would cross.

Kelley came from a poor family and had to line his shoes with newspapers to hide the holes in the soles when he was a child. He was the eldest of a family of five boys and five girls raised in West Medford, just outside Boston. His father, William, was a mailman and Kelley sometimes accompanied him on his route.

The boy was slightly built and was showing a propensity for running when other kids were playing baseball. He ran track for Medford High before the family moved to adjoining Arlington.

In 1921, when he was fourteen, his father took him to watch the marathon in Boston, which was called the American Marathon. They took the streetcar to Commonwealth Avenue, near the finish line on Exeter Street in the brick row-house boulevards in Boston's prestigious Back Bay. The boy couldn't see well, but he remembered the ephemeral look on the face of winner Frank Zuna and got excited about the idea of running for fun.

In 1923, Kelley ran the six-hundred- and thousand-yard events at Medford High before the family moved to neighboring Arlington, where he ran cross-country, the mile and two-mile events and began to do well. He achieved early success as an athlete, but after school had to go to work, pumping gas at a station just across from the high school.

When he graduated, he tried to find steady work, but the economy was heading toward a depression. He took to running road races, finding plenty of competition because many of the country's best runners were in the area.

In 1928, at 5'6" and 121 pounds, he ran his first marathon, on St. Patrick's Day, in Rhode Island. He finished seventeenth in 3:17, fading toward the end. A month later, he made his first attempt in Boston, but dropped out only a couple of miles from the finish, and quit again in 1932, this time little more than halfway into the race after staying near the lead.

He was working now in a florist shop and sharing a room with his brother in his father's house, but running gave him a drive in another direction. Because he had to work, Kelley was logging less than sixty miles a week in training, conventional for the time when runners thought more arduous training would lessen their stamina in a marathon.

In 1933, Kelley tried the Boston Marathon again, this time finishing thirty-seventh with a time of 3:03:56, hardly a world-class effort. But he was persistent.

In 1934, as Kyriakides was becoming the champion runner of countries half a world away, Kelley made a hard charge for the Boston Marathon championship. He almost chased down a Canadian immigrant from Finland, Dave Komonen, who had finished second the year before. Kelley faltered on the Newton hills of the tough Boston course and finished four minutes behind, but his time of 2:36:50 was almost a half hour faster than the year before and got him second place and notoriety as a runner to be watched.

In 1935, the field included Komonen and Kelley again, along with 1933 winner Leslie Pawson. It was a time of continuing depression in the United States and the world, even in Germany, where Adolf Hitler was starting a rise to political power amidst much unrest and economic upheaval. Running was a pleasant distraction, not just for the runners, but for the masses. It was free entertainment and high talk.

Kelley was more confident in 1935, and would have been more so if he knew the troubles that had befallen Pawson, with whom he had become good friends, and Komonen. Pawson had suffered a stress fracture earlier in the year and Komonen had missed a night of sleep driving down from Canada when his car got stuck in a blizzard. Kelley also was undergoing a new regimen of special baths and diets after consulting with specialists at a Belmont hospital, near Boston.

For the race, he had a coach who advised him to stay with the leaders through Wellesley and then break away. He had special shoes, custom-made for running by a seventy-year-old Englishman, Samuel T. A. Ritchens, who was living in Peabody, north of Boston. The STAR shoes were the inspiration too of marathoner Jock Semple, who worked for a shoe company in Beverly, the city next to Peabody, in a time when New England shoe companies were the envy of the world. Runners had only stiff, heavy shoes that had to be carefully broken in before long races. Bad shoes were a marathoner's biggest problem, not conditioning. After a lot of research, Ritchens produced shoes with a breakthrough in design and lacing and which weighed only $5^{1}/_{2}$ ounces and cost the huge sum of $7.50, but Kelley thought they would give him a huge advantage, and they would. What he didn't know was that his biggest competition in 1935 would come from a little-known marathon champion from Maryland named Pat Dengis.

A Good Friday date that April 19 cut the usual crowd of five-hundred-thousand almost in half, although the weather was ideal. Kelley started off in third place, while Dengis bided his time in thirteenth for the early part of the race. Kelley gradually moved to the lead while Dengis set his sights on him and caught him from behind near Wellesley— where Kelley had wanted to make his move.

Dengis started to pull away when he developed a stitch, a pain, in his side that stopped him like a knife. Kelley resurged and took the lead but then the stitch went away and Dengis came at him again, at the Newton hills, more than seventeen miles into the race. But Kelley held on and kept the lead as he came into Kenmore Square, the twenty-five-mile mark where there were huge crowds in a collection of streets near Fenway Park, where the Red Sox were playing. Kelley had stopped to vomit fifteen chocolate glucose tablets he had taken for energy during his long run. But then he stood up, blessed himself with the sign of the cross, and sped on to the finish, ahead of the officials so there was no tape at the line. Kelley finished first in 2:32:07 while Dengis came on strong and finished in 2:34:11, refusing medical attention and telling officials, "Hell no, let's run this thing all over again." Then he laughed exuberantly and remarked at the irony, "Where's Johnny, I've got to see Johnny! Would you imagine this: a *florist* runs twenty-six miles—for a laurel wreath."

The wreath was placed on his head by a local restaurant and hotel owner and state legislator, a Greek-American named George Demeter—who would soon become important to Kyriakides—and who had suggested the crown as a way of linking his own heritage with the history of marathon running, to put a Greek tone to it. Demeter ran alongside him at the end as the winner crossed the finish line, trying to line up the wreath with the bobbing head. Demeter longed to put the wreath on the head of a winning Greek runner.

Kelley's joy was short-lived because his somber side set in. "I know this marathon glory will be over in a few days, so I've got to make the best of it." It would take a year before he knew just how true that was.

In 1936, as Kyriakides was becoming famous in the Balkans and Europe, Kelley was the defending champion of the Boston Marathon. But the race this year would belong to Ellison Myers "Tarzan" Brown, a Narraganset Indian from Rhode Island, who devastated the split times at every checkpoint to finish in 2:33:40, while Kelley faded to fifth after trying to keep pace and expecting the fast-running Brown to burn out. It was left to William "Biddie" McMahon of Worcester to try to catch Brown. He couldn't, but his second-place time of 2:35:27 got him on the Olympic team for the games in Berlin. Kelley's place on the team was in jeopardy as he faded to fifth, behind Mel Porter, whom he'd beaten eleven of twelve times, and little-known Leo Giard.

Kelley had made a tactical mistake in the 1936 Boston Marathon, getting too exuberant when Indian followers of Brown put on Indian headdresses and beat tom-toms, spooking Kelley to try to catch up too fast on the hills in Newton. He did get Brown to slow down in the latter legs of the race and, over a three-mile period, Kelley cut Brown's lead in half. The acceleration was cutting into Kelley's stamina and reserve, and then he caught the Indian, tapped him on the shoulder, and said, "Nice running boy, now let a real man take over." It was a mistake.

Brown slipped back but bided his time and caught Kelley at the last of the Newton hills, prompting Boston Globe sportswriter Paul "Jerry" Nason to dub the more-than-slight rise "heartbreak hill" after Kelley's demise there. Within not too many blocks, Kelly was walking and looking for water and oranges, and walking side-to-side in drunken exhaustion, but not giving up. He would not repeat as champion, but his heart would take him to Berlin.

But not before he had to prove himself once again. In May, Kelley had to compete in another marathon, in Washington, D.C., and had to win or show well to get on the Olympic team. McMahon won while Kelley finished second, but Porter was third and the selection committee had to choose between Porter and Kelley for the third spot on the marathon team going to Berlin. The victories by Brown and McMahon had given them berths.

Kelley was puzzled why he wouldn't be an automatic selection with his career record, but went back to work in the florist shop where he was notified he had made the team. His tactical mistakes in Boston almost cost him. He'd made another friend in the past year though, someone who was influential and whose works would further Kelley's career.

It was Nason, who had started writing about the event in 1932, standing in a phone booth in Kenmore Square, at the twenty-five-mile mark, where he could phone in the probable winners. Nason was twenty-six in 1935 when he was assigned to be the paper's lead writer on the marathon and track. He most coveted the Boston race and wrote extensively about it in a new way, capturing the motivations of runners and covering their trials and tribulations as amateurs who ran for nothing except the love of the sport.

After Kelley's first win in 1935, Nason wrote about him as "the Arlington Irishman with the twinkling eye and the chipmunk's saucy grin," and told readers in great detail about Kelley's family and background, explaining *why* someone would want to run 26 miles, 385 yards—and do the hundreds of miles of training that led to the arduous event.

Nason was an elegant and refined man, with just a bit of a George Raft tough-guy hard look in his eye, thick black hair, and dressed impeccably, right down to his soft, wide-brimmed fedora with a silk sash, understated club ties, and long wool overcoat he wore for the frequent cool April days of the race, where he rode in a Studebaker with other *Globe* sportswriters. His writing was elevating the marathon in Boston and gaining him notoriety as a chronicler of the event and road racing.

> All that one gains by falsehood is not to be believed when he speaks the truth
>
> —Aristotle

In 1936, the world's attention was turning to the Olympic Games in Berlin. Kyriakides was aiming for them too and dedicated himself to training, showing he might be a contender when, in May, he won the five-kilometer, ten-kilometer, and the marathon in the Pan-Hellenic Games, where the Greeks were selecting their best for the Olympics.

These games were critical to establishing a persona of dominance for the Third Reich and for Adolf Hitler, especially because the Germans had never performed well, belying their image of superiority. The Americans had always dominated since the games' modern inception forty years before and it rankled the führer and German officials, who desperately wanted to win and show well. The Germans also brought a ruthless efficiency to the games, the model for much of the evil that would follow in World War II.

The Nazis were especially anxious about the presence of American blacks, whom they called Negroes and who they felt were inferior and almost subhuman. The games were also, really for the first time, designed to impress foreigners, especially the hundreds of journalists, at a time when Hitler had already begun his imperialistic plans.

He wanted to dazzle everyone with the model of organization of the Nazi state. Hitler, of course, would approve everything, but the games belonged to Dr. Carl Diem, chief of the organizing committee, and to Hitler's personal film director, a woman, Leni Riefenstahl, who would film the eleventh Olympiad.

The Germans also emulated the ancient Greeks in the sense of athleticism being crucial in a well-rounded culture featuring beauty, including its physical form and expression of the body. Winning was also paramount and repeat victors were regarded almost as gods, with statues and inscriptions of their names on columns in their home cities a commonplace tribute.

Sports had a militaristic value because they prepared young people with the rigors of sacrifice and self-discipline and behaving in step with a model set of ideals, just as for the ancient Greeks the games were much akin to battle. Hitler, for all his dementia, admired the Greeks, especially their belief in combining physical excellence with intellectual achievement. The Greeks identified the spirit as *"nous e eyees en somatee eeyee,"* which meant "a sound mind in a solid body."

The Nazis placed the games on a stage where they could symbolize what they felt was their superiority, including the ornate festivities. And, for the first time, the results were ranked, to the dismay of international Olympic officials because the Germans knew their athletes would do well outside of track and field in events such as gymnastics, shooting, and yachting, and up the medal count.

The games would try to put a mask of respectability on the evil of Hitler and his supporters. They would also bring jingoism to unprecedented heights and begin a modern era of superpatriotism in sports, interrupted by World War II. It was a bitter irony, of course, to the proposed ideal of international sports leading to world peace, and the antithesis of how the modern games had begun, in 1896.

A Frenchman, Baron Pierre de Coubertin, sought to revive the ancient Greek Olympic Games, which had begun in 776 B.C. He believed the Pheidippides story and, urged by his friend, historian Michel Breal, persuaded the Athens Organizing Committee to have a marathon race to represent Pheidippides' run and Greece's victory over Persia. That was only after the Greeks got word that the Frenchman wanted to stage the first games at the 1900 World's Fair in Paris in his home country.

With de Coubertin's urging, the marathon became one of the official nine sports of the modern Olympics of 1896 held in Athens. Breal offered a silver cup as a prize to the marathon winner who would prevail in a race that would cover the same plains, hills, and mountains Pheidippides ran, forty kilometers, or twenty-five miles.

On April 10, 1896, there were seventeen entrants, including Loues, who had fasted and prayed before the race. The hundred thousand spectators at the marble Panathenaic Stadium also included members of the Boston Athletic Association (BAA), there to watch two of their members on the U.S. team. There were nine Americans, the other seven coming from Harvard and Princeton Universities, but the competition was so stirring the BAA officials got the idea for the Boston Marathon.

Loues trailed most of the race, and an anxious crowd in the marble stadium knew little of the drama being played out on the course as he closed on the leaders. Suddenly, a horseman came galloping into the stadium and yelled, "Hellene! Hellene!" The leader at the marble entrance to the stadium appeared to exuberant shouts. "A Greek! A Greek!" It was Loues. The crowd was hysterical. Prince George and Crown Prince Constantine jumped out of the royal box, one on each side of the dusty Loues, and ran with him to the finish line, their royalty forgotten as they joined in the joy.

Loues' time was 2:58:50. The victory not only brought glory to Greece, but also served as an inspiration to keep the Olympic movement alive through the difficult times it faced over the next twelve years, and carried de Coubertin's dream into the twentieth century.

In the modern era, after the Athens games of 1896, and especially after Stockholm in 1912, the games started to become more organized and keep their high moral tone, even if they were dominated early on by men who had the money and the means to train and take time off to compete in an amateur event that was costly to them and their families, and little supported by their governments.

World War I interrupted this, and an agonized de Coubertin declared that the games he restarted would not be held in 1916 as scheduled—in Berlin. When they reconvened four years later in 1920, it was in Antwerp, although the Belgians had suffered greatly in the war. It was the first time a new Olympic flag, five rings depicting the major continents, was flown. No Germans or Austrians were invited. In these games Paavo Nurmi won double gold in the ten-thousand meters and cross-country and established himself as a legendary running star. He would build upon these victories four years later in Paris, where he won the cross-country race one day, and the next day won the fifteen hundred-meter and five thousand-meter races within two hours.

After a successful games in Amsterdam in 1928, the cash-strapped Americans, relying on contributions and government loans, were determined to make the next games in the United States a success, and built a 104,000-seat stadium in Los Angeles with the best surfaces and equipment and auditoriums, and a special new Olympic village for living accommodations, setting new standards for camaraderie among athletes. With Hollywood nearby, there was an air of celebrity too, and the studios sent movies for the competitors to enjoy and learn about American hospitality. The Americans copied an Athenian touch from 1896, releasing hundreds of white pigeons, adding a Hollywood touch—the first Olympic flame.

The Germans, despite an increased effort at improving athletic facilities in a country also torn by depression after the 1929 crash of the stock market in America, fared much poorer than expected in Los Angeles, although Arthur Jonath finished third in the hundred-meter race, behind two American black athletes, Eddie Tolan and Ralph Metcalfe. Still, the lagging performance of their athletes made German officials wring their hands in disappointment, especially because many Olympic records were smashed in the sensational American games. But it was not just sports Germans were interested in at Los Angeles.

Dr. Theodor Lewald, president of the German Olympic Committee, and Diem, a renowned sports historian, were busy observing and recording virtually every architectural and logistic aspect of the infrastructure and organization, impressed by the American zeal and cooperation and desire to please the foreign guests and officials.

The two men felt they had been robbed of the 1916 games and, as they returned to Berlin, were met again with political upheaval and the burgeoning rise of the Third Reich, making them anxious that, once again, there would be no games in Germany, although the International Olympic Committee had awarded the games to Berlin over Spain. Compounding their problem was the economic strife in Germany, with the collapse of the Weimar Republic and an unemployment rate of 20 percent in 1932.

Ignoring the rise in anti-Semitism and open railing against Jews that should have provoked a more serious warning, other countries were preoccupied with trying to overcome their own economic chaos. The virulence of the hate was powerful indeed, and extended to athletics too, first with the banning of Jewish boxers and referees and then barring Jews from all athletic endeavors, including admittance to Garmisch-Partenkirchen, which would be an Olympic site. The Nazis were not going to give any credence to athletic prowess by the Jews.

Social disruption and fear of a Communist rise led to growing support for Adolf Hitler, concurrent with a rise in militarism and a new bombast and nationalism, and a jump in membership in the Nazi party after the depression fueled by the 1929 market collapse. Even then, Hitler loved the pomp and circumstance of ceremony and attendant pageantry, which he had used in his beer hall speeches to whip crowds into a fervor. An oratory skill and genius for organization and delegating authority to zealots pushed toward the 1936 games and their intent for Germany. These Olympics would be a worldwide stage to show off Aryanism. The German people were responding with delirious acquiescence, believing they would triumph.

There was little dissension among other countries at the burgeoning anti-Semitism and totalitarianism of Germany, although Spain, which had lost its bid to host the games, said no team would be sent to Berlin. Hitler found a kindred spirit in Japan, which was using the same kind of militaristic fervor and athleticism to unite its country.

There was strong protest in the United States against Nazi policies, especially the removal of Lewald from his post as head of the German Olympic Committee because of some Jewish ancestry, although he was a Christian and widely admired by the German people. Although American officials were trying to organize support for removal of the games from Germany for discrimination against Jewish athletes, there was a strong sense that the games must go on despite governmental policies in the host country. This worried Hitler, who wanted a massive building project for the games under way.

Despite continuing unrest among the Americans about the games, they assembled a team. In Greece, Kyriakides, as his country's greatest runner, was given the honor of bringing from the daily newspaper *Kathemerini* the replica of an ancient Greek warrior's helmet to be presented to the winner of the marathon in Berlin. The award was especially significant because Greece could barely afford to send its athletes.

The games linked ancient Greece and the new Germany, fitting for a country that had a long history of Hellenophile admiration. An exhibit that opened in Berlin in 1935 included many murals of ancient Olympia and ancient Greek Olympic heroes, paralleled with the best of Germany. But the centerpiece of the 1936 games would be the new stadium, which was the nucleus of a vast complex of facilities and adjacent playing fields and sporting arenas. It was called the *Reichssportfeld* and was designed by Werner March. Hanging ominously over the five linked Olympic rings, the symbol of the games, was the heavy, foreboding sign of the Nazis, a brooding eagle.

While this was going on in Germany and Kyriakides and his team-mates were trying to prepare themselves for the competition, the Greek government on July 20 had fifteen maidens in Olympia place a huge reflector that brought the rays of the sun to a point where a torch inside ignited with the flame of the games, to be carried to Berlin, after an oration written by de Coubertin which cited the eternality of Hellenism and the Olympic spirit. A scantily clad young boy carried the torch toward Athens, starting a twelve-day odyssey of three thousand kilometers to the Berlin stadium. It was almost time for the games to begin. The torch would be carried its last leg by a blond Berliner with accompanying runners in unison until he paraded into the Olympic stadium at 6:30 P.M. on August 2, the opening day.

The Americans were sending a strong team, anchored by the great black sprinter Jesse Owens, including Johnny Kelley and Tarzan Brown, two veterans of the Boston Marathon, and the third marathoner, William McMahon. The Americans came by boat and whiled away the time running on deck and hosting talent and variety shows, where Kelley tried to persuade Owens to come on-stage. Kelley sang "Now Is the Hour," but couldn't persuade Owens to participate, although the great runner took a liking to Kelley and he came into his room to talk about the differences in running sprints and long distances.

Often though, the talk on the ship would turn to the games, to Hitler, and to the growing world tension over the ominous Nazi presence and rising tide of racism and anti-Semitism in Germany. Many of the Americans were wary and wanted to make a strong showing for the United States. For Kelley and his colleagues, though, there was time yet for levity and enjoying their experience.

Owens looked down at the three pairs of running shoes Kelley brought. "Can I try them on, Johnny?" Owens said, wanting to feel the difference from his spiked sprinters.

"Sure, Jesse," Kelley said, grinning and glad to have the team's star show an interest. Owens said, "I want to go up on the deck with them."

Kelley tried to dissuade him. "You're not supposed to. The roll of the ship will give you sore ankles," Kelley said. But Owens insisted and Kelley relented.

Owens, big and strong, tried to stretch his foot into the shoe when he heard a rip. The counter at the back of the shoe had ripped, tearing open the back of the shoe. An embarrassed Owens apologized but Kelley, unflappable as ever, told him not to worry and got help from a crew member to sew it back in place, if a little raggedly.

Later, they talked again and Owens told him how he had gotten his name and Owens said a teacher had misunderstood when he had given his name as "J. C. Owens," and the teacher replied, "Oh, you mean Jesse Owens."

When the games began, Hitler appeared in a huge open touring car, outside the stadium, and walked over to the competitors forming ranks for their entrance through a wide entrance that was called the Marathon Gate, before he entered with the fanfare of trumpets and the start of a special hymn written and orchestrated by Richard Strauss, followed by the clanging of a huge bell cast just for the event.

The Greeks, as always, entered first, the athletes wearing dark blue blazers. After the teams assembled on the parade field, the crowd heard from an ill de Coubertin, from Lausanne, over a recording played to them. "The important thing in the Olympic Games is not to win, but to take part, just as the most important thing about life is not to conquer, but to struggle well."

After a stirring ceremony with a hundred thousand people watching, a small, thin man with a proud mustache, dressed in a white-skirted *fustanella*, black vest, and black boots appeared from the Greek delegation, carrying some greenery. It was Loues, who had been near the front of the Greek team. His wizened face was wet as he cried for joy. He was led to Hitler and gave him a sprig of wild olive from Mount Olympus, home of the gods, offering it to the führer with the words "I present this to you as a symbol of love and peace. We hope that the nations will ever meet solely in such peaceful competition."

For once, Hitler was emotional and grasped Loues' hand, as a rousing performance of the "Hallelujah Chorus" reverberated throughout the stadium. It was part of the favored music of the games, which featured predominantly German composers. One display proudly boomed Beethoven's Ninth Symphony, the "Ode to Joy," and became an ironic watchword of games being conducted peacefully even as Hitler schemed for a conquest and domination of much of European mankind.

Kelley, standing with the American contingent, was flabbergasted to see Loues, one of his heroes, and he almost cried at the spectacle. He couldn't believe he was seeing the winner of the first modern Olympic marathon. It was a sight he would never forget, even down to the last detail of clothing Loues wore.

On the Greek team, Kyriakides fingered his Olympic credentials, a simple identity card that bore his picture under the title *Olympia Ausweis*, the five Olympic rings, his name, and affiliation with the Greek team. He would carry it in his pocket after the games, a memento that would let the world know he was an Olympic athlete, and one who had competed in Berlin in front of Adolf Hitler.

Now it was time for the struggling to begin.

The games would belong to Owens, who would win four gold medals, in the hundred and two-hundred-meter races, the long jump and, as a last-moment replacement, in the four-hundred-meter relay where two American Jews, Sam Stoller and Marty Glickman, fast runners indeed, were taken off for dubious reasons amidst much speculation that even the Americans did not want to offend Hitler. Stoller and Glickman had finished ahead of the men who replaced them, Ralph Metcalfe and Foy Draper, in the American trials and were bitter about the change. Some American officials thought it best to make changes and not offend Hitler. The decision split the American team. So Kelley was surprised when Owens came over to him at one point and said, "Hitler waved to me, and I waved back," and smiled impishly at the marathoner.

Led by Owens's leadoff, the American team won by so much that there was renewed anger over the replacement of Stoller and Glickman, for the Americans would have won by a large margin anyway. The anger subsided somewhat when Owens, who barely qualified for the long jump, overcame German friend Lutz Long with a monumental last jump to win the gold, and embarrass Hitler and the Nazis, who did not want a black man overcoming their Aryan heroes. Heroically, Long strolled arm-in-arm with Owens.

The marathon was still a prestige event, and Kyriakides, the champion of the Balkans, felt he would do well. Early on, he became friends with a Korean, Kee Chung Sohn, who was being forced to use a Japanese name of Kitei Son and to run under that country's flag rather than his own, for the Japanese imperialism had overtaken his Korean homeland.

The Nazi government went to great detail in preparing the games and on August 9, 1936, the marathon was conducted at 3:00 P.M. The race started in the stadium at Reichsportsfeld, following the Havel River, along Havel Chausse, turning onto Avus Sudschleife and back through Berlin. Every competitor had to turn over a certificate from a doctor before the start of the run to show they were physically qualified.

Refreshment stations included five liters each of tea, warm and cold, both unsweetened and sweetened with grape sugar, five liters of malt coffee, three liters each of orange juice and lemonade, warm gruel, and lumps of grape sugar in tablets. There were also oranges, bananas, water for drinking and washing, one washbasin, five sponges, ten towels and seventy-five drinking cups.

Kyriakides was captain of his team and the most highly regarded because of his experience throughout the Balkans. The Greeks thought he had a legitimate chance to win the Olympic marathon, although relatively little was known about many of the other competitors, including the two Koreans on the Japanese team, Sohn and Seung Yong Nam, identified by the Japanese as Shoryu Nan. There were fifty-six runners, including the American team of Johnny Kelley and Tarzan Brown from Rhode Island.

The dark-skinned Brown, an American Indian, was beset upon in a bar by a group of Nazis. He was tough and fought back furiously, but there were too many for him to take and when the police arrived, he was taken to jail along with his attackers. Kelley and American officials had to get him out so he could run and to avoid an international incident, which the Germans did not want. Brown thought he would get his revenge on the course.

Kelley was upset with the jerseys provided the runners. They were coarse and rough and rubbed the skin off the competitors and he didn't think he could stand it for twenty-six miles, through more than two

Boston Marathoner Johnny Kelley struck up a friendship with
Kyriakides at the 1936 Olympics in Berlin, where Kyriakides
took this photograph. Courtesy of the Kyriakides family.

hours of heat and sweating. Brown didn't wear his, but Kelley didn't
want to be unpatriotic and wore it, to his chagrin and discomfort.

At the starting line, milling about, Kelley noticed an intensely focused young man with jet-black curly hair. He introduced himself and
Kyriakides smiled back.

"Good luck," Kelley said shyly, holding out his hand, which was taken immediately by the Greek. They talked while waiting for the race to start. Kelley talked about the competition of the Boston Marathon and invited Kyriakides to come to Boston, and the Greek started thinking about the idea, then turned his attention back to the race.

One of the favorites was tiny Argentinian Carlos Zabala, who held the Olympic record of 2:31:36, which he set in Los Angeles four years before. There was also crafty Ernest Harper, a tight-faced Englishman, and several Finns, used to running together strategically to psychologically wear out opponents. The route would lead from the stadium, out onto Havel Chausse for thirty kilometers past the Kaiser Wilhelm turn, before turning back along the main road of Avus, a long straightaway back to the stadium, turning left only near the end at *Deutschlandhavle* to the stadium for the finish. The Germans had plenty of police and officials along the route to keep order. There would be nothing else before the eyes of Hitler and the Third Reich.

Zabala—and the American Brown—took the early lead with a fast pace, but Harper and Kitei Son hung in close. At sixteen miles, it looked as if Brown might win the gold medal, but he suddenly dropped out and later said he had a hernia. At the halfway mark, Harper and Son were chasing Zabala and Son passed Harper at a U-turn back toward the stadium, but the Finns were closing again, although they had laid off the lead for a long time, figuring on a fast finish to bring them home. Son and Harper caught Zabala, who had been running too hard, at the twenty-eight-kilometer mark, while Kyriakides was back in the pack with Kelley not far behind him. Simitsek had urged Kyriakides to keep a faster early pace than he normally liked, although the Greek preferred staying off the pace and pouring it on at the end. Early on, though, it was apparent he did not take Simitsek's advice and was staying off the lead, expecting he could charge hard at the end and still have enough time to catch the leaders. This was the first time, though he was running against Koreans and he didn't know that Son would not relent. Son kept up a driven pace and even the hard-driving finish of the Finns was not enough. Kyriakides never was able to measure up to his own hopes. Son kicked home with a new record of 2:29:12 and sprawled on the grass before getting up to run for the showers, not waiting for Harper, who came in second, 2:40 later. Nan came in third, only nine seconds behind the Englishman.

Only thirty-six runners finished the race. Kyriakides came in eleventh, while Kelley faded to seven places behind him and the two other Americans, Brown and McMahon, dropped out, as did eighteen other runners. Kelley collapsed on the grass at the end of the race and was startled when two big Germans came along to try to drag him away, following orders to get runners out of the way as soon as possible.

The little runner resisted. "Hey, put me down! Put me down!" he was yelling as they were taking him away, his scratchy shirt tearing at his chest in the sweat and heat of the finish.

It was not the finish Kyriakides envisioned, either. It got worse when Hitler shook the hands of the runners, something he did not do for black American track stars such as Owens, who had become the darling of the games—except to the Nazis. Kyriakides said his hand itched for a week. Kelley didn't like the idea either, and looked at Kyriakides and they blanched at what had happened.

Kyriakides was happy nonetheless, garnering many autographs in his official red-and-white program book, which had the insignia of the giant bell created for the games and the Nazi eagle over the Olympic rings. On the cover, it read *Ich rufe die Jugend der Welt*. It meant: I call upon the youth of the world. Kyriakides would bring it home to Athens and display it prominently in his house where everyone walking in could see he had competed in Berlin. The German language was large and visible.

On page four was a picture of Hitler and below it a slogan for the games: *Nur wer davernd nach Hoch stleistungen strebt, kann sich in der Welt durchsetzen*. "Only he who continually strives for higher accomplishments can succeed in the world."

Kyriakides, delighted in the spectacle of international competition, walked happily through the Olympic village, approaching other athletes. Among them were Owens, decathlete Glen Morris, Cornelius Johnson, John Woodruff, discus thrower Ken Carpenter, and four-hundred-meter freestyle swimmer Jack Modica, all of the United States, and many from other countries, including Chung, who signed as Kitei Son, and who was supposed to have been presented with the Spartan warrior's helmet, but never was. It disappeared, apparently expropriated by a covetous Nazi official. Chung had been slighted again.

For the Germans, the games were a riotous success and their team won the overall medal count with victories in minor sports such as gymnastics and yachting, although the Americans triumphed in the major and important categories. But Hitler, who was no athlete, saw something else in the many German wins. To him, there was a militaristic tinge to the victories. The Germans hadn't merely won the Olympic games. They had conquered the world.

Kyriakides went back to Athens disappointed with himself, but thinking there were the Balkan Games again, that he could compete in Tokyo in the next Olympics and tune his talents to be ready for international competition again.

He redeemed himself somewhat in the Balkans in October, back in Athens, winning the ten-kilometer, and taking the marathon title back from his Romanian rival, Gal. Kyriakides ran into Panathenaic Stadium, finishing before a gantlet of a hundred Evzones as an honor guard, being handed a Greek flag by a young boy who ran out to meet him, as the Greek Premier, Ioannis Metaxas, watched proudly. Kyriakides received a silver victory cup from King George. The Greeks easily won the games over Serbia.

In 1937, Kyriakides returned to London for the AAA marathon, finishing second there again. In the Pan-Hellenic Games, he won the marathon and the five-kilometer and ten-kilometer. Then Kyriakides went to Bucharest for the Balkan Games, which Greece won over Romania, where he won the marathon again on September 13, this time in 2:57:22. Then he ran around the stadium, holding an olive branch in his right hand and was hoisted on his teammates' shoulders. If not for his delayed start in 1935, he would have won four games consecutively.

Eleven days before Kyriakides' victory, de Coubertin was taking a walk in a park in Geneva, Switzerland, part of his daily routine. Suddenly, he clutched his hand to his chest, struggling with pain. He fell quickly to the ground, dead as he hit. Shortly afterward, in keeping with his wishes, he was buried in Lausanne. All except for his heart, which was taken to Greece, placed in an urn, and buried in sacred Greek soil in ancient Olympia, where the games had begun.

And now, Kyriakides started thinking about something Kelley had told him.

Come to Boston.

4

No Great Fortune Waits

Piraeus / New York / Boston 1938–Athens 1940

SEGAS, the Greek Amateur Athletic Association, wanted Kyriakides to go to Boston too, and officials made inquiries in Boston about who could host the runner. The first name that came up was that of the Demeter family, brothers who had come to the United States late in the nineteenth century and established themselves as businessmen and city leaders. Kyriakides contacted George Demeter through the Greek consulate in the city, and the series of events began that would bring the Greek runner to Boston.

The Demeter family was one of the most influential in Boston, from politics to business, and George was the most flamboyant, with his pencil-thin mustache and manicured Hollywood looks, the epitome of 1930s fashion style. Demeter loved his heritage, his Hellenism, which he fostered and promoted to anyone who would listen.

The Demeters came from the village of Vervitsa, Arcadia, in the Peloponnesus of Greece. Their family name was Demetracopoulos but was changed, as were so many others when immigrants came to the United States.

The Demeters knew the value of education too, especially George, who had a Socratic love of learning and went to the prestigious Boston Latin School, regarded as one of the finest high schools in the United States. There he led a school regiment in a parade in Boston and won the first prize, unheard of for a Greek immigrant in a city, and a school, still run by wealthy Yankee families.

With his Latin School education, George was accepted at Harvard, which he was able to afford because of the success of his brother Harry's restaurant, the Navarre Café on Columbus Avenue, a crowded avenue of brick buildings in Boston's South End.

George briefly went into the Canadian army before joining Harvard's ambulance corps during World War I, and was assigned to France, where he survived a gas attack. He returned to Harvard in 1918 to get his degree before going to Boston University Law School and then the Staley School in Brookline.

Meanwhile, the brothers were prospering in business. They were pictured standing in front of the café, next to an adjoining store, selling fruits and coffee, chocolates and cigarettes, looking like the proud Greek immigrants they were. With the success of the café, the brothers opened three restaurants along Huntington Avenue, the Irvington, St. James, and the Strand, and then, in 1929, the Minerva Hotel. The hotel, near Symphony Hall, the Christian Science Mother Church, Horticultural Hall, and the Museum of Fine Arts, was in the midst of an important social and cultural center of the city. The structure itself was one of the most beautiful in the city. There were bay windows with colorful orange awnings in front of columned arches over the windows and a light-colored stone face with gaslight-style streetlights in front. On the roof was a tall flagpole flying the American flag, which was visible throughout much of the city. The Demeters, especially George, a regal and imperial man who was somewhat aloof and austere, were becoming very prominent in Boston, and they were as proud of their American citizenship as their Hellenic heritage.

George used his growing notoriety and indefatigable style of wooing the city's politicians and elite business leaders, who liked to come to the brothers' restaurants, as a springboard into public life himself. In 1933, as a Republican, he was the first person of Greek heritage elected to a state legislature when he became a member of the Massachusetts House, immediately endearing himself to his colleagues with his bright oratory and incessant discussion about the brilliance of Greece's role in

Western civilization. He was drawn too to the Boston Marathon, which, in the 1930s, was beginning to grow in significance.

In 1931, remembering the marathon's origins, he persuaded marathon officials to let him crown the winner with a laurel wreath, the crown of victory given since ancient Olympic times. Eventually, he wanted the wreath to come directly from Greece.

In 1934, George started holding a gathering at the Lenox Hotel to greet the marathon winners. He would invite legislators and gave them names of Greek gods, mathematicians and philosophers, heroes, generals and admirals. Rep. Henry Cabot Lodge Jr., for the event in 1935, was Alcibiades, and Leverett Saltonstall won one of the top names: Pericles, the great orator of ancient Athens. After the noontime ceremony, they would go out to meet the winner at the finish line with the prized crown. Sometimes, George would run the last few yards next to the champion, to crown him as he crossed, both breathing hard now, to the amusement of his colleagues from the legislature, who had lined up to watch the end.

Harry continued to be the business leader behind the restaurants and their new prize, the Minerva. In the lobby and dining room were paintings depicting ancient Greece. On the floor were small marble tiles, and, in a small reception area, there was a statue of Demeter, the goddess of the earth. Many dignitaries, including political leaders and editors of the Greek-American newspapers *the National Herald* and the New York–based *Atlantis* would stay there and talk with the Demeters.

The dining room and hotel were also a favorite hangout of the city's political and media leaders, including robust sportswriters, such as Jerry Nason of the *Boston Globe*, who had already become a prominent chronicler of the marathon, the event he most loved. Nason wrote elegantly, with a passion about running and a flair for getting into the motivation of the runners, whose deeds and discipline he admired.

Nason looked like a Harvard man, with his good looks, smart dress, and exquisite style and way of carrying himself, but he wasn't. He had begun work at the *Globe* as a copyboy not long after graduating from Newton High School in 1927. He worked for a while as a cartoonist at the paper, but showed an immediate grasp of schoolboy sports and a writing style that brought the reader close to the subject, without the excesses that sometimes predominated among sportswriters then.

He had a prominent, strong nose, sparkling eyes, and an easy soft smile. He decided early on, after being given a chance to write about high school sports, that he liked track and running especially and kept detailed journals. Nason had a precise, almost perfect penmanship and started compiling notes about athletes he started covering, listing the events in which they competed, the dates, and their accomplishments, down to the times they ran. It helped him when he needed background about events and the athletes later.

He had fallen in love with the Boston Marathon while watching it from a bicycle not far from his house and his prose enlightened the event. Nason had taken a liking to Kelley especially because he admired the runner's pluck, but he didn't know anything about Kyriakides. He relied at first on George Demeter to provide information, who responded robustly with a ringing acclaim about his fellow Greek. It was a role Demeter liked because he didn't want to be intimately involved with the business end of the family's holdings, preferring the spotlight and hobnobbing and getting to know people such as Nason, whom he invited regularly to the Minerva and the restaurant and lounge. Demeter liked holding court.

Speare also helped run the businesses while George was the public-relations man and most visible of the family, and he kept an office in the hotel too, working there after leaving the legislature in 1937. The brothers sold their restaurants, but kept the hotel.

The marathon was Nason's favorite event, and it had natural ties between Boston and Greece. He had written often about the origins of the event, from the battlefield in ancient Greece where Pheidippides had run twenty-five hundred years before, and how officials of the Boston Athletic Association had been emotionally charged by watching the first modern Olympics in Athens in 1896, where Loues won.

The BAA officials arrived home with many gold medals, including those won by Thomas E. Burke in the hundred- and four-hundred-meter races; Ellery H. Clark, for the broad and the high jump events; and the winner of the first modern gold medal, James B. Connolly of

South Boston, in the hop, step, and jump. A top BAA official, George Brown, and the team's coach, John Graham, brought back another idea: a marathon for their city, the "Athens of America." Boston, home of Boston Latin High School, embodied the ancient Greek ideal of education and athletics. For their marathon, BAA officials wanted to re-create the same type of course as in Greece, with hills, and ventured twenty-five miles outside the city to the tiny town of Ashland for the starting point. The hills of the town of Newton were chosen to replicate the rugged hills of the Hymettus mountains, and the finish line was on the running track of the BAA at the 220-yard Irvington Street oval.

The BAA officials also decided to set the date as one of tradition: Patriots' Day, to celebrate the start of the American War of Independence in 1775. On Monday, April 19, 1897 at 12:15 P.M., eighteen men lined up on a dirt road in front of Metcalf's mill in Ashland. Thomas Burke, the Olympian, was designated to start the runners.

The Olympic champion sprinter simply drew a starting line by dragging the heel of his boot in the ground. He had no starter's pistol. He had the distinction of starting the race the same way they did in ancient Olympia by uttering one word, Απιτε!, which meant go.

The race was at first named "the American Marathon" and called that for many years. The entrants would start off on dusty roads, passing stone walls and farms, followed by people on bicycles and watched by curious crowds along the way to Boston. The first winner was John J. McDermott, a lithographer of the Pastime Athletic Club in New York, and winner of the first marathon in America, from Stamford, Connecticut, to New York in 1896.

In 1935, the year Johnny Kelley won his first of two Boston Marathons, the race was described in a column in the *Boston Post* for the arduous and unrewarding task it was. "No great fortune waits at the end of the trail for the man who breasts the tape first. The winner as a general rule comes from the obscurity that is the lot of the hard working man. It is an amateur sporting event pure and simple," the newspaper stated.

In 1938, though, no one in Boston, except for Demeter and Johnny Kelley, knew much about Kyriakides. The runners were concentrating on some warm-up races. On March 19, Kelley got some revenge on his nemesis, the Canadian Gerard Cote, beating him by 25 yards in the last 150 yards in a twenty-mile warm-up race in Kelley's hometown of North Medford. It was an unusually hot day, but Kelley was buoyed by his performance over the gritty Cote, who had seemed almost unbeatable to the little Irish-American gamer. It was Kelley's fifth victory in his hometown race, none sweeter than beating Cote.

Shortly thereafter, BAA official Tom Kanaly touted his own organization's premarathon race, the Cathedral ten-miler. "Kanaly reveals that a young Greek marathoner is coming all the way from Athens to lend genuine marathon atmosphere," Nason wrote, having already been tipped by Demeter about Kyriakides, who was bringing the laurel wreath for the winner with him. Nason provided the first real clue about Kyriakides.

Only two Europeans had won the Boston race, including Greek-born but American citizen Peter Trivoulidas in 1920-who then ran for Greece at the Olympics in Antwerp, and German Paul de Bryun, who also competed in the 1932 Olympics in Los Angeles.

Curiously, Nason wrote, "Nobody knows the name of the Greek who will travel a few thousand miles to win a wreath of laurel from his native country, but we will bet an old pipe that it is Kyriakides, who finished 11th in the Olympic race at Berlin two years ago, whipping Johnny Kelley among others. It has always been his ambition to run and win here."

Kyriakides was readying himself in Greece and looking forward to coming to the United States, where so many Greeks had come since the beginning of the century. He was running mostly on the softer ground and dirt roads of the hills around Athens, while Kelley and his rivals in the United States were running on the hard macadam of city streets, and competing in a series of premarathon races.

When Kyriakides left the port of Piraeus, outside Athens, on the steamship *Bremen*, he couldn't do any running during the voyage and had to settle for walking and light jogging on the ship, making him anxious and worried about his training. Sometimes, during the passage, he would imagine the ship was passing over the lost city of Atlantis.

On April 1, the *Bremen* arrived in New York and Kyriakides was greeted by two Greek-American athletes, Nick Giannacopoulos and Frank Vassilopoulos, and then taken to meet the Greek consul and members of the Greek-American community. He then went to the offices of the Amateur Athletic Union to show his credentials, then to McCombs Dam Park for a five-mile workout, which he did in 30:45, finally stretching the legs he had limbered on the ship with his walking routine.

Later, he was feted at a dinner at the plush St. Moritz Hotel, where Giannacopoulos and Vassilopoulos gave him some advice: "Wear old shoes for training and new shoes for the race and take a light run before the race and do not talk on race day. Do not talk to the other runners."

After dinner he was taken to the offices of the Greek-American newspaper *the Atlantis*, where he met editor Solon Vlastou, who had his picture taken with the runner and interviewed him extensively, writing a long article about Kyriakides and boosting Hellenism.

Before he arrived in Boston, the *Globe* heralded the arrival of the Balkan champion. *Athenian Boston-Bound to Run B.A.A. Marathon,* the paper reported, although misidentifying his occupation with the subhead of *Greek Auto Mechanic's Challenge Adds to International Tinge— Britisher May Come*.

For all its growing notoriety, the marathon was still a rather parochial event, with the same group of American and Canadian runners dominating: Johnny Kelley, Tarzan Brown, Les Pawson, the cocky Cote, who had finished seventh the year before, and even the aging Clarence DeMar, still regarded as the godfather of the event.

Kyriakides, Demeter believed, would change that and bring glory to the homeland of Greece. At twenty-eight, Kyriakides was in his distance-running prime with a string of Balkan championships behind him, as well as the 1936 Olympic experience in Berlin where Kyriakides felt he had not run his best, but where he had met Johnny Kelley and become friendly with him.

"I blame my defeat at Berlin in the Olympics to a poorly judged race. My trainer urged me to a faster pace at one time and I failed to follow his instructions. I felt very strong at the end," he said.

Tell me where to stand, and I will move the earth

—Archimedes

The *Globe*, like the other newspapers, immediately loved the irony of a Greek coming to Boston to run the marathon. *From the Land of the Marathon*, the paper noted of Kyriakides, and they sent a photographer to South Station to get a picture of him arriving by train from New York and being greeted by the dapper and smiling Demeter, impeccably dressed as always in a smart reversible topcoat, suit, and tie with a silk handkerchief and fedora.

Kyriakides was wearing a topcoat too and had a camera slung over his right shoulder. For the first time, he was meeting his sponsor and there was an immediate bond between the two Greeks, one an American now. Demeter wanted to put his new friend at ease and introduced himself in Greek.

Kyriakides smiled. He had brought something. It was a wreath of laurel, picked from the hills outside Athens. It was what Demeter had been placing on the heads of the winners the past few years, but this time it was hand-delivered by a man he expected would win and bring back to the country from where it had come.

Demeter was anxious to get Kyriakides settled in the Minerva and already had told his best chef, Jimmy Contanis, to ready a steady diet of steak, potatoes, milk, fruits, and vegetables. Demeter burned with the hope that Kyriakides would win the race. "Let him open any refrigerator he wants and take whatever he wants," Demeter told his chef. Contanis would sometimes look up to see Kyriakides doing just that, looking for food. The chef would laugh and say, "I have a big one for you, Stelio," pulling forth an extra large steak.

Demeter and Kyriakides took an instant liking to each other, their love for their heritage absolute, but Demeter, a formal and stolid man given to ceremony and pomp and circumstance, and a staunch believer in tradition, liked the quiet, low-keyed, and humble manner of Kyriakides. They talked casually and easily in Greek, although Demeter thought the runner would be anxious to have a meal and go to bed be-

Kyriakides (left) finally got to meet his Greek-American sponsor, Massachu-setts lawmaker George Demeter, when he arrived in Boston to prepare for the 1938 marathon. Courtesy of the *Boston Globe*.

cause he could see the weariness on Kyriakides' face, the fatigue like the raised features of a topographical map.

Demeter brought him back to the Minerva, where he had a room set aside. He first took him to his own office, a suite where he wanted Kyri-akides to meet someone especially important to the Boston Marathon. It was Nason, who took a liking to the affable, if shy, Kyriakides.

As they started to talk, slowly, Kyriakides was able to answer Nason so fluently in English that it surprised the veteran sportswriter, so he asked, "What does the Boston Marathon mean to the Hellenes?"

Kyriakides smiled, both at the question and the formality of its pres-entation, and he could sense the respect Nason had for Greece and its heritage. He returned it.

"Ah, the Boston Marathon," he smiled. "It is known to us in Greece as the greatest American athletic event. It is the only American event that is reported in our papers every year. We Greeks consider the winning of the Boston Marathon the greatest achievement in the world," Kyriakides said, as Nason took detailed notes in small handwriting so impeccable it looked as if it were typewritten. They indicated that Kyriakides was only 5'6" and weighed 140 pounds, was handsome and was wearing a wedding ring on his left hand, although he was only engaged.

"It is the custom in Greece to wear the ring upon the left hand during the period of engagement. Then wear it on the right hand when married," Kyriakides said. He said he was planning to get married later that year or the next to a woman named Fanouria Maina, and he was as happy at that prospect as running in Boston. She had brought a new serenity to his life.

Nason smiled gingerly and called him "Stanley," although Demeter explained that Stylianos translated roughly into English as "stalwart," fitting, Nason thought, for a long-distance runner. Kelley was fond of calling his friend Stanley as well, finding it easier on the tongue.

Kyriakides said he felt he had been washed ashore in America by the Fates to a land where, except for Kelley and his Greek-American comrades, he had no friends. When Nason asked about his training, Kyriakides said he had run along the original Greek marathon course and over the mountains of Hymettos, Paratha, and Stavros, the models for the Boston course.

"I have never walked along a marathon course and never failed to finish," he said, proudly. "Not even up the peak of Mount Stavros," he said, explaining it was a two-mile trek that made the Newton hills of the Boston Marathon course seem like a slight rise.

Nason's report on Kyriakides appeared the next day and said, "With pardonable pride the Greek champion points to the fact that he has never stopped to walk over those mountains . . . he has never, in fact, stopped to walk in any marathon race, and he has never failed to finish."

Nason sensed that Kyriakides had the special qualities of a champion, even through his quiet humility. Kyriakides had another admirer, the great Olympic champion Paavo Nurmi of Finland, who told Nason that "Kyriakides, should he exert all his strength to the very end, would be beaten by no man in a marathon race." It was a bold statement, underscored by Kyriakides' lack of braggadoccio.

Meanwhile, in New York on April 15, American Olympic officials were confident the 1940 Olympic Games scheduled for Tokyo would be held. American Olympic head Avery Brundage said "nothing short of a world war" would prevent it.

The runners weren't aware of that, though. They were a close-knit bunch and were thinking only of the race ahead. Gerard Cote was training hard after his seventh place finish the year before and was running a hundred miles a week. He didn't know about Kyriakides and was aiming at Kelley and Leslie Pawson. Kyriakides watched the Cathedral ten-mile race, a preliminary to the marathon, and used his other training time to walk the entire course of the marathon to guage its nuances, training only every other day.

He was quickly becoming a favorite of the local sportswriters and photographers. One picture showed him shoveling a big piece of steak into his mouth while dressed in a three-piece suit sitting next to Steward Demeter, George's brother, who oversaw his diet. Many others showed him stretching and running and working out in his favorite sweatsuit bearing the Greek name for Greece, ΕΛΛΑΣ, which in English looked like *HELLAS*. Sportswriter Arthur Duffey wrote: "He is no ordinary athlete and probably trains much harder than anyone of our American marathoners."

Duffey spent a day with Kyriakides, coming to visit him at the Minerva and watch his training. "I never saw a marathon runner put in a more strenuous day. If he does not win the Boston Marathon it won't be because he is improperly trained or he has not taken the greatest care of himself for the coming grind. Not only does Kyriakides train most scientifically as to diet and at work on the road and track, but every little detail is looked after," he wrote.

Kyriakides awoke each morning at nine o'clock, after a sleep of ten to eleven hours, but was more modest in explaining his approach to running and the marathon. "I don't suppose my diet and training system is much different from any other runner's. After a long sleep in which I always sleep soundly and go to sleep as soon as I hit the pillow, I go down for breakfast," he said. That included milk, grapefruit, and porridge. For lunch he had soup, vegetables, and steak, and for supper he had soup and chops. "The young Greek does not fear anyone in the race," Duffey said.

On April 6, the *Globe* featured three photos of Kyriakides, one rubbing his slim legs, the second in full stride around Harvard Stadium, and the third a headshot with a bright smile. "A Modern Pheidippides Visits These Shores," the paper said. Reporters and a few race veterans who watched Kyriakides train soon put out the word that the Greek champion was for real and he was becoming a favorite.

The next day Demeter and his nephew, Harry Demeter Jr., drove Kyriakides along the marathon course so the Greek could survey the landscape and the precise route, scouting for straightaways and curves and hills, all the way to Hopkinton, where Kyriakides promptly got out and said he would run back while they timed him.

He whooshed away, but not before stopping to look at some sections of the road that were different than anything he had seen. It was cement, hard as steel, it seemed to Kyriakides, and he looked at it for a long time, bending down to examine the surface, running his hand over it. This was not like the dirt of his mountains or even the hard surface of some few roads in Greece and the Balkans.

The Demeters followed, at a runner's pace, to protect and time him while he ran alone, past farms and horses and over streets where there was little traffic. George Demeter was keeping close track on a watch and, as they came into Cleveland Circle, twenty-two miles into the run and four miles from the finish, George whistled while he looked at his watch.

"I think he's running a record!" Demeter said.

Harry was so excited he drove the car up onto a curb, bounding onto adjacent trolley tracks, the tires sliding on the smooth metal. "What! Are you blind?" George shouted.

"He's going to break the record," Harry said as the car shook when they went over the curb. "Look at the time this guy is making!" he said in defense. They both laughed, but Kyriakides broke off his pace so he wouldn't wear himself out in a practice run. He was satisfied, he said, that this course could be conquered.

Demeter wasn't taking any chances though. He thought Kyriakides was still too thin so he ordered Contanis to step up the food intake for Kyriakides, to give him more steak and potatoes and high caloric foods to build him up. "Give him anything he wants. Open the refrigerator!" Demeter said.

What they couldn't foresee was that Kyriakides, who had been training in old shoes, would run in new shoes that hadn't been broken in properly. Shoes in 1938 were still a marathoner's biggest problem, apart from training, because they were stiff and heavy and led to blisters if they weren't seasoned. For all his running in Greece, Kyriakides had been running on ground, and not hardtop surfaces.

Kyriakides joined Kelley, Cote and Newfoundland champion Pat Kelly for a fun run. All were photographed jogging together, and then at Kelley's home admiring his trophies, including the 1935 medallion he received as the Boston Marathon champion. The four talked, of course, about running, laughing and joking about who might win.

A few days before the race, Nason wrote an article handicapping the event, using the Welsh runner Pat Dengis, a threat to win, as his gauge. Dengis had won virtually every important American marathon except for Boston, and made a hobby of predicting winners and analyzing the runners. He said Cote was a strong challenger, but too preoccupied with women who were attracted to his "oh-la-la" manner. He was more disparaging in his assessment of Kyriakides.

"This Mr. Kyriakides would find the profitable thing he can do on this trip to the U.S.A. would be to open up a quick-lunch restaurant down near the South Station. He is a fair-to-middling type of marathoner but is no sensation; claims he never walked in a race—and I say 'Nuts' to that." Dengis claimed that Kyriakides and Britisher A. J. Norris both had to walk part of the way during the brutal heat of the 1935 London marathon, although Kyriakides said he had staggered but not walked.

"I know my seconds," Dengis wrote. "And if our Grecian friend expects a victory in Boston he will have to first dispose of a dozen men who have been gunning for this race for six months. I'll give him fifth or no better," he wrote. Nason picked Kyriakides second.

In an interview, Kyriakides had modestly predicted he would finish in the first five and thought his friend Kelley and Pawson were the most formidable opponents, although Demeter told him to watch out for Cote, whose brash talk was often backed up with big running. Kyriakides casually mentioned that he would marry later in the year and that when he returned to Greece, would have to serve in the army for several months. No one expected Hitler's Nazism would move toward Greece, or even a war in Europe.

Part of Kyriakides' thoughts were not on the race for which he seemed so single-minded, but on Fanouria, the woman he couldn't wait to marry. She would be sitting by the radio the day of the race, waiting for news from the BBC. She knew only five words in English: her future husband's name and *first, second, and third*.

"There will be a little prayer on her lips that the name of Stylianos Kyriakides, Marathon champion of Greece and the young lady's husband-to-be, will be linked with one of them," Nason wrote after driving along the course with Kyriakides and chatting comfortably in English. Kyriakides was even more introspective, gazing out at the trees and stone walls and talking of Greece and of her. "I have told her to listen to the shortwave news broadcast, about one o'clock in the morning in Greece. Maybe the result of the race will be announced," he said, sighing.

George Demeter was driving while Nason and Kyriakides sat in the back talking. Demeter turned to Nason and said, "Say, just where do you figure this boy in next Tuesday's race?"

Nason pulled out a list that showed Kyriakides second, behind a dark-horse favorite, Duncan McCallum of Toronto, who had finished fifth the year before. Kyriakides smiled softly. "You have me for too good a place. Better move me to here," he said, pointing to fifth.

Demeter laughed. "You aren't taking him seriously?" he guffawed, knowing Kyriakides' humility, but also the Greek's supreme quiet confidence in his ability.

"The way I have it figured," Demeter said, turning his head back-and-forth from the front seat to the back, "from his record and the way he has trained he will run this course in two hours, twenty-nine minutes and forty seconds."

Nason was surprised. "That's more than a minute better than the record, George," he said.

"I know! I know! But he's going to make a record," Demeter insisted.

Kyriakides jumped in. "Record? No, it is not good to run against the record. Run to win, that is the way. I would like to be informed during the race about the leaders and my position but the time does not matter."

Kyriakides had been over the course now on foot, by car and running, and said he was aiming to make his move at the Newton hills, including the "heartbreak hill" that had broken the will of so many runners, not because of its grade, but because it came so late in the run when the nerves and heart and arms and legs wanted to stop. Kyriakides was stepping up his training the closer it got to the race, running as much as twenty kilometers a day

The Demeters and Kyriakides were confident on April 19, especially when it dawned a fair day and was seventy-four degrees by race time. Kyriakides liked the warmth of the sun. Most runners would have preferred cool or even rainy weather, to whisk away the intense heat that could build on the skin after pushing their hearts and legs so many miles.

The Demeters drove him out to Hopkinton, where the runners changed in the farmhouse of a family named Tebeau, who had given their hospitality to the event. Kyriakides was surprised to find so many Greek-Americans there cheering him on, even before the race started. It was a bucolic scene, gnarled apple trees and slim young maples along winding roads that hadn't been developed yet. If not for the runners, the only sound would have been the spring wind through the newly budded trees, near the stone walls covered with vines, and next to wild grass clumps along the roadside.

It was a wild scene as seventy-year-old Alice Tebeau, wife of "Big John the farmer," opened their home, the Lucky Rock Manor, to the runners and officials and the gawkers. The two-hundred-year-old farmhouse expected about 225 visitors in its twenty-two rambling rooms and the furniture had to be put in the attic to accommodate everyone. The Tebeaus had been giving their hospitality to the race since 1927, allowing doctors to give prerace checks and weighing-in ceremonies, and letting the runners change. The runners called her "Queen Alice" for her loving hospitality and efficient manner, and for the coffee, sizzling steaks, and fresh eggs, whose aroma filled the old house while scores of people rambled through.

"They're all nice boys, the runners," she said. "And although they wander through the whole house they're very considerate of everything . . . I don't have a bit of trouble with them," she added. As soon as the race would start, though, she and her family and some others at the start would jump to turn on the radio in her house to listen to the run.

Kelley had been staying at a home near Hopkinton to avoid all the people who would otherwise be coming by his Arlington home. He felt immense pressure as the hometown favorite and wanted to avoid well-wishers. "The result would be a constant mental turmoil. Because I went out of circulation, some have concluded that I am near the breaking point," he said. But he was down to 120 pounds and fit, and although no one predicted him to win, he felt confident.

"That's swell with me. Now I can go out and run my own race and whatever I do will be 'velvet.' I know the pressure of going to mark a favorite. I've been through that kind of mental anguish. But on previous occasions, I've been worrying about nonemployment and that isn't giving me any worry today," he said, because he was running for his new employer, the Boston Edison electric company, where he had started working as a guard after giving up his florist's job and being unemployed for a while.

Nason and other reporters would be following the runners in a Studebaker driven by C. G. Thanos, a large jovial man who had been born in Greece and had an intense interest in the race—and in Kyriakides. The *Boston Post* had named Cote, an up-and-coming runner, as the favorite along with Kelley, who was second the year before behind Young. Another choice was the hard running Dengis, who had already won his last three marathons, and then Pawson, but Kyriakides was not slighted.

Although it was hard to handicap his chances, race officials nonetheless gave him the prestige of wearing number one, which would otherwise have gone to the previous year's champion. Kyriakides knew only Kelley, who had not performed well in Berlin. No one knew that Pawson, a strong runner, had not run much because of a stress fracture he had suffered five years before when he won Boston, although his lack of success since then should have told them something.

Kyriakides was keeping to himself.

> Men pay for too much wisdom with pain
>
> —Euripides

The warm weather had brought out an estimated six hundred thousand people. At the start the gun was fired by Walter Brown, son of race founder George V. Brown, who had died in the fall. More than two hundred runners started and by the five-mile mark at Framingham, Pawson and Kelley were third and fourth while Dengis was way back in thirty-second place, Kyriakides took an early lead and was in front with a few other runners.

The Studebaker Convertible Eight driven by Thanos was carrying Nason and the other *Globe* sportswriters and was supposed to stay out front, but the driver kept back to stay alongside the somber Kyriakides and urged him to run, run, run, yelling exhortations in Greek. The sportswriters, dashingly attired in suits and wide-brimmed hats, watched in astonishment, laughing.

Over the anguished demands of the sportswriters, Thanos would stop the car periodically to get Kyriakides some water to drink. The Greek runner was content to stay toward the second pack of runners, biding his time and waiting for the Newton hills where he would make his run. For the first ten miles he stayed consistently in sixth or seventh place, close enough to the leaders to make a move when he needed to, confident he could close the gap.

The heat had spectators rushing onto the course to give the runners wet sponges, water, and fruit. Kyriakides' feet were already beginning to hurt, though, as the shoes chafed him, and by Natick, about ten miles in, Pawson and Kelley took over. Kyriakides was running loose, easy, and strong and looked to be biding his time to make his break at the Newton hills. He was refusing water at every break. But then he noticed something in his left shoe. It was the start of a blister and it started to worry him because he had never dropped out of a race. After running only a short distance, the annoyance became so strong that he stopped, pulled off the shoe, and tried to make an adjustment so there wouldn't be any more discomfort. He looked up and saw the pack running away from him and hurried back into the footwear, but there was no change in the irritation that was quickly making blisters rise on his toes.

Nason, following in an open car, noticed the slight grimace on Kyriakides and the odd way he was favoring his foot. He leaned out anxiously, and yelled, "Are you going to drop out?"

Demeter couldn't bear what he was seeing and he chimed in too. "Keep on, push on, Stelios!" he exhorted.

Kyriakides had lost some valuable time and Pawson and Kelley ran alone for the next eight miles, but then Pawson took the lead and Kelley, wearying, was looking furtively over his shoulder, expecting the loud-talking Dengis to start making a move on him. There was little water available anymore because the spectators at this point were more interested in watching and the officials had not provided stations, relying on some of them to run out and hand water to the front-runners only. The heat was sapping everyone and the sweat pouring into shoes was making blisters a worse enemy than fatigue.

The drama was playing out now without Kyriakides, whose steps were becoming ragged, blisters breaking inside his shoes, blood seeping up to his toes, the grinding chafing cutting deep into his feet, making even a slight jog a pain with every step. He gritted his teeth and kept plodding, running now more for honor than hope of victory, worried what Demeter and his new American friends would think if he failed.

By now, Thanos was desperately worried about Kyriakides. The driver was talking under his breath in Greek now, his face furrowed with anxiety, but none of the writers, even Vic Jones, a Harvard scholar who had studied Greek, could understand his mumbled words. Thanos wanted to slow down to find Kyriakides, but Nason and the others yelled, "Go to the front!"

He yielded reluctantly, mumbling angrily in Greek.

At Lake Street, almost twenty-two miles into the race, the car slowed to watch the front-runners. The driver was beside himself with worry, craning his neck over the others, looking for his Greek favorite while the huge crowds pushed up to the edge of the narrow macadam road. "Kyriakides! Where is Kyriakides!" the driver yelled loudly, this time in English. Then, to the astonishment of Nason and the others, he bounded out of the convertible and ran onto the course screaming, looking for Kyriakides.

Meanwhile, the sportswriters sat there stunned, watching the man run into the mass of teeming spectators and back along the course, looking for his hero. Nason, too, wondered where Kyriakides was because he started so strongly. Finally, one of the other writers jumped behind the wheel and drove off toward the finish line, trying to catch Kelley and Pawson and stay ahead of the oncoming runners.

Thanos wouldn't find Kyriakides, who had run until the blister had burst near Boston College, just shy of the twenty-one-mile mark. He stumbled raggedly to the side of the road, his heart and legs strong, his feet bleeding red from broken blisters that ached with heat and pain inside the tight shoes. He looked around in anguish and saw a passing bus. Kyriakides lifted his hand, embarrassed, and the bus stopped, slamming on its air brakes, and stopping just short of hitting him.

Kyriakides, sweating in his shorts and T-shirt, limped aboard to the astonished look of some passengers and a dumbstruck bus driver. This had never happened in the fifty-year history of the race. The fare was ten cents, but he carried no money. The driver looked at him. "No charge," he said, smiling. Kyriakides took a seat, his heart deflated. It was a short ride because the bus was only going as far as Lake Street. He had to sit, chagrined, defeated, sweating, bloodied, with the other passengers staring.

When the bus stopped, Kyriakides got out, looking for an official BAA car or a way to the finish line, limping and sweating. He looked down at his foot, where blood was seeping through the shoe. As the bus pulled away, a car pulled up and Kyriakides again raised his hand for help. The startled driver directed him to get in, but the car was only going as far as Washington Square on Beacon Street, just short of Coolidge Corner, and Kyriakides again had to get out.

His foot was now hurting so much he walked into a nearby drugstore as surprised customers and a pharmacist watched in bewilderment at the sight of the injured, bleeding runner coming into the store while the rest of the marathoners paraded by just outside the door.

"My foot," he said, slowly. "Can you help me?"

The pharmacist said under the law he couldn't dispense the kind of medicine Kyriakides would need. That would only be available at the finish line, where doctors and podiatrists were waiting inside the BAA headquarters across the street from the Hotel Lenox, where the race would end. A dejected Kyriakides walked back out, onto the course of the race, and alternately walked and jogged slowly until he got to Coolidge Corner, where thousands of spectators watched his anguish.

Then he saw a cab and Kyriakides stopped, put his fingers into his mouth and whistled loudly, the sound almost blowing the cap off the startled driver. Kyriakides clambered in. The driver turned around. "The finish line," Kyriakides said, slumping back. He had come five thousand miles to run and now would have to ignominiously ride in a taxi to the end where his friends and supporters were waiting. He hoped Demeter would be there to pay the fare. He wasn't alone in his dejection. Many other exhausted and blistered runners thumbed rides to the end, some hanging on to the hoods and the sides of passing cars.

Meanwhile, the runners were moving on. As they passed Cleveland Circle, the rotary that connected Commonwealth Avenue to Beacon Street, Kelley was getting overcome by the heat and stopped three times to pour water on his head while trying to keep up with Pawson, and Dengis came charging by. Ahead of both was Pawson, who slowed at Coolidge Corner, just shy of the twenty-four-mile mark and at a spot where Beacon Street takes a long downward glide.

Dengis made a last gasp charge in vain, passing a dozen runners with a furious charge, but no one would catch Pawson now. Because of excavation, the runners had to finish on a bed of planks, and Pawson rumbled across the winner in 2:35:34, a minute and seven seconds ahead of Dengis, while Kelley came up third. At least, Kelley mused, he wasn't second this time. DeMar, now fifty years old, finished seventh, ahead of the embarrassed Cote.

The well-groomed, soft-spoken, gentlemanly Pawson was a media favorite, and even Dengis acknowledged his fellow runner would not be caught that day. It was a disappointment for Dengis, who would win nine of eleven marathons in two years—his only losses at Boston.

Kyriakides was not alone in his disappointment or embarrassment either. Tarzan Brown, the former champion, finished fifty-first in 3:38, an hour slower than his best winning time, and it seemed neither he nor Kyriakides would have a chance in this race again.

Shortly, the cab carrying Kyriakides appeared at the finish line outside the Hotel Lenox. The fare was $1.25 and a sheepish-looking and hurt Kyriakides opened the door to see Demeter, his mouth agape at the sight. "Do you have $1.25?" Kyriakides asked, his head down. Inside the Lenox, some of his followers, including a young boy named Michael Dukakis, looking out a hotel window, were as dejected as he when they saw him step out of the cab. Kyriakides burned with the guilt he had let down his believers. It was a hurt deeper than the pain in his feet.

The next day, though, Nason wrote that Kyriakides' feet alone had failed him; "Accustomed to running on a softer dirt course, his underpinning became broken, smashed and bloodied, travesties of feet in the marathon. He fought on past the limits of ordinary men. He finally retired on Lake Street."

As ashamed as he felt, Kyriakides had his mashed feet tended to and spoke to the reporters and congratulated the winner and other runners. He was almost at the point of tears, but stoically held back his hurt while Thanos finally found him and consoled him. Thanos's car was left near the finish by Nason and the other reporters, who had to dash by foot to the finish line to catch the winner and front runners.

Kyriakides felt he had let down all of Greece and Greek-Americans who had counted on him. They were still relatively recent to the United States and many, like Demeter, had struggled to overcome prejudice by establishing themselves in business and other fields. They had counted vicariously on Kyriakides to bring them creditability in another important field in America: sports.

Nason wondered about Kyriakides, the charming Greek with the soft winning smile and humble manner. A dejected Kyriakides wearily packed his belongings to leave. In his bag, he packed and carefully read, again and again, the headline over Nason's story that said Pawson, not Kyriakides, had won. He took it with him, along with other articles that talked about his ignominious defeat. He would keep them forever. But before he left, he had one more visit to make in Boston.

Nason was sitting in his office on downtown Washington Street, along the newspaper row and a busy commercial street where men in suits and ties looked like a uniformed formal army, when he heard a knock on his door and looked up.

It was Kyriakides, weary but smiling, limping a little from the band-aged bloodied blisters on his left foot, but his heart and smile hurting more than his foot. Nason liked him, had thought he might even win, and listened carefully to his stories about Greece, and Kyriakides liked the sportswriter too. It would be a while before he could run another step, but he had something to say to Nason, who wondered if he'd ever see the Greek again. War seemed so imminent in Europe.

"Someday," Kyriakides said shyly, his head downcast toward the dirt-ied wooden floor. "Someday, I come back and maybe I win your marathon," he said, the smile brightening just a little.

> A ship ought not to be held by one anchor, nor life by a single hope
> —Epictetus

It took weeks for Kyriakides' foot to heal, but when it did, he ran in the Pan-Hellenic Games in Athens in the late spring, winning the five-kilometer and ten-kilometer races, but he still thought about what happened in Boston. He had something else now to take the edge off his feelings. Running wasn't his only love anymore. He had become engaged to the woman he talked about in Boston, Fanouria Maina, whom he had met several years before when he was still struggling with running and trying to make a living. He did compete again in the Balkan championships, finishing second in the marathon in Belgrade in September.

It was a difficult time for the couple, though, because he was trying to maintain a running regimen and had gone into the army in December 1938 as part of compulsory military service, leaving the room at the stadium where he lived to go to a base in Corinth, where he served as a corporal. A uniformed Kyriakides was photographed standing proudly with his comrades.

There were new tensions in the world, and even the athletes could not escape the sense that war might break out in Europe. After the technical success of the 1936 games in Berlin, Hitler had become more imperialistic, bullying England and France, moving into Austria, and starting to establish his hegemony over eastern Europe. He had real disdain for the Poles especially, because they had been instrumental in taking what he felt were German lands.

In April of 1939, Britain and France warned Hitler they would act if he attempted to move into other countries, issuing guarantees to Romania and Greece they would be protected. Mussolini, the Italian dictator, was rattling sabers with his speeches, his thirst for conquering Greece, and matching Hitler, showing visibly. The British and French stance didn't assuage Kyriakides and his fellow athletes, or many Greek citizens who feared Hitler would not be scared off by edicts from afar.

The talk of possible war spread, and, in between their workouts, the athletes talked of their own fears that their lives and country could be affected. Kyriakides was also set back by the sudden death of his father, caught in an outside shed in their village during a thunderstorm, the victim of a collapsing roof. It was a sad return to his home village, where he had to comfort his widowed mother before returning to Athens, to his job and fiancée. He was released from active duty after only a few months.

Kyriakides courted Fanouria and worked happily at the utility company, going about his rounds doing bill collecting, and enjoying the time where he was able to stop and talk to customers. He was well liked, not just for his fame, but for the shy, humble manner that especially endeared him to women. He continued his training too, aiming at the 1939 Balkan Games, which would be back in Athens.

The games were held in August of 1939, and Kyriakides again won the marathon championship—on Pheidippides' original course—with a time of 2:52:07, but he was only third in the ten-kilometer, in 33:58, far off his best. Kyriakides had other thoughts besides his running now.

Then, on September 1, came the stunning news of Germany's invasion of Poland, a blitzkrieg that shocked the Western world. Hitler, disdainful of the Western leaders, struck quickly. The Germans essentially destroyed the whole Polish air force in one day, catching most of the planes on the ground, and the world moved into war that would soon cover the whole of Europe and spread to Asia.

Kyriakides and Fanouria tried to maintain a normal life, even though they were worried about whether the Nazi aggression would reach to Greece. They liked to go to her parents' restaurant in the center of Athens, where he would enjoy the company of her large family, including her sisters Margarita, Maria, and Barbara, and brothers Nikos and Solon.

Fanouria was in the middle of the family and her parents liked Kyriakides, for his shy humility and devotion to their daughter. For a time now, Kyriakides found joy in something other than running. He loved to walk and travel with Fanouria and she brought out the smile he so often subdued.

On December 26, 1939, Kyriakides and Fanouria were married in a simple ceremony. They promptly moved into a small house in the Athens suburb of Pankrati. It was given them by her family, as part of the traditional dowry provided by the bride's family. For nine months Kyriakides felt fulfilled, his life complete with running and the marriage he had made, satisfied that this was all he would need.

While Kyriakides was running again in Greece and the Balkans, his friend Johnny Kelley was continuing to excel in the United States, winning many races over various distances, although he surprisingly finished a distant thirteenth in the 1939 Boston Marathon, which was won by Tarzan Brown, who mysteriously did not compete in the Yonkers Marathon, the second Olympic trial to determine who would be on the team in 1940.

Kelley was working for the Boston Edison utility company, a business like Kyriakides' company. Kelley was planning on getting married too, even as he—like Kyriakides—was thinking about whether the 1940 Olympic Games scheduled for Tokyo would be held.

Kelley was engaged to Mary Knowles, a stenographer for Birds Eye

Frozen Foods whom he'd met because her family lived only a block away from his. When they'd met at a subway stop, Kelley had turned to her to ask, "What time is it?" She smiled and they talked.

He showed up for the race with a short haircut, ready for marriage and taking a ribbing from his rivals. "I had it cut this way so the laurel wreath will fit better," he laughed.

Kelley was in good shape and eyeing another Olympic berth with a chance to erase the bitterness of 1936 in Berlin. The 1940 race belonged to the cocky Gerard Cote, though, the smiling Canadian who had Kelley's number. Cote won in 2:28:28, a remarkably fast time and far from his spurious effort in 1938. Kelley, for the third time in seven years, finished second, but landed a spot on the Olympic team.

On April 27, he and Mary were married in Arlington and after their honeymoon, they moved in with her mother, while he readied for the Olympic Games, not knowing what the looming war clouds in Europe and the Far East were bringing.

The people in Greece knew, though. Hitler was already rampaging through eastern Europe and the Greeks were wary of his ally Mussolini. It was grating for Mussolini, a second-rate dictator, to have to watch Hitler's successes and Il Duce was determined to emulate and surpass his ally, with eyes on Yugoslavia and his real plum, Greece, the long-hated rival in his own backyard.

Hitler could smell Mussolini's ambition, though, and he didn't want the Italians becoming too adventureous and had his military leaders warn against precipitous action at a time when the German army was already becoming too stretched across too many fronts. Hitler did not want to have to race to the rescue of any Italian fiascoes.

In April 1940, Mussolini had sent a letter to the Greek premier, Ioannis Metaxas, assuring him the Italians were not interested in Greece. Metaxas said he had received a note from Mussolini giving "categorical assurances that the Fascist government will respect the integrity of Greece as regards both her land and her sea frontiers." But Mussolini was constantly living in fear of Hitler and needed to show leadership and Metaxas didn't believe Mussolini would live up to his words of appeasement, and the Greek leader had accepted Great Britain's offer of assistance should it be necessary.

Life continued in Greece, however, even while the tensions were always there. The Greeks put together another Balkan team and in late August of 1940, Kyriakides went to Constantinople for the games again, a happily married man, more content now as he was coming out of his twenties and finding happiness with his wife. But it was also six years since his triumph in Zagreb and there were other rising stars in Greece, including a strong runner named Athanasios Ragazos, who quickly became friends with the man still regarded as Greece's best runner. Ragazos won the marathon in Turkey, while Kyriakides finished third in 2:46:43.

Then tragedy struck. Kyriakides and his new bride went to Kalamata, a famous olive town in the Peloponneseus, on a holiday to visit his brothers. They went out for a walk in the countryside and were stepping over some brush when she suddenly yelled in pain.

"What is wrong?" he asked.

"Oh nothing," she said. "I think I cut my leg on some wire." It was a nasty cut, but she didn't think about it after a while. But then Fanouria became ill suddenly, her leg hurting. The wire had been rusty and she had gotten tetanus, which spread quickly through her. She died suddenly on September 14, a distraught Kyriakides beside her, crying, his despair reaching to the heavens: she had been pregnant. He had lost a child too.

He was only thirty, a strong, respected runner with a good job, and a good wife. Life had felt so fine to him. Kyriakides returned photos of the two to her family, and reluctantly continued to live in the small house they had shared. "It doesn't really belong to me now," he said, but it had been part of the dowry of the marriage.

After that, he would go often to her grave to place flowers, but seldom talked about the tragedy. He could not do anything but grieve. He could not think about running, nor about the fear rising in Greece about war that was already at the country's doorstep. He didn't even talk about her.

Kyriakides didn't care anymore.

5

The Evil Comes to Greece

Athens, 1940–1944

Kyriakides was single again, lost without the woman he loved and who had suddenly brought some certainty to his life. He had been so happy running and being with her that he had, if only for a little while, not thought about the talk of war that seemed to settle over Greece like a shroud. He was living in the house his wife's parents had given them, but it made him feel uneasy, and he returned to the solace of long-distance running to put the pain behind him.

He also found some relief in his friends and his teammates on the Greek Olympic team, such as Mandikas and Travlos and Petropoulos, but sometimes now when they finished their workouts they would gather in the stadium in Athens and talk about the ill winds they feared would blow into their sunny land. The Nazis, the blitzkrieg had ripped through Europe and France and was aimed at England and Russia, and toward Greece. Even the traditional German affinity for Greek culture wouldn't help Greece, they knew, not even the German admiration of athletes.

There was no thought of fleeing, or surrendering, because the Greeks had never done that. They had turned back the Persians at Thermopylae and Marathon, had finally pushed out the oppressive Turks and the Ottoman Empire more than a century before after generations of occupation, and would never relent to conquest, even before the onslaught of the powerful German army and the Luftwaffe.

Hitler, however, did not want to go into the Balkans or Greece. He was already eyeing the prize of Russia, a mountainous task that would require pinpoint planning and the massive mobilization and deployment of one of the greatest armies ever assembled, at a time when the German high command would have to plan to avoid the brutality of the Russian winter. Hitler did not want Mussolini to move precipitously because the führer was not confident in the Italian armies or generals.

Italy's foreign minister, Count Galeazzo Ciano, noted in his diary of August 17, 1940, that "it is a complete order to halt all along the line," in the Balkans, which history had shown to be a place where military excursions had bogged down. Ten days later, Mussolini sent Hitler a letter indicating he had second thoughts about going into the Balkans, but the Italian leader couldn't stop thinking about a quick strike and what he thought would be an easy victory over Greece, whose small population of eight million people would never be able to stand up to the Italian army and its mobilized equipment, he thought.

Hitler did not want to invade Greece because he knew the history of the Greeks, that they would not be conquered and would never stop fighting, and he didn't want to tie up valuable divisions when he was concerned about the daunting task of confronting the Russians and their vast millions of men, especially in the dead of winter when the weather would hold back mobilization and movement of armies and supplies.

But the Italians were confident they could handle the Greeks. Mussolini especially needed the gratification of a conquest because he was intimidated by Hitler and wanted to prove to the führer that he too was a formidable leader and able to lead armies into war, if only from afar with his directions and policies. But Mussolini miscalculated.

The Italian leader had decided on October 22 that six days later he would invade Greece, despite the constant misgivings and German warnings. On October 28, he wrote Hitler a letter, backdating it to October 19, giving a vague indication about going into Greece. He did not provide enough information so that the führer could stop it, especially because Hitler several days before had a call placed to Ciano to set up a meeting of the Axis leaders. Mussolini complied and suggested October 28, without any hint to Hitler what he was planning the same day.

At 3:00 A.M. on October 28, 1940, the Italian ambassador in Athens, Emanuele Grazzi, came to the Greek leader, Ioannis Metaxas, with an ultimatum: the Greeks should surrender their country to the Italians or face the might and onslaught of the Axis powers, led by Italy.

The Italian communication stated that Greece "allow Italian forces to occupy for the duration of the present conflict with Great Britain certain strategic points in Greek territory," and said that "any resistance encountered will be put down with the force of arms." Hitler had already taken Poland, France, Holland, Belgium, Norway, and Denmark, but the Italians too had a large army that Mussolini was itching to use in a conquest, especially with setbacks in Africa and Egypt under way.

Metaxas, known as "Little Johnny," because of his 5'7" height, telephoned King George and his defense ministers and told them to expect war. He told Grazzi, "I consider this demand and the manner in which it is made a declaration of war." There was no equivocation or trepidation in his voice.

And when the Italians made their demand, Metaxas gave them the same answers his ancestors had to other would-be conquerors: Οχι.

No.

The Greeks would not allow the Italians or the Germans or anyone else to take over the country where democracy was born and where the Greeks had eventually repulsed all those who thought they could occupy their homeland. Later, the German newspaper *Berliner Borsenzeitung* would defend the invasion by stating that "by rejecting Italy's demand . . . the Greek government has taken a decision which goes against its Italian neighbor, against the new European Order and in favor of the enemy of this new order which is England. Greece had to ally itself in favor or against the European solidarity."

At 6:30 A.M., $3^1/_2$ hours after the Italian demand, two Italian infantry divisions of forty thousand men attacked Greece from Albania. Metaxas expected it. He allowed the Italians to filter through mountain passes into Thessaly almost to Ioannina, in the north central part of Greece where the Italians, to their dismay, would run into Metaxas's plan: the famed Evzones, feared mountain fighters who had been the backbone of the Greek war of independence from Turkey from 1821 to

1832 and in the Balkan wars of 1912–13, after which they exclusively became the members of the Royal Guard. They were called *palikaria*, "brave young warriors."

In ceremonial skirted *fustanellas* and tight white hosiery that belied their ferocity and fearlessness, the Evzones were recruited for their size, fighting skill, and bravery. There were about fifteen thousand of them in the Greek army but they preferred fighting as guerrillas in small units instead of in bigger divisions. They were an intimidating sight for an enemy—tall and stalwart and mustachioed, wearing deep blue velvet jackets embroided with gold, long curved swords in their sashes. In the mountains, though, their clothes were as ragged as they.

Metaxas had them ready because he didn't trust Mussolini, and he also had developed a defense strategy with Gen. Alexander Papagos, a smart field commander who knew the mountains into which the unsuspecting Italians had marched so confidently. Metaxas had seen how Mussolini had directed the building of highways through Albania and suspected they would lead to Greece for a reason.

King George of England was happy to help the Greeks, especially because his cousin sat on the throne of Greece. "In this hour of Greece's need I wish to say to the heroic Greek nation and to my cousin George, King of the Hellenes, this: We are with you in this struggle; your cause is our cause; we shall be fighting against a common foe." Hitler, already spreading himself over too many fronts, was worried whether the Italians could take or hold Greece.

Thus it was that Hitler alighted from a train on October 28 at Florence to be approached by a smug and smiling Mussolini, still chafing at all those times Hitler had driven into a country without consulting him.

His lower lip curled out defiantly, Mussolini said, "Führer, we are on the march! Victorious Italian troops crossed the Greco-Albanian frontier at dawn today!" Hitler was not happy.

So it was that the Italians walked into the Greek mountains and became quickly enveloped by crack fighting units backed by the Evzones and delivered the stunning news to the world that the Axis powers were not invulnerable when the Greeks smashed the Italian army at Metsovo Pass. The Greeks were acting almost alone, save for some British air power and mines placed along the Greek coast. They showed the differences in manpower in their country of nine million against forty-four million Italians was not too much to overcome. For now.

The Greeks were battering the Italians with a rousing show of resistance, pushing back the Italian army into Albania and taking Koritza, the principal Italian base in that country, less than a month after receiving the Italian demand. The Greeks had the Italians on the run and seemed they would push them all the way back to Italy. The Greeks taunted the Italians, painting To Rome on rocks as they pushed them back, defeating even the strong Alpine Division. Mussolini was looking silly, especially to Hitler, and the Greeks were gaining momentum.

The headlines were rocking the world, and Hitler was furious at the news that was bannered: *Greeks Push Into Albania*, and *Koritza Falls to Greeks*, and the irritating, *Greeks Trap Famed Division*. At every turn, it seemed, the Greeks were stunning the Italians and ruining Hitler's plans. He knew, even more than his generals, the truth of another headline: *Greeks To Keep Fighting No Matter What Happens*. Hitler knew history.

On November 4, Hitler convened a war conference in Berlin, summoning top generals, and he told them the Italian invasion into Greece had turned into a rout of his allies and been a "regrettable blunder" endangering Germany's position in the Balkans. The British had agreed to help the Greeks and had strengthened Crete, seventy miles off the southern coast of Greece, establishing airfields there where air strikes could hit German targets and provide troops to send to the Greek mainland. While the Greeks were enjoying their victories over the Italians, Hitler was already directing his army to prepare plans to send ten divisions into Greece on short notice. Hitler feared Greek resistance and he wanted to prevent the British from setting up a stronghold in the Mediterranean.

On December 1, 1940, the *Boston Globe* reported:

> The Italian attack on Greece has aroused the old Greek spirit of national pride, freedom and personal courage. This spirit expressed itself

in Greek philosophy, literature and arts that have been the basis of European culture. All European nations have gone to school to ancient Greek artists and philosophers. Roman art and Roman literature as well as philosophy started flourishing after the Roman armies had defeated the Greek Empire, rival of ancient Rome. Greek artists and poets were taken to Rome as teachers. Now, 2000 years later the Roman armies are on the march against Greek independence. Modern Italy may defeat the Greek army but the Greek spirit is deathless.

But it was the Italians who were being routed and embarrassed. Bitter cold and mountain fighting left the Italians looking for a way out and it was the Greeks who were yelling, "Throw them into the sea," to push them back out of Albania and all the way to the Adriatic. "Greek success may well be a turning point in the war," one newspaper wrote, and it seemed a turning point was at hand, if only the British could deliver more goods and men to continue the counteroffensive, especially with fears that the Germans might become involved as Hitler fretted. "It is inconceivable that Hitler will let his blustering ally down," one American newspaper reported.

In December, two months after the Italian demand, the Greeks were still pushing around their bigger foes. After more than six weeks of fighting, the Greeks had captured seven thousand Italians, two hundred guns, 250 cars, thousands of machine guns, tanks, and armored cars, and conquered about a quarter of Italian Albania.

The headlines in American newspapers were filled with stories of glorious Greek victories, including one story about Greek women hauling cannons up mountain tops where the Evzones had taken to taunting the Italians with cries of "aera" or "air." It meant get out! or leave our air! Another headline told disbelieving Americans, GREEK "AMAZONS" KILL FOES BY ROLLING ROCKS OFF PEAKS, about a battle in which a hundred Greek women helped trap three thousand Italians in a mountain ravine.

American leaders expressed their admiration and support for Greece, and the Greek War Relief was set up in the United States to help provide goods and commodities. On December 7, 1940, King George sent President Roosevelt a letter stating that "guardians across the seas of the ideals for which throughout the centuries Greeks have lived and died, Americans today are aware that the Greek nation is again fighting for the principles of justice, truth and liberty, without which life for us is inconceivable." Roosevelt replied promptly: "All free peoples are deeply impressed by the courage and steadfastness of the Greek nation."

There followed one Greek victory after another while Hitler fretted and fumed and Mussolini anguished over what was happening to his supposedly superior army. On January 8–9, Hitler went into the mountains at Berchtesgaden for a retreat conference where he was determined to help the Italians, without giving them too much advance notice. He decided to send $2^1/_2$ divisions into Albania to help the fleeing Italians who were being chased by the Greeks. He set up "Operation Marita," a plan to assemble up to twenty-four divisions of men in Romania to plow into Greece through Bulgaria when the brutally cold weather improved. Then he summoned Mussolini.

The quaking Italian dictator came to see Hitler on January 19 in Berghof, fearful of explaining why the Italians were being soundly defeated in Egypt and Greece. Mussolini was almost sick to his stomach at the prospect of meeting a furious führer, but he was surprised when Hitler was cordial and gentle to him and talked mostly of his worries about Russia, which he wanted to strike quickly and in great numbers.

Then came a turn no one expected. On January 29, 1941, Metaxas—who had become ill without the Greeks being told—died from complications of blood poisoning and uremia after a tonsillectomy on January 18.

By early in February, Hitler had massed an army of 680,000 men in Romania, fearful the British would strengthen the area above Salonika and jeopardize his Russian plans, providing Greece a strategic point with which to forestall even a massive German assault. But there was a caveat that surprised his top generals. Because Greece's fighting had delayed Hitler's plans even further, Russia could not be invaded for at least another month. Hitler would have to go into Greece. It may have been the worst decision he made, and it was done in a rage.

On April 6, after waves of Luftwaffe bombers had pounded Greek and Yugoslavian borders, the mighty assemblage of Nazi armies followed them into those countries.

Field Marshal List's Twelfth Army of fifteen divisions, including four armored, poured into Greece. The British sent in fifty-three thousand men to help but superior German airpower made it difficult for the Greeks and British to survive on bravery alone. The attack came at dawn on April 6 and in three days List had driven into Salonika, whose large Jewish population was now in peril and the Wehrmacht pushed on quickly toward Athens, anxious to quickly occupy the political and economic center of the country before the British could mobilize more men. The country's leaders and royalty now squabbled over the best course of action as the German air force pounded ports and cities and villages.

Northern Greek armies in Albania, who had enjoyed success, were cut off now and had to surrender to the Germans on April 23, after Hitler made sure the Italians could also accept the Greek defeat personally to avenge the insult the Greeks had given them in battle. German planes pounded, it seemed, every rock and clump of trees and shrubs where people and soldiers might hide or plan to fight, crushing everything in their path, an endless army, storming over outmanned and undergunned defenders who, unlike their ancestors, had to face the terror of technology and firepower.

The Greeks, soldiers and civilians, faced the last days before occupation as stolidly as they could and would turn sometimes to the patriotic songs of singers such as Sophia Vembo, whose plaintive laments and melancholia mixed with fervor fed them hope. Vembo would visit the wounded in hospitals, just her sight lifting the spirits of men who had lost limbs or eyes and were dying. She would stroll among them, hoping to soothe, but invariably was asked to sing.

One of the favorites was "Sons of Greece," a rousing anthem in which her strong voice would soar and she would belt, "Sons, Greece's sons, who are fighting on the tall mountains; Sons, to the sweet Virgin Mary, we are all praying for you to return." They were the words many of them had heard while slugging through the cold mountains and pushing into Albania and it made even the weary and battle-hardened veterans cry because they knew, outside the windows, the Nazis were coming.

At one hospital stop, after she had sung, a blinded veteran reached his hand up gently, trying to touch the sound. "I do not see you, my Sophia, but I hear you," he said, the singer turning with the touch. "But I thank God he took my eyes and he gave me the gift of keeping my ears so that I can listen to your sweet voice," the man said. And now it was her time to cry, and she bent down to kiss him gently and spoke to him softly, her strong voice muted with anguish. He was an officer, a proud man who had led men, and he stood up straight. "I am not crying, Sophia, that I have lost my eyes," he said. "I am crying because I do not have another two eyes that I could give for my country."

> Thoughts are mightier than strength of hand
>
> —Sophocles

It would do no good. The German armies rolled on, and on Saturday, April 26, there was a bombing raid outside Athens about 5:00 P.M. Within two hours, the last of the British convoys drove out of town in a hurry, looking for a way out of Greece. Kyriakides, like most other Greeks in Athens, could do nothing but wait for the inevitable.

On April 27, 1941, Nazi tanks rolled into Athens and hoisted the swastika over the Acropolis, the symbol of democracy for Western civilization, as British, Australian, and New Zealand troops tried desperately to escape over water, and Greek political leaders fled to Crete. They hoped to somehow resume the war from there, not knowing Hitler was assembling an unprecedented assault of armies from the air on that island. Many of the allied soldiers found themselves trapped in Greece, looking to hide in the homes of citizens whose lives were already stretched by fear.

A radio station played the Greek national anthem even as Nazi armies marched down the streets of Athens. But the music didn't last long. Stunned listeners in tavernas and their homes heard yelling in German in the background of the radio studio, and the music stopped before a breathless announcer came on to say, "We have been invaded. This is our final broadcast. People of Greece, swear on the holy gospel never to heed the tyrant's words, neither work for him nor be beguiled by his bribes." Then, it was over.

There were many acts of heroism. A soldier named Costas Koukides was guarding the Greek flag on the Acropolis when a squadron of German soldiers approached and ordered him to take it down so the swastika could rise above the Greek city. Koukides obeyed but his eyes flashed hatred and anger.

He took the flag and jumped onto a marble column, wrapping himself in the fabric and sang, "I love my country's flag as I love my life. I shall not hand it to an enemy. I prefer to die." As the startled Germans watched, Koukides jumped off the column and into space, falling two hundred meters into a rocky crevice, the Greek flag still surrounding his body.

For the Germans, who were Hellenophiles, the capture of the Acropolis was of stunning value. They had seized what Hitler himself called "the symbol of human culture," the symmetrically perfect columns and white marble rising on a hill above an ancient city where Socrates and Plato led dialogues and debate about human existence and the meaning of life. Hitler, the painter, reveled in it.

There was dismay in America too. The *Miami Herald* noted that "little Greece is done. The pitiful handful of patriots was no match for the Nazi millions and the blitzkrieg. All the glory of victory over Mussolini fades into the bitter dregs of the Hitler conquest. Even in defeat, the battle of the Greeks against the overwhelming hordes of Germany stands out as a glorious page as there is in the long history of Grecian civilization. Some day the race may raise a Homer to celebrate her 1941 exploits in imperishable epic."

Kyriakides was still not over the death of his wife, but had settled into a mind-numbing routine of rote bill collecting on his route, even forgetting for a time the running that had made him a champion. He went from house to house collecting the amounts due for the utilities.

Like his countrymen, all he could do was watch when the Germans in-vaded, and simply try to survive by working and staying out of sight of the patrols as much as possible. Because of his job, he was not ques-tioned as much as others when he went about the dirt paths of his neighborhood, house-to-house. He had become a familiar sight to the soldiers as he kept his head down and walked.

But one day in November of 1941, he came upon a house at 9 Kefkia Street in the neighborhood of Filothei and saw a small, young woman cleaning the steps outside, using a broom and a bucket of water to keep down the dust. He stopped, taken by her looks and soft demeanor. She was bending to clean when she felt his eyes on her and she looked up, shyly.

Kyriakides, for the first time in months, smiled, if only a little. "Bravo, young lady. It's nice to see someone who knows how to take care of a home." She didn't smile back, a bit indignant he had spoken to her so forwardly. Kyriakides was a bit puzzled, but not daunted. She thought, but didn't say, *What a handsome man*. Even the war hadn't yet blunted Kyriakides' lean athletic frame or sap the strength of his chiseled face or soft, inviting eyes. They looked at each other briefly, before he turned and walked away.

He went to her neighbor, Mrs. Kitsopoulos, and asked, "Who is this girl?" and she laughed and told him about Iphigenia, the young woman with light green eyes.

"She is the daughter of Mr. Katsarellos," the neighbor said, eyes twinkling, knowing what Kyriakides was already thinking.

"I would like to meet her," he said. "Someday," he added a little more slowly, "I would like to get married again. There is a war going on."

Kyriakides' heart was opening a little after the tragedy of his wife's death. He knew, in the Greek culture where the family was paramount, that he would have to approach the courting of this woman carefully, because honor was important, and he would have to ask her father for permission to marry her.

A meeting was arranged and a suited and humble Kyriakides came to the Katsarellos house again where he first met Iphigenia's father. She had never met another man before in an arranged meeting and was waiting anxiously in another room when Kyriakides came in. Mr. Katsarellos had heard of the Balkan champion, of course, but this was his daughter and he was taking no chances.

Kyriakides instantly put the man at ease with a warm smile and an earnest manner that told how serious he was about the woman he had not yet even dated.

The two men looked at each other again, their eyes locked quickly, and a casual comfort began settling in between them, a mutual respect for the great runner, and Kyriakides for the man protecting his daughter's interest. With the war raging, Kyriakides knew her family could not provide a dowry, so he took the talk into another direction that would preclude that.

"Mr. Katsarellos," he said respectfully, "you know the reason I am here. I like your daughter. Can you please ask her if she likes me so we can finish today?" Kyriakides' formality pleased the man and made him laugh just a little too. He slapped his knees and stood up proudly, looking directly at Kyriakides.

"I will go ask my daughter," he said, pretending to follow the sincerity of this ritual. Kyriakides sat nervously, fumbling slightly with his fingers, his suit chafing a bit. He looked around the sparsely furnished room and waited.

The father went to talk to his daughter. He returned to Kyriakides and said, "As you said, you like her and she likes you. Let's finish." Both men smiled. Iphigenia came in, her face down coyly, but her heart beating quickly. They gave their word to marry. In the Greek culture, this was an irrevocable promise.

He kissed her softly, formally, and gave her an embrace of promise. It was her first. They sat and talked briefly and he said there was an urgency to get married because of the war. "There are bad days ahead," he said ruefully.

The arrangement of the couple meeting, called a *proxenio*, led to their marriage a month later, on December 28, 1941, in a modest ceremony in her father's house, presided over by a favorite priest. Outside in Athens, German troops patrolled and occupied their city.

There was no dancing, no celebration in the tradition of Greek weddings, with wine and joy and exultant happiness, parties that would sometimes last several days. In smaller villages, everyone came, but the darkness of the occupation had loomed over everyday life like a shroud dropped on everyone's life and the weight was omnipresent. It was the time the Greeks called the Κατοχη, the occupation, and it was like a cobweb on the face that couldn't be rubbed away.

Life had changed for Kyriakides. He hadn't run for two years and thought his days of running were probably over. It was time to think of a family. But every so often, he thought about his triumphs and his running days and remembered Boston and George Demeter and Jerry Nason and wondered if they ever thought of him and what his life must be like in an occupied country during a world war.

There was no formal meal after the wedding. Kyriakides found some bread pieces from a local baker to eat in celebration. Their wedding gift was a silk pillow. For the next month, Kyriakides and Iphigenia lived in the house he had shared with Fanouria Maina until he, feeling the weight of the past, returned the home to her family. "It's not right," he said to his wife. "I didn't have any children with Fanouria."

He finally felt he could move on now with Iphigenia, whose small stature didn't diminish the generosity of her heart and her delight at marrying a gentle man who wanted a family. Kyriakides knew a man who had maintained his money and had a house in the neighborhood of Halandri, a working-class place, in what was still a rather rural area of Athens, with few houses and dirt roads, where almost everyone had a small garden in the back. It was more of a summer house, but it was furnished and had gas lamps and the man was afraid the Germans would take it if they saw no one was living there.

"Take it," he said. "It's better the house be occupied. You will be like the housekeepers and the Germans won't take it," he said, he too hoping for the day they believed the Allies would come and liberate the country. It would not be soon.

They had few possessions now, but he brought his many running trophies with him and set them up on a shelf, with his prized Olympic book from 1936. They had a bed in a small bedroom and one couch near a kitchen, where they would sit most of the time when he wasn't working. There was a small wash area, and a radio near the kitchen.

If they wanted to visit friends, they would use the side streets and go through the backyard and then sit in the cellar so the Germans would not know they were congregating. At home, they had only two sheets that were washed outside in a large kettle used to heat water.

A little food came from using ration cards at distribution centers, or from their own garden or trading goods. Kyriakides one day traded two shirts for them, and sometimes farmers he knew gave him a few slices of bread, or even crumbs. Rings and jewelry went for olive oil or butter or sugar. There was some electricity and Kyriakides continued to go out and collect from customers, but the usage was limited during the day. They had few clothes, only a pair of shoes each and little money or resources. He would stuff paper in his shoes when holes appeared in the soles.

At night, they would pull down a dark blue shade to hide themselves from the patrols pounding the streets, the sound of heavy heels clicking making sleep difficult because the soldiers often went house-to-house looking for suspected saboteurs.

Life had settled into an uneasy routine of worry and fear in Athens, although Kyriakides attempted to go through his daily regimen as best as he could, trying to ignore the Nazi presence everywhere on the streets, the jack-booted soldiers occupying the land where democracy was born rankling him. He was concentrating solely on surviving and getting his family through the war. Sometimes he thought the Greeks eventually would win, with the help of the allies where he knew there were many friends and Hellenophiles, including the British, some of whose soldiers were still hiding in Athens.

The sight of German soldiers, machine guns and rifles and grenades in hand, became a perverse part of everyday life, although the tension never seemed to evaporate, and there were constant reminders of the repression, men suddenly being rounded up by patrols for questioning, houses broken into by soldiers in search of loot and goods, and the unnerving sight of starving, gaunt, ghostlike figures teetering on the side-

This was the reason Kyriakides ran: to bring back food and medicine for starving Greeks, like these in a soup kitchen set up in Athens in 1941. Courtesy of Benaki Museum, Athens.

walks before toppling over, hands distended for help, people walking past them because they could offer none.

The winter of 1941 was unusually cold, and people already weakened by malnutrition succumbed to the cold and diseases as temperatures sometimes fell below freezing, which seemed colder for people used to the warmth of the Greek sun. Some homes had stoves used for heat, but it was difficult foraging for wood. The weakest, with vitamin deficiencies too, looked like zombies, walking stiffly in the streets, many with boils or tumors on their hands, feet, and faces. The Greeks hid what little food they had, to feed their families, or would carefully watch their little gardens so no one would take the few vegetables they needed to sustain themselves.

Iphigenia's father still worked for the National Bank of Greece, but this was no longer under Greek control, and she could not rely on him to sustain her family. It would be up to her husband, and he would some-how find a way to deliver food, if only a green cabbage called λα–χαυιδες, or the corn bread called μπομποτα. Often though, it was only a potato, or just a few peas.

Even Kyriakides' resolve withered on the days when he saw what he thought was the worst of war. People were eating out of trash cans, pick-ing through, scrounging quickly like squirrels or rats afraid another creature would catch them when they were vulnerable, not daring to look up, and walking away quickly when they had a crumb, discreetly trying to shove it into their mouths, fearing they would appear too furtive and attract the attention of the ever present Nazi patrols.

> War loves to seek its victims in the young
>
> —Sophocles

The famine began in the winter of 1941–42, and by 1943 an esti-mated 250,000 people would die of starvation. The lucky were able to eat dead dogs and donkeys or find scraps of sustenance. Cries of "I'm hungry" filled the air and children's swollen bellies were an uneasy sight. The Germans had tried to take every weapon away and the penalty for having one was death—for the entire family. From Athens to small vil-lages, though, from the Greek islands to Crete, where old women with pitchforks had bayoneted landing German paratroopers, Greeks fought with the weapons at hand, including their teeth and words.

German reprisals did little to stop the organized Resistance, not even the common sights of men hanging from trees in the streets of Athens, and the massacre of civilians, of women and children, in small mountain villages. In Athens, Kyriakides and his Olympic teammates could do nothing but wait and try to stay alive. He still had to work his bill-collecting route as the Greeks tried to maintain some semblance of normal life, and the Germans needed utilities to operate. But there was little spirit now to do anything but stay alive.

Back in the United States, Kelley ran again in the 1942 Boston Marathon, on a cool forty-four-degree April day, oblivious to what Kyr-iakides was going through. Kelley was happy because his second wedding anniversary was approaching and he felt fit and prime at thirty-four years old. The war had stripped the running field of many competitors and one of the leading candidates was forty-year-old schoolmaster Lou Gregory, the national champion at ten, twenty, and thirty kilometers, and Medford milkman Joe Smith, who'd won the 1941 national championship at Yonkers.

The 1941 Boston Marathon champ, Les Pawson, was out because he'd been hit by a car while running a race a few months before, an accident that pained his good friend Kelley, who had finished second to him in the 1941 marathon. Still, Smith sailed to victory over Gregory, and Kelley had to settle for fifth. It wasn't his worst moment.

That came two months later when his wife, Mary, whom he had married just two years before after the 1940 marathon, suddenly became ill. They were still living in Arlington with her mother, trying to save money to buy their own home. On a Sunday morning in June, Kelley was sitting in the living room reading the paper when he suddenly heard his mother-in-law shriek, "Get the ambulance! Get the ambulance!" Mary had taken deathly ill.

She was rushed to the hospital where doctors said she had cancer. Three days later, on June 6, as Kelley held her in his arms, she looked up at him wanly and repeated the first words he had ever said to her, when they met on the streetcar. "What time is it?" she said sweetly. And she passed away, slipping away from Kelley and taking with him, he thought, his hopes and plans and desires.

It was the kind of loss Kyriakides saw every day in Greece. Then one day came word that shocked him just when he thought there was no shock left. Petropoulos, the strong shot putter who was a member of the Olympic team, had died. Petropoulos's death was followed by that of Skiadas, the hurdler, then Travlos, the pole vaulter, and Lycopoulos, the javelin thrower, strong men who succumbed, like so many others, to starvation and illness. "If men like these, Olympic athletes, die, what hope do we have?" Kyriakides asked.

The Greeks had many enemies now: the omnipresent Germans, the lack of food, and not knowing when they might simply be rounded up for questioning, to disappear from their families, to be shot or hanged and left on a tree branch for everyone to see, as an example the Germans hoped would stem reprisals. Everyone avoided going near Haidari, the prison, and Kaisariani, the shooting range in Athens, where victims would be lined up and gunned down, falling with the shrieks of their families echoing in their ears, a final executioner walking up and administering the *coup de grâce*, a bullet to the head of those who still moved.

A still Kyriakides came home one day looking withdrawn.

"What is it?" Iphigenia asked.

He paused. "I saw someone I know hanging today," Kyriakides said. She winced, but he suddenly embraced her, seeing the fear and hopelessness. "The day will come when the Germans will leave, so Greece can get back on the right road and see the light again," he said. The Germans, trying to isolate Athens, destroyed bridges and trams and roads, keeping the countryside towns and their populations away from the country's largest city. If the Germans didn't destroy a bridge or a road, often the Greek Resistance would, trying to keep the Germans from moving supplies. The Germans tried to prevent retaliation by the Greeks by imposing severe restrictions on movements of civilians, including a dusk-to-dawn curfew. To be seen on the streets at night could mean death.

The Greeks knew that resistance was their only hope as they waited for the Allies to wear down the German might. Kyriakides would sometimes sing to his wife softly too, patriotic songs of Cyprus, where he wondered how his family lived now, and of the Greek freedom fighters of the war of independence from the Ottoman Empire.

As he walked his bill-collecting route, Kyriakides' heart ached with the sight of children sitting on the streets, some with scabies on their feet so bad they could not walk. Their distended bellies were swollen from lack of food, making him feel guilty he was trying to scrape together enough food for his own family. The sight burned into him. During the occupation, fifty thousand children were becoming orphaned, some left to wander on their own on streets that a few years before had brimmed with scenes of happy families strolling. Some people lived in caves or rock crevices outside the city, the worst with lined faces, talking in monotone voices about torture, starvation, and deprivation.

Kyriakides had to make a living, too, working as a bill collector for a utility company in Athens, where he went door-to-door every day. Courtesy of the Kyriakides family.

Soldiers sometimes would just come into people's homes and loot, take what they wanted for their own needs or those of their comrades. Iphigenia worried about that too, especially with Kyriakides on his daily rounds of bill collecting in a country where the economy was wasting away. As the days went on, Iphigenia worried whether Greece would ever be free again. Kyriakides was more optimistic. "Have patience," he told her. "When the war ends, the Allies will come and they will see the sacrifices the Greek people have made," he added.

It was not easy to have patience. They saw tragedy everywhere during the war, including the horrific execution of some young men lined up outside a high school gymnasium and machine-gunned.

The initial horror of death was soon overcome by an inability by many to feel compassion anymore because they fought for their own survival and the sight of death was too commonplace. Compassion gave way to weariness and indifference, while the level of outrage fell among many.

Horse-drawn carts would pick up bodies for burial in mass graves. The bodies would be piled up on top of one another in the back of the cart and, after a while, the horrifying sight ceased to be so and the carts went by like another bus carrying commuters. Some families simply dumped their deceased in cemeteries at night so that they would not lose their ration cards for food. A piece of bread became a delicacy, to gulp instead of savor, a lemon peel a mainstay, mother's milk the last, best food of those who had some.

The evil and brutality couldn't be overstated, nor the cold-bloodedness of the German military hierarchy, epitomized by an order from Field Marshal Hermann Goering to military leaders in Greece, on August 6, 1942: "I could not care less when you say that people under your administration are dying of hunger. Let them perish so long as no German starves." Some believed this was part of a deliberate German policy of genocide by starvation, the extermination of the Greeks through hunger.

But there was a sound Iphigenia and the Greeks never got used to, even over the keening of people crying for their dead and the moaning of those dying for food. It was the dreaded, jack-booted goose step of German soldiers locked in unison with one another, their heels clicking loudly on the stone streets, the pounding matching the fear of racing hearts in residents hiding in their homes.

The sound was more ominous one night when Kyriakides came home and quickly scurried into his house. He had three soldiers with him. They were British and as frightened as the Greeks. Besides hiding fugitives, many Greek families had been given possessions by Jewish neighbors, including money, jewelry, and cosmetics to hold, but now Iphigenia had Allied soldiers in her house, a death sentence for all if a German patrol found them. Her heart raced and her eyes widened and she could not swallow. She was terrified.

Kyriakides saw the fear in her face. "Do not worry, Iphigenia. They will only be here for a short time. It is our duty to hide them," he said, trying not to let his voice show his own worry as he gripped her shoulders. "Don't worry, it will only be for a few hours," he said. Over his shoulder, Iphigenia could see the plaintive look in the eyes of the soldiers, young men.

The frightened soldiers were quickly escorted into the cellar by Kyriakides while the worried family upstairs hoped this would not be the night a German patrol would knock on the door and yell in harsh, guttural tones for Kyriakides to open up and let them in.

Kyriakides felt, because he was not in the mountains fighting, that he had to do what he could for the Resistance. After a sleepless night, the soldiers left before dawn, when a Resistance fighter came from the nearby mountains and led them away.

The Greek Jews, of course, were special targets. The Greeks, especially church leaders, tried to protect them. By war's end, though, more than fifty-six thousand of them would be sent to concentration camps and be killed. There were many militants among the Jews too, especially in Thessalonika, and they headed into the mountains to join the *andartes*. Those who remained behind were persecuted before they were sent to concentration camps such as Auschwitz, and faced the gas chambers as soon as they arrived. Many Greeks tried, at the risk of their own lives, to hide and protect their Jewish neighbors.

In Athens and Piraeus, the police chief, Angelos Evert, whose grandfather emigrated from Germany to Greece, ordered twenty-two hundred forged identity cards be issued to help Jews escape. Because of his German name, he was not kept under close surveillance by German officials. But it didn't keep the Germans from sending thousands of Greek Jews to concentration camps and from executing Greeks who were found to harbor them. One of the Greeks who got Evert's order to help forge the identity cards was a high-ranking Athenian police official, Ioannis Tsiotos, a wounded veteran of the Bolshevik wars in Russia. He was stationed in the Kolonaki section, the third police district, which had been well-to-do before the war. He was told to provide Greek Resistance fighters and Jews with false Greek passports, for Egypt, Palestine, or the Middle East. It was a dangerous undertaking because the Germans would kill those collaborating with the Resistance or Jews, and the Gestapo was feared everywhere.

To protect him, the Greek intelligence service told him to put photos of Hitler and literature about the Nazis and Germany in his house, anticipating he would be questioned. Frightened Jews sneaked to him and he changed their names on identity cards. One, a prominent attorney named Cohen, received a card that gave his name as Pavlos Panopoulos. It saved his life when he was stopped.

One day, an Italian officer who said he was sent by the Greek underground came to Tsiotos and said he wanted an identity card to get out of the country. Within a half hour, the Gestapo showed up. The Italian was working for them. Tsiotos was arrested and taken to jail for serious questioning. He wondered whether he too would be taken to the firing range at Kaisariani, but he was resigned to his fate and had survived too many fearful settings to show any trepidation.

He was interrogated aggressively, and told he would be taken to the shooting range, but Tsiotos surprised the Gestapo officers when he said sharply, in German, "I respect Hitler. Go to my house and see who I am!"

He had set up an elaborate ruse. Then he grabbed a telephone in front of the interrogators and yelled. As they looked on astonished, he had told them, "Give me the phone. I will speak to Hitler myself!" Even the Gestapo officers didn't know how to take this action, so he was thrown back into jail and two SS officers were sent to Tsiotos's home.

When they returned, they said they had found what Tsiotos said they would: his house was filled with literature about Germany and the Third Reich, maps and photos of Hitler and high-ranking German officials. A Gestapo secretary went to Tsiotos's cell and told him that he would be released in the morning. She was a spy for the British. When Tsiotos got out, he kept issuing false identity cards, and the Greek Resistance had him follow SS Officer Hans Sandl.

While the Germans were Hellenophiles and admired the history of Greece, they were nonetheless ruthless in trying to maintain order in a country where freedom was more valued than life. Nothing, it seemed, could stop the Resistance, neither trying to appease the citizens nor killing them indiscriminately. Hanged Resistance fighters dangled from trees in Athens while their comrades made plans to keep killing Germans at night, even when orders came down that for every German killed, 100, then 150, then 200, then 250, or 300 Greeks would be killed in retaliation. Still, the Greeks fought.

Living with occupation was a dread, a fear living inside Iphigenia like a venomous snake that poisoned from the inside, terror rising to her throat when she would see German soldiers, wondering if her husband would come home every day after work. When she did go out, she would look away from the soldiers or dash into a doorway entrance to avoid them. The sound of the boots was horror, but what was worse, she thought, was the icy stare of the strong, strapping blond young men with cocked rifles and cold hearts who were ready to kill at an instant.

Exiles feed on hope

—Aeschylus

But Kyriakides wanted to do more than just survive. He wanted to help. The Germans had sealed the civilian radios so they could not receive the BBC or news from other countries. But, huddled in the dark at night in their home, Kyriakides had found a way to unseal the radio so he could hear the news, and in the next day as he walked his bill-collecting rounds, a familiar sight now to the usual German patrols, he could stop in a doorway and say hello to a customer, and pass on news from Great Britain or the United States and, in return, carry oral messages to members of the Greek Resistance.

To be caught meant a death sentence or prison, and the routine carried with it now the heart-pounding fear of a collaborator turning him in, or a sharp-eyed German officer noticing something different. But Kyriakides had a heart used to struggle and adversity, and to a tempo of tension.

Although the utility company was still in business, there was little electricity available to the residents of Athens, who relied on a hot plate or a potbellied stove with a fire to cook what little food they had. Homes were heated with stoves or fireplaces on chilly nights. The electricity was not allowed on during the day, and at night, the residents drew their blue shades to prevent any light from escaping.

There was tension in the night in the dark house. There was a bed in a small room and one couch near a kitchen where the two of them would often sit. There was a small wash area where he could clean up, and often it was of her worry he would be caught while delivering messages for the Resistance, or that the Germans would hear the radio or suspect them and burst into their house in the middle of the night and detain them, or shoot them. He would hear none of the objections. "I'm doing my patriotic duty for my country," he said simply. "The andartes are in the mountains fighting and I'm not there, but I can do this here. What I'm doing is my part," he said. Information, he knew, was as important as ammunition, even if it were as volatile as a hand grenade in his pocket.

Kyriakides tried to go through his daily routine, including delivering information for the Resistance, and just hope for the war's end. He was not working out and his weight was falling with the lack of food, but what pained him as much were the sights he saw every day, the wan, thin figures wandering aimlessly on the streets, drawn pale faces making them look like tragic figures in an ancient play. He was out of the house at 7:30 A.M. to do his rounds, anxious to get back to his wife, who was now pregnant with their first child.

After he left for work, Iphigenia stayed behind, mostly to care for herself because travel was so closely restricted that it was difficult even for family members to get around without being questioned by the German patrols that controlled the streets. Because utilities were required, even in an occupied land, Kyriakides was allowed to move about on his job, but he would return promptly at 4 P.M. to care for his wife, going to the garden to bring in what was available, carrots, potatoes, peas. They were like prisoners in their own home and had only a few pieces of clothing that had to be washed regularly.

Occasionally, Kyriakides let himself think of his running days, which seemed to be evaporating in the mist of the past now, as he came into his thirties. He had wanted only to be an athlete and run for the glory of his country when he was young, and now he worried whether the country would survive, and what was happening back on Cyprus.

All the talk was of war, and was whispered. No one cared anymore about the Balkan Games or the trivialities of running, and Kyriakides' celebrity, it seemed, had disappeared. On December 3, 1942, Iphigenia gave birth to their first child: a girl they named Eleni. She was born at Helena Venizelou Hospital, far from Halandri and one of the few still operating for civilians, with few supplies and decrepit rooms. Kyriakides came back to see her and was angry to find there was no milk for his wife. He saw Iphigenia in the bed, still weak from the delivery and hungry too.

Kyriakides wasn't sure where to go, but he walked back through the streets, farther and farther, until he got to the home of a man he knew had a goat, and asked him for some milk. "Please," he said. "It's for my wife." Even milk was a precious commodity, but the farmer agreed.

With the lack of food, Kyriakides' face had taken on a hollow look. The few products they got from the tomatoes and potatoes and beans he had planted barely sustained them, although occasionally he would find some bread on his deliveries and a little milk, which would be given to his wife and child. Walking kept him in shape, despite his hunger.

Sometimes, there would be a treat: an egg he might come upon during his rounds, the gift of those a little better off who held him in high esteem for his running accomplishments. He took the offerings reluctantly, shyly, thinking of his family having only scraps, usually just a few peas to eat. He ripped bedsheets to make diapers for his daughter, tore the wood off the bed frame to make a makeshift crib, and chopped trees to get wood to fire the pot-bellied stove.

It was a time of sacrifice, but one was more difficult for him than others. He took one of their most precious belongings, the silk pillow he received for his wedding gift, and traded it for a carriage for his daughter.

From time to time, he would walk a short distance away to another neighborhood where Simitsek, his coach, was living. They didn't talk about running or the old victories, or even if there would be new ones. All that was on everyone's mind now was the war and the constant, ceaseless dread of the Nazi presence and the fear that anyone could simply be executed for no reason.

On a warm spring day in 1943, in late afternoon, Kyriakides and his wife pushed the battered carriage carrying young Eleni on their long way back from Iphigenia's parents' house in Filothei when they got to the main square near their home in the Halandri district. They were talking easily, feeling a respite from the war around them, happy with each other and their family, when they suddenly stopped, feeling uneasy because of what they saw ahead. Anxious people were milling about, being directed by German soldiers with drawn weapons, shoved almost in the square. Now some cries were going up as men were being separated from their wives, pushed away by the jumpy young soldiers under orders. Kyriakides and his wife looked at each other in fear, but now there was no way out. It was one of the routine stops that often led to the imprisonment or execution of so many Greeks that the human roadblock was called a "blocco," a roundup sifting for troublemakers. It was a sight that chilled the hardest of men, because no one knew whether they would ever return to their families. The word they did not want to hear was *kaput!* the German declaration that they were finished, they would soon be dead.

Suddenly, they heard the screech of a truck's brakes. The Germans had blocked off the streets, looking for insurgents and those who might have been involved in the shooting of some soldiers the night before by members of the Resistance.

Kyriakides was worried too, remembering the night he had hidden the British soldiers in their home. He didn't know if the patrols would be used to find out what he had done, if he would be questioned, or even imprisoned or killed. Now the soldiers were looking at them.

"*Halt!*" a soldier shouted, his face a mixture of fear and anger, the tension visible under his steel helmet, his anxiety making him wave the rifle like a baton. Patrols frequently stopped citizens, but Kyriakides could see past the soldier to where his friends and neighbors were being aggressively moved and his heart started beating fast, sweat coming to his palms. He was worried for his wife and daughter. They were on Agia Paraskevi street, so close to the sanctuary of their home.

Now the screaming became louder as women reached for their husbands, who were being torn from them, and soldiers raced off in trucks and around the square, trying to corral the nervous Greeks. Several more soldiers and an officer came around Kyriakides. The officer pointed at Iphigenia.

"*Heraus! Geb nach hause!*" he said, pointing to her and Eleni. *Leave! Go home!* She didn't understand, and she was immobilized with fear. The German looked again, and barked it again, this time in Greek. She couldn't move. She put her head down toward the ground, afraid to look the officer in his eyes. She started sobbing, the fear rushing through her intravenously, her heart pounding so hard she thought the officer could hear it. Now she looked up suddenly at her husband, who reached for her protectively.

"Have courage and go home, and wait for me," he said softly, trying to calm her fears. But Iphigenia couldn't move. Her eyes locked on Stelio, whose own pleaded with her to leave. She looked back at the officer and the soldiers, nervous and waiting for orders. They were tall and strong and brutishly fearsome, eyes unblinking. She knew they feared and despised the Resistance because the Greeks were not intimidated by the soldiers, who worried if they would be killed by guerrillas in the night as their colleagues had.

Finally, she walked away a few feet, pushing the carriage, but her feet moved slowly and suddenly stopped again. She looked again at her husband, who stood stock still, rifles pointed at him. A warm breeze swirled past. The officer snapped at her now.

"Heraus! Heraus!" he yelled. "Go! Go!"

Kyriakides' eyes became harder now as he looked at her, signaling for her to leave. His eyes told her, *I will be all right. Leave now. Take our daughter.* Then, he said quickly, "Courage, Iphigenia." She looked piercingly into his face, summoning strength not to show fear to the soldiers, who grabbed him roughly by the arm and took him away.

She saw other women walking away crying, their husbands taken away too, into the government hall that had been commandeered by the Germans after the invasion. She could see collaborators helping the Germans and now hate filled her too at the men who had turned on their own, but she moved quickly now to get their daughter away, home to wait, to see if her husband would ever return.

Kyriakides and scores of other men were ushered into the town hall, shoved up narrow stairs amidst shouts and bedlam, officers screaming orders to soldiers, who shoved the Greeks into tiny, cramped rooms full of men full of fear and fury. They said little, looking around at one another nervously, listening intently for hours to their own silence and the screams of others taken out to be interrogated. Kyriakides recognized some of them. Then the door opened and he was summoned out, along with some others.

Kyriakides was taken to an officer, listening to the Germans talk about a soldier who had been shot. The officer was infuriated because his superiors were angry that the Greeks continued to sabotage and assassinated soldiers.

"Take out your papers!" the men were told, their identification demanded. Now Kyriakides was worried because he knew that men would sometimes summarily be shot in reprisal, especially after a German had been killed. The Germans, who found it almost impossible to fight against the guerrilla tactics of men hiding in the mountains outside the cities, wanted to contain and control Athens at all costs.

It was a warm night and Kyriakides tried not to sweat or show the fear that was beginning to envelop him. In a race, he controlled his own destiny and the events. Here he could do nothing, especially show fear or anger, submissiveness or aggression.

Before he could empty his pockets, he was questioned by an officer, who looked at him sharply.

"What do you do for work?"

"What time did you get home today?"

"Where were you today?"

The questions came out like bullets from a machine gun, guttural in their Germanic tone, and for a moment Kyriakides reeled, his mind working fast, hoping his fear would not show.

Kyriakides emptied his pockets slowly and the papers were looked at by the officer, who was expecting perfunctory work papers or official identification. He abruptly stopped when he saw a card that had some familiar writing from his homeland. It was headed OLYMPIA AUSWEIS, and showed the German seal of an eagle above five Olympic rings.

Underneath was a photo of Kyriakides, and on either side were phrases: *Gultig bist. Oktober 1946 und XI Olympiade* Berlin 1936. Above the photograph was a number: 04418. Under the picture was his name, birthdate, birthplace, and two signatures that chilled the German officer: Dr. Theodor Lewald and Dr. Carl Diem. Lewald was the president of the German Olympic Committee in 1936 and Diem was the head organizer, and they were monumental figures in the Third Reich.

"What is this?" the officer asked, frozen with trepidation. "Is that you in this photograph?" he asked to be sure because Kyriakides, like most other Greeks, had lost so much weight and his face and body were drawn and taut from hunger.

"It is my Olympic pass for the 1936 games at Berlin," Kyriakides said.

"Were you there?" the German asked.

"Yes," said a nervous Kyriakides, worried if he'd see his wife and children again.

"What did you do?" the German asked, his sternness breaking a bit.

"Marathon," Kyriakides said stiffly.

"Ah, marathon. An athlete. Why didn't you tell me that? Here, take your clothes. Go," the German said.

Kyriakides was surprised, and worried too. He was happy to be free, but worried about his friends who were being kept, but he could not show it. Kyriakides knew he hadn't been responsible for the death of the German soldiers, but his heart and mind raced together, trying not to show his fear about his neighbors who were being held. There were hundreds of them still in the building, their fates sealed as tightly as the doors that held them there.

Still shaken, and worried for his countrymen, Kyriakides hustled back through the dark streets to his home. It was midnight, nearly seven hours after the fateful stop, when he knocked on the door and came in to his wife. She was still sitting, sobbing and worrying. She had been like that for hours.

They ran into each other's arms, grateful to live another day with each other.

He said, "Praise the Lord and the Virgin Mary," trying now to stem tears too. They looked at each other intently, their embrace tightening, and kissed quickly, fervently. He pulled his head back to talk. "I saw people I knew when they were being interrogated, the ones they thought were guilty or could have collaborated were put in separate rooms and kept there," he said, between labored breaths. Kyriakides was angry too that a Greek collaborator had helped point out people for death.

They huddled tightly that night, not letting go of each other. Kyriakides found sleep difficult and, as he tossed and turned, he wondered about the men in the building who were not let go. He remembered the fear and, even worse, the resignation in some of their eyes. They knew it was their last night on earth.

The next morning, anxious about what he would see, Kyriakides set out on his collecting route and went back past the building where he had been held. He froze. There, dangling from trees in the crossroads near the square, were some of the men he had been held with.

Some, he knew, were innocent like him but had been executed as examples. Others had been sent to the hellish Haidari prison, kept away from their families. More than a hundred of the men held that night with him were never heard from again. He turned his head away and walked, quickly, his heart pulsating with rage and sadness.

On his route, everyone wanted to know what happened, but Kyriakides was too saddened to talk much about it. He hoped, more fervently now, that somehow the war would end, that somehow the Allies could reach Greece before he and everyone was killed.

> Having done what men could, they suffered what men must
> —Thucydides

Kyriakides thought that now he could wait out the war, that his escape from death was over. He let himself think of maybe running again some day, seeing himself in the blue uniform of Greece in a Balkan Games, maybe even an Olympic Games, maybe somewhere else. Life in Athens had again settled into a routine that was at once frightening in its oppression, but bearable, as long as they didn't again run into a *"blocco,"* the human roadblock that had terrified them.

But not a month after he had narrowly missed being executed, trouble came again, this time while he was at work and his wife was at home, tending to their daughter, Eleni. Iphigenia heard the sound of a truck rattling on the street outside. She looked out the window and saw armed German soldiers jumping out the back, weapons at the ready. They looked grim and serious. There were five of them. She was startled to realize she was counting them.

The soldiers started going house-to-house and a frightened Iphigenia shrank back into her house, fearful of a knock on the door. It didn't take long. There came a loud banging and shouting outside the door as a soldier demanded she open it.

"Mach die tur auf," she heard, the bark of a German soldier. A simple, cold command that froze her. *Open the door.* With them was the most hated of all Greeks, a collaborator. And he yelled in her own language, "Ανοιξε την πορτα!" *Open the door.*

She knew what it meant. They were coming to loot, to claim the house, to occupy it and put her family out. Her heart beating fast, Iphigenia opened it. Soldiers came pouring in, looking around quickly, their steel helmets hanging over their eyes like shields. Eleni was crying and clinging to her, but all Iphigenia could do was watch as the men stomped around the room, looking for goods and furniture they could take. She held her daughter to her. The collaborator looked at her without changing expression, directing the soldiers, as her eyes fixed on her countryman with icy rage, interrupted by fear at the sight of the soldiers tearing apart her home, throwing around her cherished goods.

Then the soldiers saw her husband's trophies, medals, and photographs of Kyriakides in his running uniform and stopped.

"Whose trophies are those?" he asked loudly.

Suddenly, she summoned strength to answer, her eyes opening, her head up.

"Those," she said slowly, "are my husband's."

"What does he do?"

"He's an athlete," she said. Then she thought and waited a moment, knowing the Germans admiration of athletes. A slight smile crossed her face. "He's a marathoner." She was feeling a little stronger now, a little more defiant, and her face turned up with her lips pursed.

Then the officer noticed an elaborate book with a red stripe and white cover. It was a program from the Olympic Games in Berlin and had a cover showing Nazi insignia and the eagle of the Third Reich.

"What is this book?" a German asked, and the collaborator interpreted.

"It is my husband's," she answered. "He competed in the 1936 Olympics. And that book has the picture and autograph of Adolf Hitler," she added, opening to page four where the soldiers and officer saw the führer. They gulped and stepped back and the officer turned to the trophies on the shelf.

The officer paused and the soldiers stopped looking through the house. Iphigenia went to a drawer and took out some papers, wiping her hands on her apron, turning slowly and unfolding them. The officer grabbed them roughly from her. He looked and then gulped, his eyes rising slowly to meet hers.

The papers were Kyriakides' identification and credentials from the Olympics. They had a picture of Hitler on them, and the signatures of the Olympic Committee in Germany, including many of the top officials in the government. For a moment there was nothing but tense quiet.

Then the officer smiled and yelled to his soldiers. "Come see these!" he laughed happily. The soldiers gathered and looked at the papers and pictures and then at her. Suddenly, one came to her and grabbed her and for a moment she was afraid again, but it was only to hug her. He kissed her and the others joined, surrounding Iphigenia and laughing and kissing her. For a moment, they felt human, not mechanical men without emotions. They were young, far from their homes too, and the moment had changed them. Even though it would not last, Iphigenia was grateful for the respite from fear.

The officer was still smiling. "We don't want anything from you," he said. "When is your husband coming home?" he asked.

"He doesn't have any free time, he is always working," she said.

"Well, we are coming on Sunday to see him," the officer said.

They left, promising to return on different terms, and her dread eased.

Then Kyriakides came home and saw the look of anguish on his wife's face.

"What is it?" he asked, knowing something had happened. He looked around automatically for his daughter and saw the disarray that Iphigenia was trying to restore before he came back. Once again, they came to each other and held one another tightly, but he could not stop her shaking. The fear and dread were crushing now and he fought to keep his composure. Kyriakides knew he had to be there when they returned.

On Sunday, the soldiers came back, this time knocking on the door and asking to enter. They had a high-ranking officer with them and his look was warm, but scary in its quietness. The soldiers came into the room as the officer saw Kyriakides, snapped to attention, and strode over to him earnestly.

Kyriakides took a step back, surprised to find he was being hugged and congratulated. Iphigenia, seizing the moment, made tea and the soldiers unwrapped some black bread they had brought and sat down and ate with him. The soldiers were laughing now, but Kyriakides still felt ill at ease. He did not want to show his contempt, and his smile, a mask of Greek tragedy, was forced to protect his family.

"How did you wind up in the games in Germany?" he was asked as they crowded around, throwing more questions, eager to hear about the Olympics, which, for many of the young soldiers, was already a part of their country's history. They gave Kyriakides and Iphigenia black bread and chocolate.

For the next few days, other officers were brought to his home to meet the great runner Kyriakides, the champion of the Balkans, who had run in Germany on their soil and in front of their führer. For a time, it seemed he was safe. If only they could hold on until the war ended.

The news that came from the radio he secretly unsealed and from the Resistance was more heartening now, even if the sights on the streets of Athens were not. Kyriakides' heart grew heavier with the awful scenes of hunger and starvation before him as he tried to walk his route.

Throughout Greece, the fighting by the *andartes* had become more ferocious: they killed German soldiers in the streets of Athens, undaunted by the brutal reprisals against Greek citizens. In some places, including Crete, the Germans had embarked on a policy of *Ausrottung*, or extermination, but they hadn't counted on the ceaseless resistance, much of which was now in the mountains, controlled by the *andartes*, whose impression was intimidating: thick, busy mustaches, bandoliers strapped around their bodies, hard chiseled faces set in defiance, knives stuck in their belts, the weapons the Germans feared because they would often be used surreptitiously in the night to slit the enemy's throats.

It was the scene Hitler feared the most. He had shown great admiration for the fighting spirit of the Greeks against the Italians, and even against the overwhelming forces of his own Wehrmacht and elite units. The generals and officers and soldiers now trying to contend with the Greeks found them unyielding to either peaceful efforts or reprisals.

Kyriakides tried to keep his house up and appear normal, even in the occupied city. There was now no gas for the lamps and little electricity. The food shortages were exacerbated by the Germans assuming control of the country's food distribution system and agricultural areas.

On his daily rounds, even though he was recognized by the patrols, Kyriakides would walk around the soldiers who strolled the streets. They carried rifles and machine guns under their arms, staring sternly at suspicious persons, on edge and wary because of the many sabotage efforts and the occasional killing of soldiers that would inevitably be followed by the rounding up of Greek men.

Life in Athens was now a cycle of fear and dread, of little or no food, and the joy was out of the air in a city where once bouzouki music blared and people danced, just glad to be alive. Many were not. As the Greek resistance stiffened, so too did the German reprisals.

Kyriakides knew how close he had come to death during the fateful stop in Halandri because the word had spread among the Greeks, despite German attempts to stifle information, about the impromptu mass executions of civilians, sometimes simply for dramatic purposes and for intimidation. The Germans themselves ironically helped spread the seeds of resistance by making public some of their executions, as Kyriakides had seen with the awful sight of men hanging the day after his release.

The hangings were common: along country roads bodies were on trees everywhere. In cities, they were left dangling from makeshift gallows for everyone to see. Instead of frightening the Greeks, it hardened their hate and determination. In the town of Arta, Greeks had cut down a dozen telephone poles to cut German communications, so the Germans hung twelve men in public. It had no effect on the resistance.

On December 13, 1943, in the picturesque mountainous town of Kalávrita, near the Corinthian gulf, the freedom fighters were not the target. Kalávrita was one of the few places in Greece where it would sometimes snow and the villagers were rough-hewn people used to hard work and a changing climate. They were not daunted by much. At 6:00 A.M., the church bells rang, beckoning villagers to come to the square. There they were divided into two groups, women and children under twelve, and men and boys over twelve years old. Mothers tried to convince the soldiers their teenaged sons were too young to be put with the men. German officers said no one would be hurt.

The women and children were put into a schoolhouse. The men, some in their eighties, were taken to a field. A moment later, machine guns popped up on either side and the men were gunned down like scythes being taken to crops. The death toll was 1,621. For the next half hour, single gunshots rang out as the wounded were shot in the head. As the men were being killed, the schoolhouse was set on fire and women began throwing their children out the windows to save them. One German soldier, taking pity, opened the door and set them free before the burning roof collapsed. There was chaos in the village.

The Germans went to a monastery called Agia Lavra—where the

Greek revolution in the nineteenth century had begun—and killed all the monks because they had protested the slayings.

When Kyriakides and his wife heard about Kalávrita, they were shocked at the brutality, even after having seen the dead and the executions in Athens. Iphigenia grabbed her husband fiercely, clutching him to her breast, turning her head to his eyes, crying in anguish.

In between her gasps, as he tried to comfort her, stroking her hair while his eyes went blank with resignation at what might be all their fates, she looked at him and asked, "What evil is happening here in Greece?"

> For freedom, sons of Greece
>
> —Aeschylus

News of the massacres spread quickly, even in a country where the Germans had tried to control communications. Even the atrocities that had become too common hadn't inured the Greeks to what happened at Kalávrita. In Athens, Prime Minister Ioannis Rallis, who served at the whim of the occupiers, protested vigorously, but to no avail.

Ipighenia and Kyriakides had heard the news too, and they were as shocked, and frightened, as their neighbors. They cried for the dead, and they feared too: if the Germans could do this in the countryside, what could happen in Athens, especially if the Allies and the Americans would finally reach them? Would the Germans retaliate with last-moment massacres in the city?

It was 1944 and Kyriakides and his family were like so many others now. Even with his modest salary of $60 per month from the utility company, Kyriakides could not provide all that his family needed. He traded his suit for food, and sold much of the furniture. He worried he would have to sell the trophies he'd won in years of championship running and talked with Iphigenia about it.

"These cups represent another day, another life to me. I cannot part with them. Never again can I win so many beautiful trophies," he said. She agreed. The trophies would be the last to be sold, if they needed to survive. Kyriakides' hopes were fading now because it seemed the Germans had control of the cities and the Allies were being stalemated throughout Europe and the Mediterranean.

But German officials began sensing the inevitability of Russian and Allied intervention, especially as the Russians moved on Romania, and many Nazis moved away from Athens and desertions began in 1944. The Germans sensed the end was near in October, even as Greek Resistance units moved into Athens and there were reports the British would soon return. Kyriakides became bolder in listening to the radio now. On the night of October 11, 1944, he heard some news that made his heart leap with joy. There was a report that British units would roll into downtown Athens the next morning.

So, on the morning of Oct. 12, 1944, $3^1/_2$ years after the Nazi storm troopers rolled into Athens, hundreds of blue-and-white Greek flags suddenly and simultaneously appeared on balconies and in windows throughout the city and crowds converged on Syntagma Square, the heart of the city, to watch a German unit take down the hated Swastika.

Then began a delirious wave of joy as Resistance fighters joined ordinary citizens in a frenzied exultation that the city again belonged to the Greeks. A convoy of British troops soon arrived, and a few days later there was a repeat of the celebration in the country's second-largest city, Thessalonika, in the north. Winston Churchill came to Athens himself, the chubby little man with the big cigar and ubiquitous curious smile walking beside the towering Archbishop Damaskinos on a tour, touting the Greek spirit. The newspapers reported that he said, "Greeks no longer fight like heroes; heroes fight like greeks."

The scenes outside Athens were less jubilant, a weary and war-worn peoples staggering beside the ruins of burned out villages, shoeless and hungry children crying, adults with worn rags for clothing and eyes looking toward the distance, not caring much anymore what happened. This was the day for which they had waited, but for some it had come too late. Thousands of children were orphaned, and the adults who survived had lost spouses and brothers and sisters, and the most common look was a gaunt resignation. Whole families, and whole villages, had simply disappeared and there was nothing to liberate. On the streets of Athens, there were still lines for soup kitchens and weary men, women, and children stood stoically in line. Some would die anyway, even with the meager food they got.

There were already edgy overtones in a country still divided by politics, between loyalists and burgeoning Communists, and only two months later, insurgent Greek units were battling British contingents in Athens. America and its allies did not want to lose Greece, vital strategically, geographically, and politically, to communism, as so many other countries in the region had been lost.

It would take a long time before the city and the country would start to return from the devastation. The hunger would continue with a looming civil war. But for now, there was joy in the freedom-loving country and some American units were surprised to find that as they handed out food and relief supplies, Greeks would deposit small gifts in gratitude. A special bond developed between Americans and Greeks.

There would be fighting for control of the city as the British took on insurgent units, some of whom did not want the king to return and feared a new kind of fascism would replace the Nazi occupiers. It was bitter and divisive and led to the murder of many affluent and intellectual citizens who had become targets too.

It was a new kind of class warfare brought on by political differences that, once again, had split the Greeks as it had since ancient times when the notion of city-states often kept the Greeks apart. Now it seemed even more senseless in the aftermath of a war that had nearly destroyed their country and their heritage. Kyriakides was heartsick about the division and talked of moving his family back to Cyprus, back to the small town where he had grown up. Having barely survived the war with the Germans, Kyriakides did not want to lose his family to the Greek infighting.

The intervention of British and American forces did not stop the squabbling between the Greek factions, anxious to take control of a new country, to form Greece again from the ashes of destruction. Loyalists and Communists battled, and Greek officials struggled to reform a government.

Cyprus more and more seemed like a beacon of serenity to him, but it would have to wait, because even as he and Iphigenia wearied of another round of war, she was pregnant again, soon to deliver and worried about the lack of medical supplies. It seemed the strife would go on forever. But their first dreams after marriage were for children, even in the midst of war, because they knew someday it would end and they hoped they would survive.

In November, the Kyriakides family moved in with her parents at 9 Kefkia Street in Filothei, not too far from their home in Halandri. With one young child in tow, and another due, she wanted to be near her parents. The city was in chaos and she didn't know if she would be able to get a hospital again.

On December 10, 1944, she went into labor, with bombs and cannon fire outside, the sounds of a renewed war, the sounds of Greeks fighting Greeks. Kyriakides, remembering the difficulty of Eleni's birth, took the chance of going to a nearby British-run hospital for supplies, hoping to avoid the fighting units, especially those aligned against the British.

"Please, I need some things. My wife has just given birth." he pleaded. He was given pharmaceuticals, medicine, cotton, and hygienic goods. Shoving them into a bag, he ran back toward his house, but was stopped by a guerrilla checkpoint.

He had been seen going into the hospital and they asked him "Where did you get all those things you are carrying?"

One looked at him warily. "You must be on the British side," he said.

Kyriakides said nothing at first. "You must be punished," Kyriakides was told. He swallowed hard and, rising with dignity and defiance, he said, "I am Stelios Kyriakides, the marathoner. My wife has just given birth." The rebel's eyes searched Kyriakides' face for signs of deceit.

"If you do not believe who I am, come to my house and you will see for yourself," Kyriakides said.

"The British gave me this for my wife," he said. The rebels, realizing he was not a spy and recognizing his name, released him and went to his house. They left when they saw his story was true.

The war was over.

The war had begun.

6

The Song of Cyprus

Athens, 1944/Cyprus/Athens/New York/Boston, 1946

The second half of the twentieth century was before him, but all that
Kyriakides could think about was how to keep his family intact, even as
a civil war was starting to swirl around them. They had survived World
War II where many of their friends, and some of his teammates, had not.
He had survived near-execution and hunger and, it seemed, had lost his
running career. He was thirty-five now and had not run since the
Balkan Games in Constantinople five years before, what seemed like an
eternity. He was worn and gaunt and emaciated and thought now only
of how to raise his children, Eleni and Dimitri, and bring happiness
again to his wife, Iphigenia.

Kyriakides kept his humble demeanor and was a devoted family man
and father. He didn't smoke or drink, and was a man of moderation, not
unusually thrifty or overly extravagant, although the idea of plentiful
money seemed foreign. He found solace in his family and in music and
kept a radio constantly playing in his room now that the war was over.

At bedtime, he retired to the bedroom to read newspapers and listen
to ethnic songs, demotic songs of ordinary Greeks and the Cypriot
music on which he had been reared. He longed for meat and potatoes
and milk and fruits and greens, and especially steaks, which the family
had not seen for years.

Kyriakides kept his faith too, attending church regularly and observing all the holidays, especially name days, those named after patron saints of the Greek Orthodox Church. In church, he would sit near the chanters of Byzantine liturgies and song, although he could not sing well. Instead, he would chant under his breath because he was so enchanted by the music of the church. It kept him placid. He would often take communion, even if he had not fasted, which perplexed Iphigenia.

"You have not fasted, why are you taking communion, Stelio?" she asked once.

"I felt like going to receive communion, so I did," he answered, a little direct for her, she thought. She did not question him. But he continued. "I have done no harm to anybody, but at the moment it came to me the desire to go receive communion, so I went and now I feel better," he said, ending the talk.

His physical appearance was not improving, though, and he seemed too quiet for Iphigenia. She thought he must miss his running, but he seemed not able to go back to it, worn out mentally and physically by the rigors of just staying alive during the war and trying to keep his family fed.

He had not received a higher education and tried to compensate by reading and studying. When Iphigenia asked him about it, he would shrug his shoulders and say, "A man who is uneducated is like a piece of wood that you can just smash all day," without making an impression, he tried to explain. He wanted his children to go to college, but wondered now how they would even eat.

Kyriakides thought of that in the dark days at the end of 1944 after the Germans had gone and the civil war had begun, and decided what he would do: he would take his family back to Cyprus, back to Statos to see his mother and to let his children live on a farm and play with animals and get away from war-torn Athens, to be in the Cypriot sun and see the ocean and run with abandon and forget what the war had wrought.

From the beginning of 1945 until April, the Kyriakides struggled as did nearly everyone else in Athens, trying to feed their families. Many would go to bread lines, where people would stand with food ration cards in hand near outdoor stone stoves where bread was baking, the tantalizing smell an irresistible temptation to people whose stomachs were rumbling with hunger. Many, like Kyriakides, did not want to eat, preferring to give the food to their children. Men and women would stand after the bread was distributed, hoping to scoop some of the crumbs. The soup kitchens that had started during the war years found many new customers now: children, some with distended bellies and swollen features by starvation, hoping to find some sustenance.

Through all this, Kyriakides slowly walked his bill collecting route, trying to renew some semblance of a normal life. Dinner too often was a few peas to be shared, but occasionally, on his rounds, he would be given potatoes and lettuce by customers who remembered what his running had done for Greece before the war years had driven away thoughts of glory, replacing them with thoughts only of living.

Athens, pockmarked with ruined buildings destroyed by bombings and machine gunnings and the new internal strife between Greeks that had led to new fighting, was an eerie sight: the resplendent home of the Acropolis, bathed in Mediterranean light, but a bleak, dark neighborhood of misery, people withering before one another's eyes, the awful keening of the dying echoing in the lonely nights. The war—with the Germans—had ended, but now it seemed Greece was plunged again into a continuing nightmare. The worst sights were those of homeless children, some wandering aimlessly, others as young as ten going into the mountains, conscripting themselves to both sides of the new fight between Greeks.

It was no better in the small villages or the mountains where peasants and people could not even turn to the land for food because it had been stripped during the war. Many thousands of people, especially young men, had been killed. Those who had survived found themselves conscripted to fight against the Communists—or were Communists themselves, sometimes fighting relatives and family members from the same villages.

But many Greeks, even in their hunger, wondered how long they could last, when the peace would again be shattered, when the weariness would end.

> There is in the worst of fortune the best of chances for a happy change
>
> —Euripides

During World War II, Cyprus remained aligned with the ruling British, despite Nazi propaganda attempts to persuade Cypriots to renounce the British and take claim of their island. Instead, more than thirty thousand Cypriots joined the fight against the Nazis. It was, they said, "for freedom and Greece." The question of Cypriot independence would have to wait.

There was tension but no fighting on Cyprus and the British government was inviting back Cypriots. Kyriakides took a leave of absence in April, packed up his family, and boarded a ship back to his home island, leaving from the port of Piraeus. The cost was paid by the British on Cyprus to enable families to reunite, if even for a time.

When they got to Cyprus, though, they were surprised to find that even he, the still-revered champion runner of the island, would have to take his family into a quarantine for forty days because of fear of disease from the mainland. They were taken to an army base near Larnica, and put up in barracks and tents along with thousands of others. They had brought only a few belongings and mattresses.

They started to eat better. With government-provided food-stuffs, Kyriakides gradually started to gain some strength and a little weight, but the thoughts of what had been left behind in Greece gnawed at him. He ran barefoot along the beaches of Cyprus, joyous to be running again, the sand helping him rebuild the strength in his legs, the sun shining on the sea, his family away from the war-torn images of a glorious city under siege again.

He was happy to have his family away from Athens, especially the children, who had been growing up against the background din of war and death and with little joy. Now that he was back where his running had changed his life, he began to think of how his running could save his country too. He remembered the awful night in Halandri where he had almost been executed and thought his salvation was a sign.

Kyriakides, always private, was even more pensive now, his thoughts making him more introspective. He could not forget the images of death. He came to Iphigenia with an idea, approaching her gingerly as they waited through their quarantine.

She looked at him, sensing something.

"What is it, Stelio?"

He paused. "I am going to start to train to go to America, to Boston, to win for Greece," he said, waiting for her reply. She wasn't sure what he meant, but she put the thought aside, thinking he was just happy to be back where he could run again, sure he didn't mean what he had said. She would find out later how strong his resolve was.

After the quarantine, he moved his family to Limassol, where he had lived as a young boy and where he had many relatives to help them. They first stayed at his aunt's house, where they were welcomed, although few mentioned his running exploits anymore because everyone was trying to resurrect their lives and many had lost so much during the war. Kyriakides' aunt had two daughters who immediately took to caring for Dimitri and Eleni. The families sang and danced and ate well for the first time in years. The joy was coming back to life.

Kyriakides' name was well known on Cyprus too, unlike when he was a young man trying to make his way. His running fame had preceded him, even to the small villages of the island.

Later, they rented a two-room house, supported by a temporary job he got with the city of Limassol. Relatives brought food and clothing to help. Kyriakides also planned a visit to Statos, to see his mother and show her his wife and children.

It was a poignant short trip back to the village where he had grown up and where his mother was waiting to see him. She delighted in seeing her grandchildren, and the son who was famous throughout Cyprus and all of Greece; even the war had not diminished that.

To renew the training he had started on the beaches, he worked out now also in a gymnasium in Limassol, but he could not regain the weight or strength of his prewar conditioning, as hard as he worked. But often, after a workout and shower, came a special time: the family would sit together on the sands of the beaches to eat and just talk and gaze at the land and sea around them.

In September, they returned to Athens, because he had to go back to his job and had established their home. Cyprus had regenerated his spirit, but his body had still not come back. Iphigenia sensed something was bothering her husband. He saw that Greece was still in turmoil and that people were dying in the streets. He saw it when he went to work on his rounds. The sick had little hope of medical attention, the hungry little hope of food. Routine infections or illnesses became deadly for those who had not eaten or had medical care.

Still, Greece was struggling to return to some semblance of normal life and routine of business. The country had been decimated by a world war and the brief civil war that seemed ready to restart, even as the country tried to rebuild itself. Bridges were still blown up, roads ruined, the countryside ravaged, transportation at a standstill. Some villages were eerily empty, their populations killed or starved. In others, people tried to renew their lives or had fled to Athens hoping for food and help. They would find neither.

For Kyriakides, coming back to Athens meant that his family would not eat as well as in Cyprus, but his job at the utility company offered him a better future and more benefits. He returned to work, but the thoughts that had plagued him since Cyprus grew stronger now as he saw that Greece was still not well, and the new civil war worrying him.

As he walked his route again, his heart ached with the sight of little children sitting in the streets, hands out, looking for food, and the too-common scene of adults just dropping as they walked in the streets, fainting from lack of food, and too often left to die. He knew what he wanted to do, and he had to talk with Iphigenia again because it was now near the start of winter.

He came to her in their home, the same look on his face she had seen in Cyprus when he talked of a mission that she somehow dismissed then. He stopped and looked away hesitantly. He often found it difficult to look directly at his wife because of his tenderness for her, and her eyes gleamed with love for him. It was sometimes difficult to explain hard decisions.

"I want to run again in Boston," he said, looking back at her for just a moment, trying to gauge what her reaction might be. She was puzzled and afraid. She looked at him long and hard and saw the sinew in his body was not as it was, but he still had heart. She smiled for he was irrepressible.

"We have been eating better, Iphigenia," he said. "But many in Greece are not. If I go to Boston and win, the world will know what has happened to Greece. I have to do it. That is my dream, and Greece's dream, for me to go to Boston." He looked at her again longingly, hoping for her approval. "This . . ." he trailed off softly, reaching up to her, "is my life's dream."

Iphigenia paused. She loved him and supported him, but she was worried about his health. He was barely 130 pounds now on a narrow 5'7" frame and his legs were so thin she wondered how he could sustain himself over a short run, never mind twenty-six miles of pounding. She remembered, too, how he had come home broken in 1938, his bloodied feet keeping him from running for three months. The concrete of Boston had worn out the feet that had carried him to so many victories, and that was eight years before!

"You're crazy!" she said.

"I'm worried, Stelio. I'm worried something will happen to you. I'm worried you will die in the streets of Boston," she said with more passion, and his heart welled with hurt that he had frightened her.

"Do not worry," he said, smiling, his own eyes taking on a new light now, trying to lessen her fear and buoy himself. "I will train with Otto, I will train hard and do it right and prepare myself." Then he told her something else.

"I've had a premonition that I'm going to win." She loved him fervently, but had to speak.

"You can't run, you can't win, you haven't eaten and you haven't trained. You will die in the streets," she said, trying to keep from crying, her deep eyes black with worry. They never argued much, but Iphigenia felt fear deep in her heart. She hadn't lost her husband to German armies and German patrols, and she did not want to lose him to running.

"You can't go to America. You are half starved," she said, in a high voice pierced with anxiety. She looked at him intently, seeing his pale, yellow weakness, and her heart sank. His dream was unattainable, she thought. But he looked at her almost as if reading her mind, and a slight smile formed on his lips.

"Something is driving me, I feel I can win," he said.

"What makes you think that?" Iphigenia asked.

"I hope," he smiled, then reassured her with the melody of his words. "Don't worry. God is great. Don't worry."

"How will you get there? Who will pay for it? You don't even have enough food to train for a marathon. We don't have enough money," she implored.

"I have been writing to George Demeter in Boston," he said. "They want me to come back. I am going to ask Mr. Kemp if the company will bring me back to Boston. And we have things that we can sell, Iphigenia, but only if you agree with me."

"Stelio, it's almost December. The race is only four months away. You haven't run a race for six years. You haven't trained. You can't do it! You can't do it!" she said, almost crying now. "You're crazy," she said, sighing in exasperation.

"I want to win the Boston Marathon. I know I can do it," he said. "This is the most important race in the world and people will pay attention if I win and they will know what is happening in Greece. I want them to remember what happened and what happened to my teammates and to us and to Greece," he said, searching for words to soothe her.

Then he gathered his strength and held her forearms and looked directly at her. "I want the name of Greece to be heard."

Iphigenia looked down for a moment and then at her husband. "Yes, Stelio," she said. He knew she was worried about their finances and food. "We might have to sell some things," he said. "Maybe the radio and the stove even." Iphigenia blanched, but laughed just a little.

She knew how much he loved listening to the radio at night, but kidded him. "I don't mind you selling the radio, but don't sell the stove. How am I going to cook?" she laughed, and he looked back, laughing at the same time, the relief from the tension good to feel. But then it subsided and he became serious as he thought of his mission.

"It doesn't matter. We're going to make this sacrifice," he said.

"When I come back from Boston as the victor, I will buy you a new stove and thank you for the sacrifices you have made," he said. His face hardened with determination and his black eyes envisioned Boston, the course, and the concrete, and the few months he would have to train. He had to contact George Demeter again, he knew, and Tom Pappas, a rich man who could help him and Greece. Pappas had numerous business contacts in the United States and Greece. As head of a major food company in Boston, he and his family were politically well connected.

Saying no more, Iphigenia bowed her head and looked back up for a fleeting moment, acknowledging her husband.

The next day Kyriakides went to see his boss, Leslie Kemp, who had always backed him before when he was training to run to represent Greece. Kyriakides' friend Greg Lazarides, an official at the company, had already been talking to Kemp about him.

Kemp was familiar with the officials of SEGAS, and he liked the celebrity that Kyriakides' fame brought to the company. Like Dr. Cheverton years before on Cyprus, he was an English Hellenophile and he and Kyriakides had an easy rapport. But now Kyriakides had to ask for what seemed like a fortune.

"Come in Stelio," Kemp said, motioning him to sit in a chair. Kemp was a big man, heavyset, with thin wire-rimmed glasses and a wide, inexpressive face, and he favored light-colored suits. He had a British air of distinction and liked to get right to the point in a conversation, but he had come to like and admire Kyriakides for his devotion to his work and discipline for running. Kyriakides sat and fidgeted just for a moment while Kemp reclined easily. "What do you need, Stelio?" he said, trying to put him at ease.

"Mr. Kemp," he said just a bit hesitantly, "I want to return to Boston to run in the marathon. I know I can win it." Kemp paused a moment, looking wonderingly at Kyriakides. He too saw only a shadow of the strong man who had failed in Boston in 1938, and wondered why he wanted to go back.

"Why, Stelio?" he said directly. "Why do you want to run in Boston?"

"I have seen what the war has done to Greece and still see people dying in the streets and I want to help. I am only a runner, but that is what I do and what I can still do and I know if I train right this time that I can win. I know the course and I know what happened last time."

"What do you want from us?" Kemp asked.

"I have Greek-American friends in Boston, Mr. Demeter. They can help me there, but I need help to get to Boston. I need the money to get there," he said, his heart beating as fast as if he were in the finish of a marathon, wondering what Kemp would say.

The Englishman paused, his mouth pursed, his lower lip curling up to cover the top as he thought. "This will cost a lot of money, Stelio, maybe a million drachmas or more," the equivalent of more than $1,000. "Do you think you can win?" he asked.

"Yes, I do," Kyriakides said. Kemp knew he meant it, but doubted he could win. Kyriakides paused. "Mr. Kemp, I'm willing to sell almost everything I have, including my stove and radio, to help pay for this because I know I can win. I have had a premonition."

Kemp paused again. He liked Kyriakides but he was worried. "Stelios, I know you've been worried because you've had to drink some of the milk your children are given through the rations. Your salary does not allow you to eat. I will give you some extra money to buy fruit and milk."

Now Kyriakides wondered why Kemp would do that. He didn't wait long.

"Stelio," Kemp smiled. "All I ask is that you finish in the top three."

They looked at each other for a moment without speaking. Kemp started again. "I will pay for your expenses and I'm going to give you a little extra money so when you return you can bring a couple of presents for your family."

Kyriakides' heart nearly burst with joy and he jumped to his feet to shake Kemp's hand. "I will run for Greece," he said, his eyes glistening. Their hands locked hard and they looked into each other's eyes. Kyriakides turned and left, his feet barely touching the floor because he was so anxious to see Iphigenia.

He would have to work his normal workday and still find time to run a hundred miles or more a week to get in shape, and this time over tough terrain that would harden his feet to inure him to Boston's concrete, but he vowed to run until he dropped and to bring glory to Greece, as well as food and medicine. Kyriakides hurried home to tell his wife. He burst into the door, his smile lighting the room. She looked at him in wonder, seeing a man she thought had lost his logic.

"I can't believe what Mr. Kemp said," he told her. "I'm like crazy today. God was with me. He helped me again," he said, his face looking odd to her.

"What's wrong with you?" she asked him, upbraiding just a bit. "I thought you were sick."

"There's nothing wrong with me. I just insured my trip to Boston," he said proudly, and they embraced in joy, hugging and laughing and spinning around the room. Iphigenia felt his happiness, but inside she worried still that his dream would end as it had eight years before, or even worse. She couldn't let him see the anxiety that was trying to spread to her face and eyes and she gripped him tightly.

"Yes, Stelio, you are going to Boston, but you must train for it. You must eat right and sleep right." He paused again for a moment, knowing the family's diet sometimes was only some vegetables and only a little milk, not nearly enough protein or carbohydrates needed to keep a marathon runner in condition. He wondered about his stamina and strength and how much he had lost by not running in the last few prime years of his life, even after the Cyprus hiatus.

"Stelio, it's almost Christmas," she said. "Wait until then and you can start to run." She had given in because she saw what had happened to Greece and what was still going on outside their door.

There was still poverty and destitution in the streets, and it was not uncommon to see old women picking through the remains of rubbish or trying to collect a few sticks for firewood. Burnt-out trolleys were being used to carry passengers through the streets after the end of the Nazi occupation. Kyriakides' heart ached when he walked his route and saw children with swollen bellies and old men and women walking awkwardly, some suddenly dying, their bodies to be collected by men on carts who would travel the city to pick up the dead. They were scenes Kyriakides passed every day and each time his heart ached and his resolution grew to go back to Boston.

He went to see Simitsek, who was living nearby. The track coach had managed to survive the war but there had not been the opportunity to do his life's work, to work with athletes, and he wanted another challenge, another chance to win.

He walked creakily to the door when he heard the knock and his eyes opened wide with astonishment to see Kyriakides, who looked like he had a secret he needed to tell. Kyriakides' face was bright with delight and he rushed into the house to tell Simitsek he had a way to go back to running, back to Boston. Simitsek started to smile slightly, and then it grew as he thought of how to train his protégé again.

"This time, Otto, I need to toughen my feet. I will run in the mountains outside the city."

"Yes, Stelio, and I will time you. You need to improve with each run because there is not much time for training. Boston is only a few months away." He was worried too because he knew Kyriakides had been a world-class runner, but that was before the war and his loss of weight. Much of the strength he had regained in Cyprus was lost again now with the lack of meat and proper nutrition.

"And there is something else, Stelio," Simitsek said, a wry grin turning up at the edge of his mouth. "No sex. Sex will sap your strength. You will have to abstain from sex until after the race," he said, this time seriously. That was more than four months but Kyriakides just nodded in affirmation. *Iphigenia will understand*, he thought.

> Thinking is the talking of the soul with itself
>
> —Plato

Kyriakides was troubled. It was an overwhelming task, returning to Boston where he hadn't been for eight years. He was no longer young and at the peak of his abilities, and he hadn't trained really at all for years now. He hadn't eaten right or stayed in shape, and he was worried too about the mental toughness that had sustained him. There was a place he could go, however, to think and draw strength: Thermopylae.

He loved to stand there, just to imagine the battle that had taken place in 480 B.C. when King Leonidas and his three hundred Spartans held off a vast Persian army and King Xerxes for two days, armed with their spears and plumed helmets and blazing red capes with the Greek letter Λ, lambda, the "L" that symbolized the ancient name for his city, Lacadaemon. The capes and soldiers uniforms were red so they would not show blood to the enemy when they were wounded, and the Spartans bravery and ferocity were legendary, even to the seemingly unconquerable Persians.

Kyriakides stood in the pass, at the point midway between northern and southern Greece on its eastern shores, the spot where invading armies would have to enter, and thought what it was like twenty-five hundred years before when the pass, now almost three miles wide because of centuries of alluvial deposits, was only fifty feet wide and guarded by the Spartans standing shield-to-shield.

He drew courage and strength and could feel what the Spartans felt, the warm winds of the hot sulfur springs that gave the pass its name blowing lightly over his curly black hair and rigid high-cheeked face that made him look like so many of the men who perished on the spot. He could look out and hear the sounds of swords clashing and the close-ranked Spartans luring in Xerxes' fabled personal guard, the Immortals, slaying them and driving the Persian king to bewilderment and fear. Every Greek knew the story and how Leonidas's words and the deeds of the men who died had stood the centuries and become a watchword even in the recent end of World War II, when Greeks refused to give up their resistance to the Nazi occupation that had killed so many people. Kyriakides knew he had to do something and had come here, as he had so many times before, to find peace and inspiration. He loved the soil of his country.

He remembered standing in the pass trying to feel the vibrations of the battle that had raged there, trying to sense what Leonidas and the Spartans had felt, knowing they would die, but never deserting their duty to Greece. He could feel his chest swell with fear and desire to be as strong, looking at the pass and the heights around it and wondering what the Greeks had felt looking out across the land and water to where Xerxes was encamped with his scores of thousands of warriors. He remembered the words they left behind: "Stranger, announce to the Spar-

tans that we lie here dead, obedient to their words." He drew resolve
from their deed and wondered if he could stand as tall for Greece in
what he wanted to do now: train his starved body hard enough in a few
months to go to Boston to win the city's famous marathon, not for glory
or honor, but to let the world understand how his fellow Greeks were
starving in the streets. He stood there for a long time, closing his eyes,
seeing Leonidas, and then whooshed in his breath like a man about to
dive into a pool of cold water, his chest heaving in anticipation and
anxiety, but knowing he would do it anyway. Like the Spartans, he had
to win or die.

> The beginning is the most important part of the work
>
> —Plato

On a warm winter day, Kyriakides put on his running shoes, shorts,
and shirt, and ran out through his neighborhood, past the few white-
stuccoed houses with blue fringes, and up, up, toward the hills of
Filothei, to the mountains outside Athens, where he wanted the incline
and the hard-graveled course. He sweated and strained and his legs
ached with the loss of his training as he propelled himself up steep
grades, head down, sweat pasting the black wavy hair to his forehead,
his eyes riveted on the ground, thoughts of Boston forcing him forward
with the strain, pebbles sliding away under his shoes, sticking to the
bottom, making him slip and sometimes stumble as he churned his arms
for balance. At first he had the sun of the Greek sky, but the higher he
ran, the cooler it got; and as the winter wore on, one day he ran into
snow in the higher elevations, the cool wind whipping his slim frame as
he ran alone in the mountains, only the echo of his breathing and the
slashing slide of his steps pounding the gravel and the stones and the
snow keeping him company, a tympani of rhythm; the running music.
He was alone now, away even from Simitsek and his wife, and from the
curious who would see him running in the populated neighborhoods
that led to the hills. Mostly, he ran through the sweet-smelling orange
and lemon trees and past ubiquitous olive trees. It was hard going be-

cause he was not gaining weight. His appearance was worrying Iphigenia. He seemed pale and weak, despite the running.

But Kyriakides alone knew how well his training was going in the mountains, where he was accustoming himself to the hardness of the terrain and toughening his heart and spirit at the same time, even if he didn't look well. He was driven, running when it hurt so much he wanted to stop, heart pounding and legs burning and head bowed as he ran through the Greek winter. When he wasn't running on the streets or in the mountains, Kyriakides took to the tracks for speed training. The training program was one he had used for years, and did so for Boston: a mix of stamina and speed workouts. Sometimes, of course, it had involved Simitsek following him on a bicycle or in a car, shouting encouragement and advice. But usually, the regimen would involve running ten to fifteen miles a day, stepping it up to fifteen to twenty miles a day before major races, sometimes on soft ground to strengthen his leg muscles, but other times on hard ground or rocks for his feet. At least twice during every season, he would walk the National Marathon course in Athens at four to five miles per hour to help him remember each rise or dip in the course. In Boston in 1938, he had been able to do that only briefly and as he went through his workouts now, he tried to concentrate and remember the hills of Boston.

He remembered Boston in 1938. "This time, I'll win," he kept repeating. It was a mantra. Kyriakides was a driven man and he used the same energy that helped him learn English in such a short time so many years before in Cyprus. "When I set out to do something, I do it!" he said confidently. Kyriakides running was not an unusual sight, but few knew why he was working out so hard now. His friends and neighbors yelled words of encouragement at the start of his training runs, carrying him under the trees of his own street. Those who knew what he was doing would hand him vegetables, a cucumber, a head of cabbage, extra beans, as he walked his bill-collecting route. It was food he did not want to take because he knew it was a hardship, a deep sacrifice, and often the food would go instead to his family.

He ran wearing blue shoes with four spikes to help grip the hillsides.

He ran on asphalt too, with Simitsek watching that part of the course, along the original route of the marathon, before Kyriakides would disappear into the hills and mountains, carried only by his discipline and desire, running sometimes past the ravages of the ruined city and the bodies of people who had collapsed from hunger. It ate at him like the losses in Boston and in Berlin, both which he felt he could have won.

As he walked his rounds, his hamstrings and leg muscles aching with hurt, he would be soothed by customers as he went door-to-door. "Tell them in America, say to every American, 'Thank you,'" Kyriakides heard almost everywhere he went, the grateful Greeks happy that American intervention had helped end the Nazi occupation of their country. He had to balance eating and sleeping with his workouts and his work too, and the mental anguish of carrying the burden for seven million people, none of them knowing yet why he was running. He wondered about Demeter and his old friend Johnny Kelley, who was the defending champion. It would be hard to run against a friend, he thought, but this race was not for sport or even personal triumph.

Every day, Kyriakides would don the same running gear and trump onto the street, trying to gain speed and working so hard he would sweat, even in the cool mountain air of the Greek winter. It was such a day when he was sliding on the rocks up a hill when he stopped suddenly, removed his shoes and put them in his hand, and decided to run barefoot over the pebbles and gravel to toughen his feet, remembering 1938 again, and the loss in Boston.

He ran higher, turning around and coming back down the mountains outside Athens in his bare feet, running back into the city where curious residents spotted him, head down, running possessed, the shoes waving in his hands, up and down and back and forth like the hands of a metronome gone awry, until he spotted a railroad track and suddenly jumped between the tracks, running barefoot on the fine stone ballast, blasting his feet into callused hardness. It was six miles along the tracks and Kyriakides picked up the pace as he picked up his head, running faster and faster, imagining a train behind him, until one started to close on him and he leaped off to the side, nearly stumbling, now trying to keep pace with the passing train as passersby applauded and cheered and urged him on.

"Run, Stelio!"

You are an eagle.

As he started his daily runs, there would be Simitsek, watch in hand and advice pouring out, telling Kyriakides how to pace, how fast to run, what to watch for. But he wouldn't let Kyriakides run only for distance, breaking the training into alternate routines of long-distance running with sprints of one-thousand- and five-thousand-meters, speed training to build his ability to break away from a field at the end of a marathon. Even in winter, the Mediterranean sun baked his body as he ran, sweat pouring under his arms, the heat rising to his skin, his legs aching with the tight burning feeling of muscles contracted, but being pushed, the automatic metronome swing of his arms the only thing propelling him besides his spirit. Perspiration ran into his eyes as he looked—always as Simitsek said—at the watch. He thought of the ocean near Limassol in Cyprus and longed to be running again by the beach there so he could turn and jump into the cool water.

Kyriakides occasionally worked out in the gym in the College of Athens where he still enjoyed some celebrity as a champion of the Balkans. He ran in the fields and the mountains because the neighborhoods hadn't been built up yet after the war. Sometimes, he would run through the towns of Galatsi and Kalaogresa and back to the mountains and back to Filothei. One time he lost his shirt and had to run barechested, the sight amusing people going about their business, shaking their heads at the man without a shirt.

One day a man came by and saw him running in the snow, wearing only his shorts and T-shirt. "Kyriakides, you are crazy," the man said. It was Apostolos Nikolaides, the president of SEGAS, which had sent him to Boston in 1938. The word was passed about Kyriakides' obsession. He kept running, though, until one day he was visited again by Nikolaides, worried he was training too hard.

"Something is telling me to persevere and not stop at a difficult moment," Kyriakides said.

And so, through December and January, Kyriakides trained and wrote to George Demeter, asking his help in being sponsored again to come to Boston, telling him that he had found a way to get there, but needed help, a place to stay and train. Demeter was delighted, happy Kyriakides had survived the war and wanted to come back. Kyriakides was working harder now, and the arduous training was taking its toll. He still wasn't eating enough and the race was only two months away. On February 21, 1946, he received a telegram from Demeter, telling him to work hard because he would be getting an invitation from the Boston Athletic Association. YOUR LETTER ARRIVED TODAY. BOTH INVITATIONS MAILED TOMORROW. GET READY. TRAIN HARD AND WIN FIFTIETH AN-NIVERSARY BOSTON MARATHON RACE.

Not until March 7 did Kyriakides get a letter from BAA president Walter Brown, though, telling him that an official invitation was on its way: "We all remember well the splendid showing you turned in the last time you came to this country to compete in this race and realize your sterling qualities as a marathon runner and champion in your own country and we would be very happy to accept your entry." Kyriakides felt reenergized and smiled as he read the letter and showed it to Iphigenia. Her smile was less certain because he still didn't look strong enough to compete.

A week later came an edgy advisory from Demeter, who too remembered what had happened in 1938 when he was so sure Kyriakides would take the Boston race. The telegram stated: TRAIN SAFELY ONLY ON CONCRETE CEMENT PLACES AS MARATHON COURSES FOR STRONG HARD TOUGH VICTORIOUS FEET, remembering the 1938 problems Kyriakides had with blisters that required him to drop out of the running.

Kyriakides' face hardened as he read the words. *They don't think I can win*, he thought. He had seen the telltale glances in the eyes of his wife, and even in Simitsek when the training started. He began to have some doubts himself. Why wasn't his hard work bringing swifter results in his times and in his body's reaction to the work?

After a hard run one night, exhausted and feet hurting, he fell to his knees about a mile from his home, suddenly losing the strength to get up and continue. Breathing hard, on his hands and knees in the dirt, he felt afraid, his breath coming in great sobbing gasps, the fear evaporating his courage. At night, Kyriakides would go into the bedroom, sometimes looking longingly at the bed and his wife, wanting to be intimate but heeding Simitsek's words. Her eyes told him she missed him too, but the words were unspoken about their need for each other, and he was tired and mentally worn out, watching the calendar and trying to think of Boston coming up so fast now. He would be asleep by 10:00 P.M., sometimes bypassing the little milk and bread they had for his family, his heart worn by the sight of the too-common meal: a few peas.

Near the first of April, Kyriakides began to gather his belongings for the trip. The ticket was paid by his company, and he had some spending money, but he worried now about what would happen to his family when he was gone. "If I win, I will be staying in the United States. I will go anywhere to talk about how there is no food and what has happened to our country. I may be gone a month or more," he said.

Five days before coming to the United States, he had eaten little, giving away most of the food to his wife and two children. He couldn't stand to see the look of yearning for food in their faces. His own was drawn and his long, slender fingers exacerbated the look of a hungry bird, eyes agog but not seeing. His friends and family discouraged him again from even trying to compete in Boston because they were so worried about his health.

"At least this time I don't have to go by ship," Kyriakides smiled brightly, trying to lift their spirits. The trip in 1938 on the *Bremen* had cost him valuable training time and Kyriakides now was booked on the first TWA flight out of Athens after the war, luckily replacing another person who could not go.

On April 2, the day before he was set to leave, Kyriakides had to explain to his in-laws and other relatives why, again, he was going to Boston. They didn't think he had a chance. They were upset with him, and his father-in-law flashed anger. "I think that man is crazy," he told his daughter about her husband. "He is not thinking that he has a family. Why does he think he is going to America? He is not in any kind of athletic shape. How is he going to run against those giants in America?"

That's when Kyriakides flashed with his own anger, rare for him.

"I will make you eat your traditional lamb with joy this Easter. You will have a second Resurrection in Greece with my victory," he said, the usually calm black eyes flashing. The kidding stopped. There was a resolution in his voice that froze them.

That night was difficult. His flight was in the morning and he slowly packed in the bedroom, Iphigenia watching. In the big brown suitcase was a pair of plain leather running shoes with small spikes, and the black suit he was married in, with a white shirt and a black bow tie. "Why are you bringing that, Stelio?" she asked.

Kyriakides looked over from the bag on the bed, turned to her, and smiled, his black eyes brightening. "I'm going to wear it after I win," he said. Her heart leaped with hope.

That night, as they were in bed together, Kyriakides fidgeted, finding sleep difficult. He was worried about his wife and children, who didn't fully understand where their father was going and why he was leaving. In the past few days, the smallest disturbances had upset him because he was so concentrated and fretful about the race, knowing the burden he was carrying. His shyness had become deep introspection, mixed with a slight agitation. He had to win, he knew. He had to win. He turned to Iphigenia and told her gently what to do on the night of the race. This year, the religious calendar followed by the Greek Orthodox Church and the Roman Catholics would coincide and Easter would fall on the same day, Sunday, April 21, for both churches. Because Good Friday would be on April 19, the traditional day of the Boston Marathon's running, the race was being pushed back to Saturday, April 20.

The time difference meant that the race would not end in Greece until late on the night before Easter, after the joyous Resurrection liturgy in the church, and Iphigenia would not know what had happened in Boston until the next morning when radio broadcasts would begin. "When I win, you will hear it on the BBC on Easter morning at seven-thirty. I want you to hear what has happened to me in Boston," he whispered.

He tossed next to her, worried about her and anxious to get to Boston at the same time. "I cannot rest until I reach America," he said, his words bonding them in the dark. "This has been bothering me night and day. I hope to find Greeks who will help me. From the letters I received, they will help me," he said, his body moving, sleep not coming.

"Calm down, Stelio," she said tenderly, a hand touching him, calming him, supporting him. She was worried too, but she could not let him know. "Now that you have decided to go, with the help of God, you will do your best. Stay cool, stay calm." Then they stopped talking, taking comfort just in lying next to each other, their bodies touching, each knowing the other would not sleep.

> Life is short, the art long, opportunity fleeting, experience treacherous, judgment difficult
>
> —Hippocrates

The next morning, April 3, Kyriakides had breakfast with his wife and children and waited for Simitsek so they could all take a coal-powered bus to the TWA office downtown, where he would be taken to the airport outside Athens and board the airline's first postwar flight to America. He would be on a flight filled with influential people and wondered if he was dressed well enough. Only Iphigenia and Simitsek would be going with him, and Kyriakides and his wife awakened at five o'clock to get ready. In the early morning hour, Kyriakides had stopped to look at his sleeping children, his heart skipping with hope and worry. Relatives would watch them while he headed to the airport.

Kyriakides had included a little lunch and had his ticket for flight 931 tucked in his pocket. The flight, paid by his company, was $646.30 to New York, an astounding sum for the time, a fortune beyond his reach. It was an 8:30 A.M. flight but he had to be at the office early. He ate an egg, tea with milk, and a little bread, but his thoughts were not on food now. Kyriakides kissed his children good-bye and stepped into the bus with his wife and Simitsek. No words were said as they left each other alone with their thoughts, until Simitsek leaned over to give Kyriakides some last-minute advice. "Don't look back," he smiled, repeating the mantra he had delivered during Kyriakides' training. "And practice your sprints."

When they got to the TWA office on Stadiou Street, they were surprised to find no one there except some carpenters trying to finish work. There were no passengers and no airline officials. The other passengers were at the airport and Kyriakides' heart skipped again with fear he might miss his flight.

They looked around at each other, wondering what to do, when suddenly a car pulled up and a driver got out and said, "Mr. Kyriakides?"

Kyriakides acknowledged himself. This was his ride to the airport and America. They relaxed and Simitsek grabbed him by the shoulders, smiled, and said nothing for a moment. Kyriakides looked back, a gentle ease in his face, one arm holding onto a light brown suitcase that would be his only luggage, wondering how to respond, when Simitsek hugged him ferociously and the two men held each other, their bond going back to the first days they had met.

Their eyes almost brimmed when Simitsek blurted, "Watch your time at five-thousand and ten-thousand meters. Check and make sure they are good," he said, stepping back to give Kyriakides his last moment with Iphigenia, who stood a step away, her own heart alternately sinking with worry and hope that he would prevail over such long odds. He still looked too weak, she thought. Kyriakides turned to his wife, so much shorter than he, looking down into her face, its serenity broken by her concern. She looked up into his eyes. Clutching his arms, she pulled him to her and put her lips to his ear.

"My thoughts will be with you. I will pray to God for your victory and to see your dream come true," she whispered, his fingers tightening on the shoulders of his suit. "You have the love from within my heart," she said, her voice breaking. "May you have good success," and they embraced. He kissed her tenderly, his thoughts floating with his closed eyes.

He stepped back, looked at Simitsek again, back to his wife, and stepped into the waiting car, the driver holding the door. The car pulled away and he looked straight ahead before turning back to look out the window at his coach and wife, standing on the sidewalk, waving good-bye.

He rode to the airport quietly, slowly pulling his thoughts away from Greece and toward the United States and Boston. The flight, in stages, would take fifty-six hours and take him to Rome, Paris, Shannon, and

New Brunswick before landing in New York, where he would meet some Greek-American friends and athletes before taking a train to Boston, where Demeter would be waiting. He thought of his old friend Jerry Nason, and what he would say when they met again after eight years. And he thought of his mission, of Kemp, and of his Olympic teammates, those who had died during the war, and of his friend Ragazos, the great runner who had beat him in Constantinople in 1940. He was running for all of them now, for all of Greece.

At the airport, Kyriakides stepped slowly out of the car, holding the brown suitcase, and looked at the airplane and the important-looking people who were boarding, and for just a moment, he doubted himself. It had been eight years since Boston and so much had happened. He swallowed and crossed the tarmac to the plane that would take him back to his dream, to the place where he had failed, when the only prize was glory.

This time it was survival.

New York City, April 5

Kyriakides was weary after the long plane ride, but happy to see some familiar faces when he arrived in New York, friends who had greeted him in 1938. He took a deep breath and looked around America, glad to be back. Then came the four-hour train ride to Boston, where Demeter was waiting, once again at South Station. In 1938, the greetings had been jaunty, with smiles and formalities and pictures of the two shaking hands, and fluffy features on "the Modern Pheidippides," about the Greek with the broad smile and easy manner.

This time, there were no photographers or newsmen waiting in Boston. No one thought Kyriakides could win.

He wondered himself now.

7

Nike

Boston, April 8, 1946, Monday night

The fiftieth anniversary of the Boston Marathon was only ten days off
and *Boston Globe* sports editor Jerry Nason was sitting back in the chair
of his office in the newspaper's downtown headquarters on busy Washington Street, a crowded, narrow street of brick buildings housing the
city's shopping district and string of newspapers competing with one another for readers and advertisers. The newspapers were adjacent to "Pi
Alley," a narrow corridor where the jumbled-up letters known as "pied
type" would sometimes be unceremoniously dumped and left, cluttering
the dirty alley with messy piles that made walking there difficult. You
could look out the front windows and see men in hats and suits and
well-dressed women hustling about. The city had a new air of optimism
and commerce in the first year after World War II, and Nason sensed
there was a big change coming in society.

He could tell from the way sports were changing, a growing feeling
that professionals might usurp the college games that had ruled headlines for so long, and that even his beloved Boston Marathon would
take on a new look in a new postwar world. The war was over and the
world was changing.

There was a lot of attention on the race this year and writers were
looking for new angles for the event, which had become the world's
most prestigious marathon, but which had still not attracted a full

150

world-class international field. Nason was wondering what he would write about this year.

Nason loved the marathon, the characters who ran it, and the sheer amateurism and purity of an event in which there was no ball, no puck, no devices. The only object was to run, to put one foot in front of the other to test yourself and to try to beat others. Boston was a bustling newspaper town, and the *Globe's* competitors were close by in the section of Washington Street that became known as "newspaper row" and Nason would often see his colleagues and rivals on the street, men who preferred formal dress and hats and loved to talk about sports. In April in Boston, that meant the marathon. It had been fifty years since the first modern Olympic Games in Athens in 1896, where Spiridon Loues had salvaged the pride of his country by winning the gold medal in the marathon. A Bostonian, George Brown, had seen the games and brought back the idea of the marathon to Boston, quickly selling the idea to the affluent members of the BAA, who decided to start their own race in 1897.

They tied it to another tradition: April 19, Patriots' Day, the day New England revolutionaries in 1775 had begun their battle for independence from Great Britain, when Paul Revere had made his ride through the Boston countryside to Lexington and Concord, and where embattled farmers stood and fired the shot heard 'round the world. In the next century, Boston developed a blue-blooded sense of culture, of universities and learning, that found the city dubbed "the Athens of America."

The event was especially important for the BAA and for Nason, who was quickly becoming one of the most important chroniclers of the race. He had a generous demeanor and compassionate stance for amateurs, men, he thought, who still typified the best of sports because they gave of themselves and still had a sense of sportsmanship.

Nason especially loved covering the event because it brought a wide range of characters. This year there would be the shy, slender defending champion and local favorite Johnny Kelley, who had finished second six times before; and three previous winners, the cocky, cigar-smoking Canadian, Gerard Cote, who was back from World War II; the 58-year-old seven-time winner Clarence DeMar, more loved by the fans than his rivals, who thought him arrogant and distant; and the poverty-stricken American Indian Tarzan Brown from Rhode Island. Nason was contemplating the race, wondering whom he would pick this year. The writers loved the prognostication game.

Suddenly, there was a sharp knock on the door. Nason jerked his head up to look. He saw the gaunt figure of a man whose sharp, angular face and hawklike eyes were nonetheless softened by a calm demeanor, although nothing could hide the weariness he wore like a cloak, or conceal how tight the yellow parchment of his skin was across his hollow-cheeked features. It was a face Nason had seen before. This man had aged quickly, had seen horror. This was a man who had a deep mission on his mind and had closed out all other thoughts. The eyes showed a back-lit blaze of determination, but a curious probing sadness as well. Nason was still trying to figure out where he had seen him before when the man spoke, almost timidly.

"Jerry Nason?" he said, now sounding apologetic, a thin foreign accent showing he knew English well but hadn't spoken it much recently. Nason stared at him.

"I am Stylianos Kyriakides," the man said proudly, even while seeing the disbelieving look on Nason's face. "And you are shocked," he said, his voice trailing off before picking up. "For this you are not to blame. Few will recognize me now."

Nason couldn't believe it. The last time he'd seen Kyriakides was when the Greek came to Boston to run in 1938, a handsome, strong, twenty-eight-year-old favorite who looked like a California collegian and had charmed him and the rest of the sportswriting crew, who had called him "a modern Pheidippides" after the Greek who had run from the plains of Marathon to Athens to announce victory over the Persians twenty-five hundred years before, and giving the long-distance race its name.

Kyriakides tried to put at ease the man who had befriended him eight years before when the Greek had come to Boston as the champion of the Balkans and one of the first from another country to contest for one of the world's most prestigious prizes. Nason remembered Kyriakides' ignominious defeat and the Greek's vow the last time he had seen him to come back and win the marathon. But Kyriakides was now thirty-six and weak from lack of food and training. Nason thought Kyriakides would fall down where he stood, he looked so frail, and the writer's heart sank at the sight.

Then Kyriakides smiled. The grin didn't jump from his mouth so much as slowly spread, like the slow-motion ripple of a quiet body of water suddenly disturbed by the drop of a pebble. Nason relaxed too, glad to see again the man whose humility had surprised the sportswriter so used to the brashness of some athletes. Nason recognized Kyriakides now, even through the brown-travailed features and worn face and the added weariness of a 5,000-mile plane ride from Greece and a 220-mile train ride from New York that had taken Kyriakides back to Boston.

Slowly, Kyriakides sat in one of the hard wooden chairs, across the desk and the typewriter where they'd last spoken in 1938. And he then quietly unfolded the story of horror and death that had overtaken Greece during World War II, and how he had barely survived with his own life. He asked Nason to tell Americans not of himself, but of what had happened to Greece.

"So many people have starved to death," said Kyriakides, who was down to a little more than 130 pounds and seemed even thinner because of his tiny 5'7" stature. Through his too-big clothes, he seemed smaller than the handsome and gallant man who had been a prerace favorite in 1938. Kyriakides talked of people dropping dead in the streets of Athens, of those starving to death in rural areas where there was nothing but dirt, how some of his Olympic teammates had died from lack of food and medicine. Nason listened intently as Kyriakides talked about how he had to sell his clothes and shirts and footwear, furniture, and belongings to keep his family alive.

"It was necessary to do this, to keep food in the bellies of my wife and children," Kyriakides said.

His soft, graveled voice was slow but never faltered as he described the ravages of war, the loss of life, and the destruction of the cradle of democracy. Nason leaned back and looked carefully into the slender, black-eyed Greek's face. This was not a story of sports or a typical feature story about another runner.

Kyriakides continued and sighed. "In Greece today there is nothing—absolutely nothing! We have known three enemies. There are no roads, no bridges, no railroads, no harbors, no trams. There is nothing, nothing except the soil of Greece and a people determined to survive and be great again." Nason wondered how he'd survived, or trained, especially on a salary of $60 a month as a bill collector for an Athens utility company, at a time when good running shoes cost as much as $30.

But Kyriakides spelled the tale of Greece like Socrates delivering a soliloquy. "You see, we haven't much in Greece today. We haven't enough food or clothing, or any of the necessities of living. But, what we have we owe to Americans." Before he left Athens, he said many Greeks came up to him and said, "All the people, the poor and hungry people say to me: tell them in America, say to every American, 'Thanks!'" The Greeks appreciated the American assistance during and after the war, even though it had not fully stopped the spread of famine.

Nason asked, worried, "Do you have the stamina to run, Stelio?" It was not a sportswriter's probing question, but the concern of a friend. Kyriakides paused.

"My company has helped me," he said. "I had rations to train." He didn't tell Nason he had given much of the food to his family and had been training only a few months. He looked carefully at Nason, trying to gauge the writer's reaction. Kyriakides didn't want pity. He wanted to show strength and resolve and remembered how close the two had become in 1938 before Kyriakides had quit the race.

"I think I have the strength for it," Kyriakides said. "If not in my legs," he paused, "then maybe here," pointing to his chest, "in my heart."

Then he started to talk about the night in Athens a few years before when it seemed his life would end at the hands of a German patrol, before his Olympic credentials, stuffed in a pocket, had saved him. That was only a few years after Nason had last seen him, and the sports editor almost shriveled at the thought of what nearly happened.

Nason sat back in his chair and thought Kyriakides had punished

himself as only a Greek could, a stoic within whom was burning a bon-
fire of intensity. Kyriakides talked about pounding his feet on rocky
grounds and gravelly railroad tracks, including running barefoot to
toughen his feet, remembering what happened eight years before when
he said his feet couldn't stand up to the macadam of the Boston
Marathon route. Nason's heart ached because he felt such admiration
and a closeness to Kyriakides, but the Greek looked too worn out and
weak to even compete, never mind win, the grueling marathon. The
sports editor thought to himself the words he would later write: "Little
man, you have made a long, long journey in vain. You are hungry and
the war has etched its miserable years on your face. You have the
strength of heart but not the power of body to beat back the twenty-six
miles and win the marathon."

World War II had ended and the United States was helping rebuild
Europe, but Greece was still rocked by a savage civil war that had split
families and intensified a worldwide food crisis. It was especially difficult in Greece, where the Germans had ravaged the industry and the
agriculture, leaving many people with nothing more to eat than boiled
dandelion greens.

Gnawing at Kyriakides too was the knowledge that his family, his
wife, Iphigenia, and young children, Eleni and Dimitri, often had only a
few peas to eat while he was training to win. It would do no good to finish second, he knew. He had to win so the world would know what was
happening in Greece, and for this he had to force himself to accept the
worst kind of sacrifice—not of self, but of his family. It burned him.

Nason was struck by the quiet humility of Kyriakides, who again was
being helped by Boston's vast Greek-American community, especially
the Demeter family, George, Speare, and Pan, who owned the Hotel
Minerva where Kyriakides was their guest, and where chef Jimmy Contanis was being ordered to feed Kyriakides a steady diet of milk and
steaks. Kyriakides' mission wasn't the athletic triumph that was moti-
vating most of the other front-runners, but the survival of his country
and people.

When he was training under the eyes of the Demeters, he was scien-
tific in his approach. He slept as much as he could, ten to eleven hours a

night, and when he was awake thought only of training and running. For breakfast, he had milk, grapefruit, coffee, and porridge. For lunch, there was soup with plenty of vegetables, including string beans, but no pies or fattening desserts. For supper, there was soup every night and occasionally a pork chop, and the first steaks he had seen in six years.

After their long talk with Nason, Kyriakides left because he had much to do.

"Thank you . . . my friend," Kyriakides said, rising slowly, his thin frame making him look like he would topple. He smiled at Nason and left. The sportswriter turned to his typewriter. He knew now what his story was.

That night, at midnight, Kyriakides went on WNAC radio to talk about the race, and what was happening in his country. The station's Gus Saunders did the radio announcement for the race and gave Kyriakides a chance to tell people why he was in the United States. Kyriakides would not make a prediction where he would finish, but said the Greeks, who founded the Olympics, considered the Boston Marathon almost as important, especially this year.

"Seven million people. They all eagerly await the results of this race," he said. It was a simpler time without worldwide television and people had to rely on telegrams and radio and relayed word to reach them about international events, especially in the hills and small villages of Greece and Cyprus.

"This year they will, of course, want to know where I finish," he said, not underestimating the importance of his participation. It was a tremendous burden.

Kyriakides was growing in strength and confidence, even if it was not reflected in his face yet. At one prerace conference where he was questioned by reporters, he became a little bolder in his feelings and, after talking about how the Demeters had arranged to sponsor him, predicted how he would do. He would, he said, triumph no matter the cost.

One reporter questioned him, "What are you saying, you're going to come in first? You may come in second, you may come in third."

"No," Kyriakides said softly. "I'm going to come in first."

He remembered a conversation with his wife when, a few months before, he'd first told her he would come to Boston to run, to let the world know of Greece's fight for survival. "If you run, you'll die," she'd said fearfully.

"And if I die, I'm going to run," he said. "I came to run for Greece, my country."

Then he told her how it would be, despite her fears and protest. "And I'm going to run," he said adamantly. But then he paused to look at her pleading eyes and tried to comfort her. "Whatever God wills, I hope to come in first, to win."

Kyriakides was confident in his abilities, even through his modesty. The great Olympic long-distance running champion Paavo Nurmi had said that when Kyriakides put his mind to it, perhaps no one in the world could beat the Greek in a marathon. Now Kyriakides was familiar with the Boston course and had prepared his feet for it. He tried to downplay the difficulty as he spoke to the American sportswriters, eager for a story about a challenge to Kelley, the defending champion, and seizing on the American's friendship and rivalry with the Greek.

"Running in the marathon is really easier here than it is in my country. Here you do have some stiff hills over the Marathon course, but at home it is all hills and mountains," he said. But he said he was glad he had flown rather than taken a boat, which would have interrupted his training. He had run up until he had left Athens only a few days before and this time he knew the field too.

"I know I have some good men to beat and I regard the Canadian, Cote, and your own local boy, Johnny Kelley, as the men to watch if they are both in good condition," he said. Kyriakides was looking forward to seeing Kelley again too. They had met at the Olympics in Berlin in 1936 and then again in Boston two years later, when Kelley had given him a photograph wearing his U.S.A. uniform in Berlin. Kyriakides' presence in Boston in 1946 made the race a truly international event for the first time. He said his goal was to bring back at least $250,000 in aid for Greece. He was representing the Olympic Athletic Club of Athens, but said his real allegiance remained with his sporting club in Cyprus.

The next day, still moved by his meeting, Nason wrote a column that was entitled GREEK HOPES TO WIN MORE THAN MARATHON—HELP

FOR HIS PEOPLE. He told of Kyriakides' failure in 1938 in Boston, and his relationship to George Demeter, who had brought him back again. He lamented too, remembering the Kyriakides of twenty-eight years old, eight years before. "Now he is 36. The Germans have come and gone. Greece has been ravished. And Kyriakides, a bill collector whose monthly salary is $60, has been forced to sell his home, his fine clothes, his boots, furniture—all but his precious running trophies—to keep his wife and two kiddies from starvation," Nason wrote. "He is the marathoner with a mission; and the gift he hopes to bear back to Greece is the generosity of a rich nation for a poor and starving one."

Kyriakides carried something else with him on this trip too. It was the laurel wreath from Greece that would crown the champion, put on the winner's head by George Demeter, the suave former state legislator who was demonstrative about his heritage. In 1945, Demeter had put the wreath on the crown of Johnny Kelley. This time, said Kyriakides, "I hope I shall be the lucky one to be crowned with the laurel wreath by my good friend." He was no longer a state legislator, but Demeter, who favored a pencil-thin mustache and fine suits, had authored a widely accepted book on rules of parliamentary procedure that was used by many legislative bodies and enjoyed wide popularity in Boston, where he had championed Hellenic causes and constantly pushed Greece's links to Western democracy. As did Kyriakides, Demeter still felt the weight of the 1938 disappointment and this time he was keen that Kyriakides would have every amenity. With his nephew, Harry Demeter, he would drive Kyriakides to the course once again to familiarize him with the route. Kyriakides had assured him that this time there would be no question as to the toughness of his feet because he had trained so hard on hard surfaces.

The race was only twelve days off and this year would be run not on Patriots' Day, April 19, its traditional time, but on Saturday, April 20, because April 19 was Good Friday. The Greek Orthodox calendar differed from that used by other Christians and only about every four years did the Easters of the different churches coincide, including this year. That meant the runners would be racing on Holy Saturday and Kyriakides, a devout man, had planned to attend Easter eve mass at the cathedral in Roxbury, the largest Greek church in the area, which was overseen by a young and rising ecumenical leader in the church, Rev. James Coucouzes.

Still frail from years of a poor diet, Kyriakides was trying to gain weight with his steak-and-milk diet, and liked to sleep for lengthy periods. This meant he would have little time for anything else before the race except training, eating, and sleeping. But it gnawed at him that while he was enjoying a good life in Boston, his family and friends were still suffering, and that despite efforts in the United States such as the Greek War Relief led by Boston businessman Thomas Pappas and Hollywood tycoon Spyros Skouras, few Americans knew of the deep deprivation of his countrymen.

Kyriakides was humble, and did not want to let the Americans know of his confidence. He had received a lot of advice from his trainer, Otto Simitsek, and supporters urging him not to be boastful, easy for the quiet man to take, because he didn't like to talk much anyway. Nason was following him now too, because of the bond that had developed between the two men. But Nason didn't like what he saw, the aging and the withering of the body that seemed so strong eight years before, even though Kyriakides had been stopped then by his feet, and not by his heart. The world was different now, though, and Nason wondered whether Kyriakides' determination could carry his worn body over the course that had defeated the Greek when he was in his prime as the champion of the Balkans and seemed to fly over the course before his feet gave out. But if Nason was worried, Kyriakides wasn't.

He had to win, he knew.

Fame is the perfume of heroic deeds

—Socrates

There would be an early test. On April 13, Kyriakides ran in the Boston Cathedral ten-mile tune-up race, a handicap event in which some runners were allowed to start several minutes ahead of the more elite field. This would give him a chance to test his speed and endurance in a race in which he wouldn't feel any pressure to win, because only

Kelley and Brown knew much about him. Kyriakides ran loosely and easily and finished third in a time of 51:40 behind Lloyd Bairstow and American marathon champion Charlie Robbins, who were better at the shorter distance.

After the race, Kyriakides telegrammed his family: I FELT FINE, FINE . . . THE ROADS, THE CLIMATE, EVERYTHING IS DIFFERENT FROM GREECE. I SET MY TIME BEFOREHAND AT 53 MINUTES. I RUN MUCH BETTER THAN THAT, SO I'M PLEASED.

He also sent a telegram to Athens and one of his company's sponsors, Greg Lazarides, and said he was happy because Robbins was a tenmile national champion in the United States and hadn't been able to really shake Kyriakides, who was not pushing himself. "I feel fit and confident," he said. While he was doing that, Cote was taking a ride over the marathon course in a press car, playing to his friends in the media and smoking a cigar and seeming cocky about his chances, his happygo-lucky smile so different from the singular obsession of Kyriakides' set face. His eyes were already locked onto the race and there rarely was anything approaching levity or happiness in his visage, the remembrance of what was happening in Greece steeping him in the sobriety of his mission. Leslie Kemp, the director of the Athens utility company who had approved the company sponsorship and helped pay the five million drachmas, or $1,000, for the cost of the trip, hoped Kyriakides would come in only in the top three in such a tough field. BAA officials were fearful too, and Demeter and Kyriakides had to reassure them the Greek was fit enough to run, something which his strong showing in the 10-mile race had helped prove.

But that was ten miles in a practice race, not the twenty-six miles, 385 yards of the marathon, and a route that took the runners from rolling countryside up the steep hills of Newton, including the infamous "heartbreak hill," which had broken the spirit of many determined runners before, men who'd not suffered near-starvation. Kyriakides hadn't felt the course unusually tough, even when he had to drop out in 1938. But then he was not running with the burden of his country's salvation and the route had its treacherous points, especially leading into the hills, which soon turned to the leg-busting downhills from Cleveland

Circle, about six miles from the finish, down a long decline of road past
the brownstones of Beacon Street in the well-to-do town of Brookline,
into the bustle of Kenmore Square, near Fenway Park, where the Red
Sox had a game scheduled, through the thick crowds lining the streets
toward the finish. By the time you reached the downhills, an athlete
had already run himself into the ground and, if there were a chance to
win, he would have to push himself past the sweat and thirst and pain
bursts in his legs and arms and body, take on the challenge if another
runner was testing him, and then try to *speed up* a pace that was already
nearly five minutes a mile. He would need more than training and desire
to carry him and the worry of a family and a country would be like another weight on his shoulders, Kyriakides knew.

Kyriakides *was* worried about what was happening to Greece, thinking often of the time difference and what his wife and children were
doing. He pictured them as he ran. There were few telephones and no
way to contact her besides telegrams and letters, and he would assidu-
ously sit down and write her, hoping the volume of his words would
communicate his feelings. A few days before the race, Iphigenia's heart
raced as a letter arrived from her husband.

She ran into her home and sat by herself, opening the letter slowly at
first, pausing for breath, then tearing the envelope and saving the
American stamps. She couldn't hear his voice, but she wanted to see his
handwriting. She closed her eyes for a moment, blinked to clear them,
and started to read, feeling the pulse in her wrist rise like a tide and tick
her heart.

Dear Iphigenia,

I was very well received by the Greek-American community. My
hopes for winning for Greece have been uplifted more. The Greeks of
America are true Greeks, like the ancient Greeks. One reporter told me
if I finish second or third, I have done well. I was weak and they fed me.
They were very concerned about me being weak. I am staying at the
Hotel Minerva again. I gained strength and I told myself no matter
what, I must win the marathon.

The BAA did not want me to run because they thought I could not finish the marathon. But I ran in a 10-mile race and I did well and that's when they believed I could run the marathon.

The letter continued, not with running or the marathon, but with his thoughts of her and their children and Greece. She put it down and let her thoughts drift to Boston, imagining him sitting at his desk in the hotel, thinking of her. On April 17, three days before the race, George and Harry Demeter were watching Kyriakides train on roads near the hotel when they saw he was in some pain and they took off his shoe to reveal a bloody sock. "Stelios, what is that?" George said, his face furrowed.

"It's okay, it's okay," Kyriakides said. "It's just the shoes. My feet are okay." Demeter, remembering his own pain eight years before in watching his countryman fall, wanted to be sure and took him to a foot doctor who said indeed it was just that the shoes were too tight. They went to a cobbler for some repairs. The cobbler looked at the bottom of the shoes. There were tiny pebbles stuck in the grooves and he wanted to take them out. "No," said Kyriakides. "These came from the mountains of Greece where I trained and they will bring me good luck," he said.

The sportswriters were building up the race now, and Bostonians and New Englanders, glad to be shed of the weariness of the war years, were embracing the event with new gusto and enthusiasm. The city was energized with the start of a new postwar resurgence in the economy and the energy of so many young men back from war, eager to start their real lives. Downtown Boston was alive with people eager to see spring too, and the streets bustled with workers and a new era of big Detroit automobiles, stylish convertibles and sedans, while the many downtown movie houses carried an optimistic new brand of films. Even the ubiquitous brick of the city couldn't quell the color of the coming spring or dull the confidence of people eager to embrace a new time. It seemed so different from the depression of Athens, Kyriakides thought. He was as much an ambassador as a runner he knew, and he tried to carry himself like a diplomat and a messenger, careful to dress well when he was in public and weigh his words.

Demeter explained why, telling reporters why the Greek was so single-minded and serious. "Kyriakides is a representative of Greek athleticism, and while he is here as an athlete, his efforts in the marathon mean much more. As an athlete, he has been commissioned to pick up some athletic supplies to take back to Greece. It's almost pathetic how much they want back there. Three or four discuses, some shot for shot-putting, javelins, track shoes, spiked shoes, track suits," he said. Demeter said Kyriakides would be traveling to help raise money for the Greek Relief. "A victory might mean, by the time he finishes his tour, a whole ship of supplies that are so desperately needed back in his home country. It's a terrible burden for just one small man. But Kyriakides is a Greek and he's proud that he's the man to carry that burden. That's why he may be a bit more serious Saturday, since he's running for food and clothing—even medicine—for millions of his countrymen," he added. It was a story line irresistible to the sportswriters, for whom sports could become cavalier. Not for Kyriakides. He said he also wanted to bring back some sweat suits for young athletes to begin their training. "They want to interest the young boys and girls in track. After all, that was of Greek origin," he said proudly.

The next day, sportswriter Arthur Siegel was as taken as was Nason by this story. In the *Boston Traveler,* under the headline, GREEK FOOD RE-LIEF RIDES ON MARATHON, he wrote that although the race itself was a sporting event that was taken light-heartedly by many people, despite its fierce competition, Kyriakides' quest had brought dramatic human urgency to the event. "If Stylianos Kyriakides of Greece can win, or be right there at the finish, that achievement will mean more food and clothing for impoverished Greece," Siegel wrote. And, he added, "the average competitor this Saturday will be thinking of what it means to him personally. There may be the national pride. But Kyriakides has a whole nation depending on him." That was a lot different, Siegel noted, from seeking personal glory. "He came over here once before, merely as a competitor. This time he's here as a life-saving patriot."

Indeed, Kyriakides' most important message here was to make the world aware of just how desperate the straits were for Greeks, even more so than in other places in the world where there were food shortages. Americans could understand that from reading their newspapers, but few of them had ever experienced the deep rumbling hunger that personified, for the first time, what that word meant, he knew. For all the wartime sacrifice of Americans, not many knew the hollow emptiness of going to bed hungry almost every night and of craving the simplest basic foods that had suddenly become gourmet items. Until you knew what hunger meant, you didn't know what it meant, he knew, and he thought of it every time he sat down to a steak at the Hotel Minerva and wondered what Iphigenia was eating, what his children were having.

Then came some news that he hoped would make Americans understand the plight of the Greeks. President Harry Truman on April 18 said he was calling home from Europe former president Herbert Hoover, who was overseeing an international commission on food shortages. Truman appeared before three-hundred newspaper editors in Washington, D.C., and said grimly that "the world food shortage is worse than has been painted." World War II had ended less than a year before. There was yet no plan to rebuild Europe, and there were more immediate problems of food and medicine and survival.

The Department of Agriculture estimated that one slice of bread in every loaf was being wasted and urged Americans not to throw away any, noting that saving that single piece alone would have given 2.5 million people in Europe three-fourths of a pound of bread every day. "Remember that people are starving and many will die unless help comes soon. And remember that help comes only from you," a department directorate stated. An international food board provided thicker bread slices for distribution overseas, but director Fiorello LaGuardia said the allowance was still far short of "desperate needs."

Truman said, "America cannot remain healthy and happy in the same world where millions of human beings are starving. A sound world order can never be built upon a foundation of human misery." He added, "We would all be better off spiritually and physically if we ate less . . . One day a week let us reduce our food consumption to that of the average person in the hungry lands. We cannot doubt that at this moment many people in the famine-stricken homes of Europe and Asia are dying of hunger." It was the American's duty and obligation to help.

Now we cannot ignore the cry of hungry children. Surely we will not turn our backs on the millions of human beings begging for just a crust of bread. The warm heart of America will respond to the greatest threat of mass starvation in the history of mankind. Once again I appeal to all Americans to sacrifice so that others may live. Millions will surely die unless we eat less. Again I strongly urge all Americans to save bread and to conserve oils and fats. These are our most essential weapons at our disposal to fight famine abroad. Every slice of bread, every ounce of fat and oil saved by your voluntary sacrifice will help keep starving people alive.

America, and the world, were in transition, but the past and its link, the aftermath of World War II, were making the change difficult. While Kyriakides was helping to bring a real international presence to the Boston Marathon, black baseball star Jackie Robinson was breaking the color line. In Montreal, in a minor league game that marked his first professional appearance for the AAA farm team of the Brooklyn Dodgers, Robinson caused a sensation April 18, opening the season with a three-run home run and becoming an instant attraction. A crowd of almost twenty-five thousand nearly pulled off his shirt in adoration of his exploits, which also included two stolen bases. There were almost twice as many tickets sold as there were seats.

In Boston, the Bruins were fighting a losing battle for the Stanley Cup in the National Hockey League to the perennial champions, the Montreal Canadiens, who were each paid $2,100 for their triumph. In downtown Boston, where movie theaters were still plentiful, the Paramount and Fenway were showing Joel McCrea and Sonny Tufts in *The Virginian*, while the Tremont and Majestic were showing the more risqué *Diary of a Chambermaid* with Paulette Goddard. Ballroom dancing was being advertised in the age before televisions were commonplace. Ingrid Bergman and Bing Crosby were starring in *The Bells of St. Mary's*, and drive-in theaters were opening for the season. The Patio Room advertised a complete fried chicken dinner for $1.35 with two vegetables, dessert, and coffee. In America, at least, food was plentiful, and that's what Kyriakides saw, even as he ate well and worried about those back home who did not. There were other burgeoning signs of prosperity in the United States, and signs there was about to be a sweeping change throughout the world in the postwar era.

While American GIs were settling back into a peacetime existence and Congress mulled benefits and plans to reintegrate them into a prospering society, much of the world was still ravaged by years of war. The unprecedented devastation of new bombs and weapons brought a mass level of destruction from which it would take years to rebuild. It was worse in an agriculturally based country such as Greece, which even before the war was far behind other industrial countries in its infrastructure and ability to raise and distribute mass amounts of food.

Even while he was eating and sleeping properly and gaining a little weight, Kyriakides' countenance still carried a grim mirror of what he had seen and suffered, along with the weight of worrying about his wife, Iphigenia, daughter, Eleni, three, and son, Dimitri, who was only sixteen months. Without instant communication, he had to rely on letters or expensive telegrams and he was bowed by missing them and trying to think about his double-edged mission. At night, after his training and supper, he would sit quietly at his desk, writing letters, or lie back on the bed looking at the ceiling before sleeping.

Kyriakides had been training for this race only since just after Christmas in 1945, six years after his last competitive race at Constantinople. His wife worried about his conditioning and his strength, and the Demeters were concerned too. He was gaunt and undernourished, but his soul burned like coal and he was determined to erase the horror of the war years and fulfill his pledge to Nason to come back to Boston and win the race. Even Kyriakides' strong run in the Cathedral ten-mile race didn't fully assuage the fears of George Demeter and of Nason, though.

Each day, Kyriakides would awaken and run, quietly consumed by what he had to accomplish. He would run and run and run, an automaton on a quest. He said little and although Nason and other sportswriters now began to write more expansively of his story, Kyriakides kept his words closer, preferring to run alone and talk only with the Demeters.

Already, he was beginning to feel the crushing weight of what he had to do. He looked forward to letters from Iphigenia, who said she was praying for him. He hadn't heard her voice because there was no phone in his home, only a radio tuned to the BBC for news of the Boston Marathon. Kyriakides, though, wrote again to her of his growing belief in his words and feelings.

"When I win the race, part of the victory has to go to the Greek-American patriots of Boston," who had helped him so much, he wrote. Kyriakides wrote that he was very enthusiastic about the reception he was getting from the strong Greek-American community in greater Boston, a tight-knit group despite their regional differences and the various associations representing where they had come from in Greece. He was the primary news to them now, although a young schoolboy in nearby Lynn, Harry Agganis, was attracting a lot of attention with his burgeoning exploits as a star in baseball and football. Kyriakides talked warmly of the Demeters, and Tom Pappas, whose company's business in foodstuffs was becoming one of the largest in the region, giving their family growing influence.

Demeter, though, was still anxious about Kyriakides' appearance and directed his hotel chef, Contanis, to make sure the runner had all the food he wanted. "Cook just for him," Demeter said. Kyriakides would come to the dining room in the Hotel Minerva and sit next to the kitchen at the same table where he could be quickly served, and where he was treated royally.

"What you want, Stelios?" Contanis laughed. "Steak?"

There was plenty of it and while Kyriakides grew in strength, few could see it. One competitor did, though. Francis Darrah, a war veteran from Manchester, New Hampshire was the only one picking Kyriakides in some prerace polls. He had written Nason the week before, stating that "I really think the Greek runner can do it. I pick Kyriakides first."

Nason predicted the winner would be Tarzan Brown, although the Indian had not been running seriously for several years and had dropped out of the 1936 Olympics in Berlin. Brown was still a formidable runner, despite the poverty that had overtaken his family and left him hungry to win again. He was a Narraganset Indian brave who had won the race ten years before and in 1939, but his running abilities hadn't brought him any fortune. He lived in Charlestown, Rhode Island, in a shack with five other people, including four children. He was running for a reason too.

"Look around at this place where I live. See for yourself! You'll know why I've got to do the only thing left to do—win the Boston Marathon race in world record time," he told reporters who tracked him down. Brown said he had been training hard and thought he had a good chance to win. "If I'm up there at twenty miles, no one is going to beat me." Brown said he was an angry runner too, because all his fame in the marathon hadn't made his life easier, nor stopped prejudice. He said he couldn't even get a haircut near where he lived because of discrimination against Indians. He had worked as a tree surgeon, stone mason, wood chopper, handyman, and in a coal yard in Westerly, Rhode Island, and would haul trash and junk away for little money, but had turned to training and desperately wanted to win this year. Brown said he was being paid $20 to remove trees while others were paid as much as $75 and the discrimination grated on him, drove him.

Nason picked former champion Bairstow, a well-educated, mild-mannered man, for second and then Cote and Kelley, and picked Kyriakides for fifth but couched it this way: "Cote is the guy to beat and a lot of people here figure Johnny Kelley is the one to do it." Although Kelley had won in 1935 and 1945, his six second-place finishes and his nervous over-the-shoulder glancing style of wondering where other runners were made him a hesitant favorite. Cote had beaten him three times, including 1943 and 1944. World War II made him miss the 1945 race and a chance to win three consecutive times, but Kelley had seen Kyriakides' strength in Boston in 1938 and knew the Greek had a deadly kick down the stretch.

Kelley was a curious runner, who had so much experience it seemed unlikely he'd be rattled. But he was a mixture of confidence and anxiety although he had run literally scores of races at every distance—and had won many of them, from ten-kilometer tuneups to fifteen-kilometer and twenty-mile runs and marathons everywhere it seemed. He was a natural runner but despite his two victories in Boston, many of the scribes were ascribing to him the mantle of an also-ran, an impression

Kelley was running away from. Even his triumph in 1945-when Cote was away in the war—didn't assuage some of his critics. Kelley was thirty-eight now, two years older than Kyriakides, and his perpetual grin sometimes seemed to mask an air of apprehension that running wouldn't take away.

In 1945, after the race, Nason wrote of Kelley's surprise strong showing in beating Bairstow and Don Heinicke in that "he did not stagger one solitary step of the way . . . he did not fret or fume or worry his way over the macadam. He did not, in fact, do any of the things Kelley was supposed to do—including finishing second!" It was a brief moment of real joy for Kelley. He was, in fact, a premier runner and American athletic icon, a role that seemed to put him ill at ease and sometimes affected his performance.

The Kelley of 1946 seemed rejuvenated, though, by his win the year before when, Nason wrote, Kelley had positively exploded during the grueling jaunt through the Newton hills, "like a string of firecrackers popping off." Kelley himself said he had never felt so happy in a run when he came into Kenmore Square, a mile from the end, and saw only an adoring audience. "What a feeling to come over the bridge there and see nobody in sight. Hot damn!" he said. It was an expression of relief from a great runner who often looked as if he expected to lose, despite the fierce introspective competitiveness that was rarely uttered. Indeed, the expression of pure, unadulterated joy on his face when he crossed the finish in 1945 seemed to personify the hope and erase the dread of so many also-ran races. Kelley's face tilted up, mouth agape as if invisible demons were being exorcised, his arms akimbo, the number "1" on his shirt carrying him across. Nason had described the scene as "the wiry little man, his smile bigger than his stride." On that day it was.

Like his friend Kyriakides, though, Kelley had had another weight on his mind during the war years. It was the death of his first wife, Mary Elizabeth Knowles, not long after they'd married in 1940. He'd even had to file a suit trying to recover from her mother some of his wedding gifts and athletic trophies that she'd wanted to keep while he was in the army.

Why did Kelley run so much if it seemed to pain him in some ways? "I just love it, that's all," he said. By 1942, he'd already finished twenty-seven marathons, but his slight 123-pound physique seemed ill-equipped to withstand the rigors. He couldn't stop doing it, though. "When the time comes to quit, it will be with regrets because I've had a lot of fun and won a lot of races and associated with the swellest bunch of athletes in the world," he said.

The long-distance running world in the 1930s and 1940s was a small coterie of those who knew one another well in the United States, mostly easterners, and some Canadians. The same names kept popping up at events everywhere. It was a group familiar to the few sportswriters too, and Kyriakides' return seemed to open new horizons for them and the event. Nason described Kelley as a mild but nervous battling veteran and Cote as suave and confident. They had last met two years before when Cote won by sixty yards. In 1943, the smiling Cote, with the grin of an irrepressible rogue who was impossible not to like, had buried Kelley by four-hundred yards, and the Canadian's cockiness often backed up his ability to do what he said he would. Unlike Kelley, who ran looking over his shoulder for rivals, Cote's vision was straight ahead and he always seemed surprised someone was ahead of him or would have the audacity to try to pass him.

Nason sensed something was going on inside the quiet Kyriakides and wrote that the Greek "had the vision of 7 million destitute Greeks spurring him on." He had perceived the smoldering intensity of Kyriakides' determination but wondered how the small and fragile body could propel him over Boston's notoriously harsh course. Despite the good food and rest, Kyriakides' 5'7" frame still carried only 134 pounds, only a few pounds more than when he'd arrived a couple of weeks before. He just didn't look like he could win.

> Self conquest is the greatest of all victories
>
> —Plato

After a quiet Good Friday, where Greek-Americans had carried the symbolic tomb of Christ, the *Epitaphios* through the streets around their churches, Kyriakides awoke on the day of the race, Saturday, April 20, set for a steak breakfast, when a letter arrived. It was from his wife. He sat at his desk in his room and carefully and slowly unfolded the paper, reading it deliberately, feeling his heart swell at the sign.

He had missed her so much, never so much perhaps as now. Outside was waiting the greatest race of his life and he had steeled himself to try to win, to try to not let emotion or love for his family and country interfere with his thoughts, to interrupt his singular concentration. He was worried about Cote, who was a fearless runner, and about Kelley, whose shyness was the opposite of the Canadian champion, but who—if he could keep his concentration—could run away from anyone in the field. Kyriakides turned back to the letter.

> My dear Stelio,
> I wake up every morning and I see you in front of me. I ask God to help you become a victor and that you fulfill your dream for Hellas. The day you run, I will go to church with the children and pray to God and I will light a candle that you will return to Greece a victor. I am sending you the love from within my heart and wishes and blessings from our children.

> Iphigenia

She signed too the name of their daughter, Eleni. Neither had known the letter would arrive the same day he would take onto the historic course the hopes of a nation. In their home in Athens, Iphigenia was tending to Eleni and Dimitri, and readying the household for Easter morning. It was Holy Saturday and Boston was six hours behind as evening approached in Greece and she felt forlorn. Her husband was five thousand miles away and she was nearly overcome with anxiety and worry. She took her children to church and lit a *lambatha*, a giant white candle, and knelt to pray while her children watched. In the church, Agia Filothei, everyone saw and knelt with her and prayed for Stylianos Kyriakides and Greece. Then they went home to prepare their families for the next morning, for Easter and the news of how he had done. Kyriakides remembered too that while he was eating well, his family was not. Nor was much of the rest of the world.

If there was any doubt about how serious the food shortages in the world, and Greece, had become, Americans didn't have to look further than the front page of the *Boston Globe* the morning of April 20, 1946, the day of the race. While Kyriakides and his competitors slept, the early morning editions hit the streets with grim news.

The front-page banner headline in the *Boston Globe* the day of the race told of Truman's growing concerns: TRUMAN ASKS STARVATION DAYS.

It was his plea for Americans to help, underscored by the drama of the subheadings: "U.S. Urged to Go on Rations Twice a Week," and "Hoover Says Millions Face Death in Europe."

United Press International reported the story, in a broadcast relayed around the world: "The United States assumed almost half the world's famine relief load effort tonight with a series of sweeping pronouncements by President Truman and his aides calling for two 'starvation days' a week in the American home and a vast export of grains to Europe and the Orient between now and mid-Summer." Truman was blunt: "The time for talk has passed. The time for action is here."

Federal agriculture officials said millers had been asked to cut their production of flour for domestic use to 75 percent of the 1945 output, even though the soldiers had returned home. All food manufacturers were told they could not carry more than a twenty-one-day inventory. Agriculture secretary Anderson said, "These measures have been taken only out of dire necessity to make urgent relief needs," around the world. Truman said the United States would export one million tons of wheat a month to help out. Former president Herbert Hoover, honorary chairman of the President's Famine Emergency Committee, came back from Cairo to be with the president. Truman outlined a six-part relief proposal to end what he said was the world's worst food crisis ever. The appeal came deliberately on Good Friday, a fast day for millions of Catholics and other worshipers. "Our reserve stocks of wheat are low. We are going to whittle that reserve even lower," he said in a sacrificial tone.

That came with an appeal to the heart of American humanity. "Bread has a reality as the symbol of life. As never before in history it is now the symbol of life of nations themselves. To reduce the bread ration has become the symbol of calamity," he said. It may have been hard for

Americans, even as they remembered their own rationing during World War II, to think that the essence of life itself was not available. But Kyriakides knew it.

Against that backdrop, and the constant worry over his family and the self-imposed pressure to win the race nobody had thought he could, Kyriakides had a breakfast steak about 9:15 A.M. and prepared himself mentally. A light rain had fallen and it seemed like a good day for a long run. There was an air of expectation and tension as Kyriakides got into the car, a Hudson, and sat in the back seat with the laurel wreath that George Demeter would carry to the finish line and place on the winner's head, as he had done to Kelley the year before. Demeter had decorated the wreath with blue-and-white ribbons, the colors of Greece. It was almost an hour's ride over secondary roads to the tiny town of Hopkinton, a picture postcard New England village twenty-six miles west of the city, and little was said on the way. Kyriakides was focusing on the race now.

Iphigenia's letter had affected him and he was contemplative. George Demeter told him, "This is your day. We are sure you can do it," and they talked about the race and the training and Kyriakides' confidence. Kyriakides spoke about how he wanted to win, not for the victory, but for Greece and to show Americans what was happening in his country.

"The weather is with us," George said. "This is a good omen." But he wished he could do something more to spur on Kyriakides, whose natural introverted state was compounded now by the nearness of the starting line for the noontime race. It was 7:00 P.M. in Greece and Kyriakides wondered where his wife was, if she were on her way to church for the beginning of the Easter eve service. The next morning was the most solemn of the religious holidays for the Orthodox Church, starting with services at midnight.

There was a field of 102 runners for the first postwar marathon, the race's fiftieth anniversary. In the past, the runners had changed at the farmhouse of a family named Tebeau, but this year there were too many runners and the Tebeau family had grown, so the participants were moved to a town community center, where the men changed in the open inside. Kyriakides came in and was met quickly by Kelley, smiling broadly at the sight of his old friend, the gap in his grin making him seem only more sincere.

"Stelios, did you take my advice on the shoes and socks to wear?" Kelley said, warmly extendings his hand. Kyriakides, for a moment, smiled back too and greeted the man against whom he'd raced in 1936 and 1938. "Thank you, Jonnee," he said, just a speck of accent and nervous energy starting to appear. Just a few days before, Demeter had called Kelley asking for some advice to help Kyriakides. "What kind of shoes are best? How about socks? How many miles should be run in the last real training test? What should he eat?" Demeter asked, and Kelley gave his best answers. Kelley was a little edgy, worried about the race and Cote's way of digging him, and he had another concern now too. He had read the articles about Kyriakides and it had affected him, but he was trying not to think about it now because he wanted to win, even though he was close to the Greek.

Kelley and Cote then dressed together in a corner of the gymnasium, a nervous tension between them amid reports this would be a grudge match between the shy and reticent Irish-American and the bold and brash Canadian. Little attention was paid to Tarzan Brown, although DeMar was attracting reporters and friends, and crowds had gathered for the start.

Cote had fought with the Canadian army during World War II and his experiences had done little to diminish his extroverted manner and constant beaming smile. He said he was in his best shape and said he was more worried about the veteran Don Heinicke from Baltimore than anyone else. He didn't know that Heinicke had become a father a few days before and was more worried about his wife and new child than the race coming up. Another favorite, John Kernason, was a thirty-four-year-old father of two children and was stenographer to the postmaster in New York. He wore glasses and was in his second Boston Marathon. And there was a black competitor, Dr. G. J. Gaither, a doctor from Maryland. He was representing the Twelfth Street YMCA in Brentwood, Maryland, but was sixty-five years old.

In the growing euphoria of the first race in the postwar world, crowds spilled out in enormous numbers, an estimated five-hundred thousand lining the long route, so deep in some places that the event would be billed as "the race nobody saw" because those in the back couldn't see the course. But, of course, most everyone did because they would surge to the front as the leaders came by the checkpoints, and the buzz of the close contest that would come rippled through them.

At the starting line, officials were dressed in suits and ties and trench coats and fedoras. The start would carry the runners past farmland as they ran on macadam along New England stone walls. There had been showers that morning, but then the weather turned ideal, if a little cool. Some of the favorites had other things on their mind too. DeMar, now fifty-eight, for some inexplicable reason, put some coins in his pocket and they jingled as he moved. Outside, officials and spectators and a fleet of cars were already preparing for the start and race officials were concerned because of the many cars that had gathered. There were many unofficial "official cars" ready to follow the runners. It was tough enough for the runners to go over narrow and winding roads, and would be more difficult now with the exhaust of so many vehicles on the route.

Police motorcycles had been supplemented by new police cars, to help control the crowd of motorists and bicyclists. For the first time too, the contestants were herded into a penned-off area, behind a slatted snow fence corral. The runners, wearing only thin clothes and smelling of liniment, were kept separate but could chat with fans over the fence. It was still cool and there was a relaxed air for most, but not for the top competitors, whose chests were starting to tighten.

Inside the town center, near a weigh-in area where doctors were checking the runners, Kyriakides had changed into his running outfit, loose shorts with pockets and a heavy white cotton T-shirt with the hand-embroidered blue letters "GREECE" in a slight semicircle over his chest. Underneath was the symbol of the winged goddess of victory, Nike, on a cross. Under that was a more important symbol. It was the number 77, obtained by Demeter. Kelley, as the defending champion, would have the honor of wearing number 1.

Before the race, Demeter told BAA officials he wanted Kyriakides to have the double seven. "Seven is a lucky number for Greeks and double seven is doubly lucky," he said. It was an odd number because the top runners had low numbers to signify their seeding. In 1938, Kyriakides had number 1. And 77 was the number of an all-American college football star, Red Grange, "the Galloping Ghost," a favorite of Demeter's. Kyriakides liked it and said he would wear the number for his people and his country and his gratitude to the Americans for the help they had given Greece.

"He's going to be not only all-American but all-Greek and all-world athlete," Demeter said. How Kyriakides got the shirt was another story. Two days before the race, Kyriakides and Demeter went by the garment shop of Oliver Lewis, the black owner of New York Art Embroidery Company on Tremont Street, across from the Boston Common. It was a third floor walk-up and Lewis had been given a white T-shirt earlier in the week. He had crookedly printed the outline of "Greece" on the front. A sixteen-year-old stitcher, Helen Primpas, a Greek-American, was given the shirt to sew. "Ollie, this is crooked," she said. "Let me straighten it out."

"Go ahead, finish it up," he said impatiently. "You don't think he's going to win, do you?"

"Ollie, wouldn't it be funny if he did. He would be splattered all over the *Boston Globe*," she said.

Kyriakides walked in, and picked up the shirt when she'd finished sewing on the name of his country and the number and the figure of Nike.

"Ευχαριστω πολυ," he said. Thank you, very much. The girl smiled timidly and said, "Καλη τυχη," for good luck. It was a formality, because Primpas thought to herself, "How is he going to win the race? He looks like Greek War Relief. He is so scrawny." Kyriakides was not an imposing figure.

Drs. Thomas Kelley, Nicholas King, and M. A. Cohen, were at the starting line, making sure the runners were fit and ready. Now it was only a few minutes before the race and although most of the runners were already in the corral outside, Kyriakides was sitting for the prerace weigh-in, talking casually with Demeter when one of the BAA doctors came up and looked at him gravely.

"I'm sorry," the doctor said. "You can't run." He wasn't going to let a competitor die under his aegis.

Kyriakides, stunned, raised his head uncertainly, wondering what the words meant. He had traveled five thousand miles and survived war, only to be told a few moments before the race that he could not run? He looked toward Demeter. The doctor shook his head. "You are too thin and weak. You are going to die if you run," he said. Kyriakides was still wondering how to respond when Demeter jumped up sharply, a formidable figure in his suit and topcoat, summoning up his stentorian legislative stance and voice and the skills of a parliamentarian and debater. Kyriakides, who had seen war and horror, was stunned silent. *Not now. Not here. Not after so much.* Demeter would not let the race be taken away from Kyriakides, and he whirled in anger at the doctor.

"He is a Greek! He has a letter from his athletic club and Greece is responsible if something happens to him. You cannot keep him out of this race!" He stood his ground, challenging the doctor, who looked at him for a moment, Demeter looking like a Spartan at the pass of Thermopylae. The doctor paused and shrugged. Kyriakides would run.

Outside, Demeter and Kyriakides talked with Kelley and Cote and the legendary DeMar, still one of the most sought-after figures. Kyriakides was reserved and, with Demeter, wished good luck to his rivals. The Demeters had to leave to get back to the finish line in Boston, outside the Lenox Hotel on Exeter Street, but George fiddled with a last moment thought to give inspiration to Kyriakides. The runners were headed to the starting line when Demeter reached into his pocket and pulled out a ragged piece of paper and scribbled something on it. He walked over to Kyriakides and pulled him aside. "Open your hand, Stelios," he said. Demeter pressed the paper into his left hand.

"There is something written on both sides. Read the top side now but do not read the back until you come to the finish line," he said, smiling and looking into his friend's eyes. Then he walked away and got into his car to drive back to the finish line with the laurel wreath that had been carried from Greece by Kyriakides. Kyriakides looked down at the note on the yellowed paper, at the top side. It said Η Ταν Η Επι Τας— it was *e tan e epi tas*, the words uttered by Spartan mothers to their sons as they handed them their shields before going off to battle.

It meant "with it or on it," the admonition that they should come home victorious, with their shields, or dead on them. To Kyriakides, the meaning was clear.

Win or die.

> A man's character is his fate
>
> —Heraclitus

When the gun sounded at the start, Kyriakides could see around him a field of topflight runners and officials, and a crowd of spectators that would grow larger the closer the runners got to Boston. They would go through checkpoints in rural Ashland, the larger towns of Framingham and Natick, to Wellesley, past the women's college where some would traditionally join the race for a short distance, up onto the hills of Newton, and then into the large rotary known as Cleveland Circle, the start of the last dash down the crowded thoroughfare of brownstone homes on a trolley line and the wide boulevard of Beacon Street. That would lead into Kenmore Square and past Fenway Park, where the Boston Red Sox were playing. The baseball crowds would mingle with the marathon crowds when the game ended, although Kenmore Square already was a cauldron of excitement. At the moment he read Demeter's note and clutched it into his left hand, leaving the back side for the end of the race more than two hours off, Kyriakides felt Θελησις, the Greek name for the will to succeed, swell in his chest. Kyriakides thought of his wife and children and fellow Greeks sitting around their radios listening and waiting for news from the BBC. He was running for seven million people.

Kyriakides had taken to an unusual device for a runner in 1946. He was wearing a timing watch on his left wrist and would use it to check his pace every five miles. He had bought the watch before the London Marathon, when he had been a young and strong marathoner thought to be one of the best in the world. But he was thirty-six now and only a dark horse challenger.

The BAA had placed volunteers along the route to help the runners, and Demeter had also put a friend, a Greek man, in the crowd to urge on Kyriakides near the finish. Almost immediately, though, the runners' first concern was the number of official cars on the course, in front of and behind them. They had to weave between the cars and bicycles and pedestrians and police motorcycles trying to keep a path open and order on the course. One of the race cars was a 1946 Ford Sportsman's Convertible carrying two of the city's best-known sportswriters, Gerry Hern and Joe McKenney of the *Boston Post*, while politicians, officials, and friends and sportswriters were in other cars. On WNAC radio, Gus Saunders, one of the city's best-known radio figures, was calling the race. Standing in the crowd along Beacon Street near Kenmore Square was a ten-year-old boy from Brookline, Michael Dukakis, a Greek-American who had felt pride that he could watch a Greek run in the race. Dukakis came from a family where his heritage mattered and his father, a doctor, and mother instilled in him a sense of culture and history.

There were a lot of Greek-Americans in the crowd that intensified from Cleveland Circle, down Beacon Street to Kenmore Square—near Boston University, where Greek-American students had turned out to watch and cheer Kyriakides. From there, the race would head onto Commonwealth Avenue, a broad boulevard with a tree-shaded mall in the middle, past European-style brownstones and brick homes of distinctive design, to a right turn onto Exeter Street, three blocks over to the finish line where Demeter and BAA officials and the largest crowd was waiting at the Hotel Lenox.

At the start, though, Kyriakides was thinking only of his wife and family and how little they had to eat, and not so much about Kelley or Cote or the strong field, which included schoolmaster Lou Gregory, who in 1942 had finished second to record-holder Joe Smith. Gregory had run the second fastest sub–2:30 time in the race's history, a 2:28:03, and although he was forty, was still considered a threat. There was also national ten-kilometer and marathon champion Robbins, and Kernason, who was representing the Millrose Athletic Association in New York.

At the gun, fired by George V. Brown Jr., Robbins jumped out front, hoping to get his picture taken because he knew cameramen would be on the rocks snapping shots of the early leaders. Gregory then took the early lead with little known Ruben Meyer of Chicago. With only 102 runners, there was plenty of room for everyone. It was an eclectic field too, including eighteen-year-old calypso singer Oswald Kissoon of Canada. And scores of unwanted vehicles, including official cars, bicyclists, motorcyclists, sedans, Jeeps, and people just wandering across the runner's path trying to be close.

Kyriakides decided he would sit back in the pack, as he had done in 1938. The first checkpoint was in Framingham, about 5.3 miles away, and he felt comfortable laying off the lead. By Framingham, Gregory held a fifty-yard lead, helped by a brisk and cold tailwind that nonetheless made for good running weather. Still, the time was two minutes slower than the record as the wary runners jockeyed for position and none, it seemed, wanted to go out too fast. None knew either of the Kyriakides kick and penchant for running down front-runners at the end of a race. In his left hand, he held the dirty scrap of paper that bore Demeter's message and he clutched it like a trophy. But he looked straight ahead, eyes unwavering.

There were about ten-thousand spectators in Framingham when Gregory came by in 32:21, just ahead of Kernason and seventy-five yards ahead of a group—that did not include Kyriakides, still biding his time in the middle of the field, looking only at his watch now, and not at the leaders. There was, after all, more than twenty miles to go and Kyriakides kept his thoughts on his family and country. By this time, Kyriakides had positioned himself with Kelley, knowing that the former year's champion would likely lay off the pace for a while and gradually try to stretch out a lead somewhere around Coolidge Corner, only a few miles from the finish.

For all his respect for his good friend Kelley, Kyriakides was more concerned with the lithe and cocky cigar-smoking Cote. He kept a close eye on Cote, but only for the first few miles because the wily Kyriakides saw that Cote didn't have it this day and looked to Robbins to be a front-runner, as he stayed slightly behind. Cote had suffered a stitch in his side that threw him off the lead. Kyriakides' heart pounded and he was starting to sweat, as much from the mental fatigue as the physical exertion. The spectators were into the race, yelling and cheering, the course crowded with cars and bicyclists and the odd person who would dash onto the course.

The next checkpoint was the town of Natick, 9.7 miles from the start. By then, Gregory had faded into the pack while Kernason, a tall, skinny man with thick glasses, took over. He was known for his fast starts, so the other runners weren't too surprised he was leading now, although the pace still was slow. In the pack with Gregory were Robbins, Cote, Heinicke, Ab Morton, Bairstow, and Kyriakides, who was running fourth. Kernason's time was 53:43:05, but the race wasn't even at the halfway mark yet. For the first time, though, Cote saw the back of Kyriakides. The Greek was looking at his watch and here he announced the time to those running around him. They were puzzled or befuddled, wondering why he was even wearing a watch and giving them the time. He kept track of the runners from the colors of their shorts and started to close the gap, passing them one at a time.

The closest checkpoint to a halfway mark was Wellesley, at 12.5 miles. The runners were following the still mostly rural road past farms and a few houses as they came up to the college, where a gaggle of coeds was waiting, some of whom would jump out in old-fashioned running attire and follow a tradition of galloping with the leaders, although women were not allowed to formally enter and run.

A lot more cars were now following the leaders, creating almost a traffic jam on the road. It seemed everyone from Mayor James Michael Curley to Gov. Maurice Tobin, and assorted hangers-on had permits allowing their cars to be on the roads with the runners. It was becoming unwieldy. Spectators leaned out of car windows only a few yards from their favorites, cheering them on. Kernason had opened a 150-yard lead and was looking brisk and confident, with Gregory moving back into second and—350 yards behind the leader—were Kelley, Cote, Kyriakides, Robbins, and Bairstow. It was evident one of these seven men would win the fiftieth Boston Marathon, even as they tried to maneuver through the cars and motorcycles and bicycles and the now thickening throngs of people who sometimes just wandered onto the course. The runners could hear the suddenly swelling sound of the exhortations of the watchers too, those who had picked out their favorites. Kelley, from nearby West Acton and a worker at a Boston Edison plant, was a target of "Go Johnny!" cries. There were none yet for Kyriakides, hard behind Kernason and Kelley, who was not looking over his shoulder yet.

Here Kyriakides decided to try to close the gap, chasing Kernason down and closing on Kelley's heels. He wasn't looking at Kernason now, though, only at Kelley, his friend. Kernason had stepped up the pace from Natick and now his time, as the leader was 1:11:07, thirteen seconds ahead of Kelley's mark the year before. Then Kyriakides ran into something no one could have expected. He heard someone in the crowd yelling in Greek, and then looked behind him to see a man running, exhorting him in his native language and trying to catch him. He was holding an orange. Kyriakides' heart skidded, but he halted briefly to take the orange.

The man started to hug and kiss him, caught up in the passion and the drama. Kyriakides looked up and saw Kelley had taken a forty-yard lead over him. He wondered how he would make up the distance and the time without losing strength, especially because the others were picking up the pace. Kyriakides burst into an overdrive to close the gap, but worried whether he had burnt out his reserves, especially with so much left in the race. The adrenaline and enthusiasm had propelled him forward, but his strategy of laying off the front had enabled him not to expend all his energy. But he caught Kelley and the two started a series of duels, sprinting ahead and falling back, only a few feet apart laterally, and alternately running ahead of, and then behind, each other. It was in deadly earnestness now and both men's faces tightened, realizing that it might end up this way, the two of them pulling away from the field and trying to chase each other down in the last yards of the long race.

The next checkpoint would be Woodland Park, almost seventeen miles in and approaching the dreaded hills of Newton, next to Brookline, the town adjacent to Cleveland Circle and the finishing stretch into Kenmore Square and then to the finish line where a nervous Demeter was waiting, listening to Saunders's report on the radio. Kyriakides' name was not being mentioned much, and Gregory had resurged and taken the lead and would hold it going into the Newton hills, his time of 1:36:18 putting him fifty yards ahead of the sudden duo of Kelley and Kyriakides taking aim at his back. No one knew the real drama was unfolding with the two "K" boys.

Heinicke dropped out with a bad back at the eighteen-mile mark and Bairstow was fading, feeling ill. He suddenly dropped out at Newton Falls and Kernason dropped behind shortly thereafter and fell further behind at Newton Hospital. Kelley, Robbins, and Kyriakides were close behind the leader.

Cote faltered at Auburndale, where Kyriakides and Kelley were next to each other, anticipating a rush to the front, wondering when the other would try to take the lead. They moved together as one, catching Gregory, who, faltering under the sudden pounding of Kelley and Kyri-akides, had fallen to fourth by now, with badly blistered feet and a lame knee, which was forcing him to slow and walk. Gregory was forty years old, the holder of nineteen national championships at distances from ten-thousand meters to thirty kilometers, and was a formidable foe and champion. He was a schoolteacher formerly and had been released from the navy three months earlier, as a lieutenant commander, but his age had caught him.

There was another enemy now: the automobiles surrounding the runners. The "official" cars and those that had crowded onto the course had ejected a haze of blue fumes that looked like a hazy gas cloud in places, almost putting the runners behind a face of smoky exhaust that made it hard for them to breathe right, the noxious odors filtering into their noses and open mouths agape for air. And now, the first of the Newton hills was ahead.

Kyriakides and Kelley had passed Gregory on the first upgrade of the first hill, and Robbins had moved into third, but then Kyriakides and Kelley started running alone by the Braeburn Country Club as Robbins fell off the pace too. It was now Kyriakides and Kelley, one and then the other inching ahead, breathing hard, vision obscured by sweat, warily eyeing each other, trying not to let their heads down. The two were shoulder-to-shoulder after twenty miles approaching the steepest of the Newton hills, where they were surrounded by bicycles, Jeeps, motor-bikes, police cars, and motorcars and what was described as "the largest

Kyriakides (no. 77) and 1945 champion Johnny Kelley ran stride-for-stride and shoulder-to-shoulder up the famed "heartbreak hill" as they broke away from the pack, and had to fight for position with vehicles too. Courtesy of the *Boston Globe*.

flotilla of freeloaders and officials that ever convoyed two small runners down the drama-drenched road." They passed the spires of Boston College in gothic drama.

Now, for the first time, it was Kelley and Kyriakides, the two friends, not even glancing to the side to acknowledge each other, their hearts racing with anxiety and desire while the crowds screamed as the two ran like thoroughbred horses down a home stretch. But they were still six miles from the finish. They were almost stride-for-stride as they came up a Newton hill, crowded only by a few cars and motorcycles, each looking straight ahead and not toward each other. It was left to the two of them as the word of Kyriakides' challenge began spreading through the crowd, who pronounced his name awkwardly and finally settled on the buzz, "*The Greek!*'

Both looked fresh and full of running, but Kelley had finished second too many times and that was weighing on him as he could see the deadly earnestness of his friend Kyriakides' face and pace. Kyriakides looked like a bronzed figure, an automaton whose expression never changed from a stoic mask of determination, while the more animated Kelley had changes in his expression that told of his worry. Kyriakides had put Demeter's note in his pocket now, but the words burned through and he hadn't yet read the back—that would have to wait for the finish.

The Newton hills were like a wall to many runners, who just couldn't put their feet in front of them with the same determination anymore at this point. Kyriakides' face didn't show it and Kelley's clockwork motion of his legs, which kept the same pace like a grandfather clock, didn't show it, but the two men were feeling the strain of thousands of rapid steps, the marathon contorting their muscles with pain and burning and making them reach into adrenaline and desire to outfight each other.

Their steps were synchronous, millimeters of air under their heels as their feet left the pavement and they tried to stare straight ahead. Kyriakides was succeeding, locked into looking at the visions of famine and ghosts and his ancestors urging him on, from Thermopylae to World War II. For Kyriakides, this was a race for life or death. Then Kyriakides heard a voice in a language he understood. It came from somewhere in the crowd and reenergized him with new desire. It was a cry Kyriakides understood: "For Greece!" He weaved slightly with the words and thought of his starving people and his face took on an even more determined gaze.

At the finish, Demeter nervously held the wreath, standing near the finish line while trying to listen to the radio. Kyriakides, heart aching with desire, was now near the spot where he'd had to drop out with blisters in 1938. That moment had led him into Nason's office eight years before with a promise to return and win.

Behind lay the other favorites, Cote still suffering a siege of cramps that kept him off the lead, Heinicke's bad back forcing him out, and Bairstow, a strong runner, hurting from stomach cramps from a bad pork pie he had eaten a couple of nights before. Bairstow went through four attacks of nausea before he finally had to drop out. Kelley had won the duel of the Newton hills, taking a slight lead at the Lake Street check-point, at the bottom of the Newton hills, only five miles from the finish. Kyriakides was hard on his heels, though, and Kelley couldn't relax and his face was showing the strain. He didn't want to finish second again, not even to his friend. The cries of the crowd alternated now, their numbers thickening along crowded Beacon Street, at Cleveland Circle, where the crowd grew thick. "Go Johnny!" was heard frequently from his hometown fans. But now more people were stumbling to support the Greek and Kyriakides heard sputtered awkward yells of *"Keeklees,"* until finally they changed to "The Greek is coming!"

Now there was a duel in the crowd too, Kelley's legions of supporters spurring him on, yelling, "Go Johnny!" and the single repeated beat of "Kelley! Kelley! Kelley!" It was, after all, still the American Marathon and Kelley was the hometown hero and defending champion.

Then, simply, a pulse beat that started to reverberate like a sound wave carried through the lines of crowds, rippling and becoming alive, the noise darkening Kelley's face.

"The Greek!"

"The Greek!"

From Cleveland Circle, where trolleys would turn around in a rotary, Beacon Street turned downhill for a while, and then up a steep grade leading toward the major intersection in Brookline of Coolidge Corner, where an S. S. Pierce Tudor-style store graced a corner and where a major throng of people waited. This was the gateway to the finish, little more than three miles from the end where Demeter and celebrities waited anxiously. Kelley came out of Cleveland Circle with a lead and sportswriters said they "kissed the Greek good-bye," figuring no one was going to catch the fleet Irishman. Then the bronze turned fluid and Kyriakides came after Kelley like a man chasing a dream, for a purpose that was greater than life. Kelley was running confidently and smiling easily, but even as he glanced over his shoulder, he couldn't see the stern de-termination of the pursuing Kyriakides. Yhen he heard the warning shouts of the crowd, *"The Greek is coming!"* Kelley started taking more anxious and frightened glances over his shoulder, where Kyriakides was stalking him like Achilles circling Troy.

Down Beacon they went, heartbeat-for-heartbeat, Kelley hoping to stave off yet another second-place finish and defend his championship, Kyriakides running for seven million people. In Greece, it was early evening and his wife and family and friends fretted, readying for Easter and hoping to hear something from the BBC about the race. Kyriakides' black hair was plastered with sweat, while Kelley's arms ached and his shirt was wet throughout. Strain was showing on his face. Kelley was holding a sixty-yard lead, but Kyriakides was looking strong and he heard Greeks yelling encouragement to him in his native language, spurring him: "You're doing well, you're going to finish second!"

But Kyriakides hadn't come five-thousand miles to finish second. His mission was too important. He hadn't broken a smile or, it seemed, even a sweat for nearly twenty-four miles, but this moved him to speak for the only time during his stoic run. He answered, strong and seriously, looking at the man who had yelled. Kyriakides said, "No, not second! I'm going to finish first!" Kyriakides had not held the lead at any of the official checkpoints, but was in a position to win—if he could outkick the determined Kelley. For the past couple of miles, after breaking away at the Newton hills, they'd traded the lead a half dozen times, but Kelley had moved out a little more comfortably after Cleveland Circle, opening the gap at Coolidge Corner, heading down the hill toward the homestretch that would begin in Kenmore Square, where scores of thousands of people were waiting. It looked like Kelley would repeat as champion.

Kyriakides' mind was reeling now, fatigue catching him too as he saw Kelley's back, and for the first time he worried whether he could win. His heart sank to his feet and spirit drained out of him. *Win or die*. Then Kyriakides looked into the crowd, which was becoming louder and more excited watching the sudden sprint of the two left alone in the home stretch of the world's most prestigious race. He saw the face of an old Greek man who was watching him like a sentinel. It was the man Demeter had put there. The steps became slow motion and the soaring sounds deadened, like murmurs under water, and Kyriakides saw the old man's mouth slowly, syllable-by-syllable, utter a phrase that made his heart at once stop and start rapidly and made goose bumps race across his flesh.

The old man shouted, in Greek, like a god from Mount Olympus sending down an order. "For Greece! For your children!" He clutched his hair in anguish as he yelled and Kyriakides, weary and worried, was lifted by the raw charge of emotion. Kyriakides became Hermes, wings on his feet and his head turned back to the run and the charging Kelley, who thought he might have finished his Greek friend two miles from the end. Kelley was a champion too and he did not want to be denied, no matter how important the cause for Kyriakides, who felt he was running with the gods now, and his mind saw something else, above the faces of the crowd. It was the vision of the blue-and-white Greek flag urging him on. It was torches burning on the Acropolis not far from his house. He thought of his wife and children having only peas to eat, of the work of Simitsek, who'd pushed him to win.

Kyriakides thought of the letter from his wife and daughter and how they wanted him to win, and he remembered his countrymen and his face became hard with determination. His company leaders had wanted him to be among the first three. He looked again at his wristwatch, as he had done so often, and thought of the mountains where he had trained so hard his shoes had become pockmarked from stones. Kyriakides, in his passion and fatigue, saw something else: his crying countrymen, their tears falling and voices in union rising and imploring. It was a simple exhortation: "Win! Win for us!" And a moment later, another Greek-American, exulting at seeing Kyriakides' burst to the lead, tore up a newspaper into confetti-size pieces and threw them at him as he passed, yelling encouragement in Greek: "Here. Take this for flowers!"

At the same time, Kyriakides could not believe what his ears were hearing. Here in Boston, in the backyard of his friend and rival Johnny Kelley, the Americans were cheering for a foreigner, they were cheering for the Greek runner so many had embraced eight years before, when he had stepped, crestfallen, out of a car at the finish line, unable even to walk with bloodied and blistered feet that didn't hurt so much as did his heart. He didn't even want to look at anyone then, especially the thousands of Greek-Americans who embraced him nonetheless, even as Kyriakides felt he had let them down.

This crowd let him know that he hadn't. The crescendo of sound that came from the scores of thousands of fans along the route sounded to him like the battle cry of the Spartans at Thermopylae, fighting—like Kyriakides—to help save Greece. The sound of the Boston Marathon crowd was a victory cry for Kyriakides—if only he could catch Kelley. And then he saw him, only a few yards ahead as they came down Beacon Street toward the entrance to Kenmore Square, where thousands of students, many from nearby Boston University, had picked up the buzz of the crowd as it swept down the street like a wave. A death sprint began, Kelley pushing himself hard now and delighted he wasn't slowing, thinking that he would repeat as the champion and prouder still because he was not fading. But Kyriakides was running with millions now, their faces too superimposed in his mind's eye, and he was catching Kelley quickly. Kelley looked first over his right shoulder, then back over his left, his lithe little body struggling to keep rhythm as he heard the cries of the crowd: "The Greek is coming!"

As they approached Kenmore Square, little more than a mile from the end, near St. Mary's Street, the spot where subway cars emerged from underground and rode along a median that split the fashionable street of brick homes, Stylianos Kyriakides passed Johnny Kelley, who couldn't believe it. Not second. Not again. He pushed himself, but Kyriakides went by him as if he were tied to a tree. Kelley's eyes widened and he tried to keep up, but Kyriakides was running above the ground now, pulling away. Kelley was so tired he thought he could not even finish now because Kyriakides had broken his spirit as much as his pace, but his champion's heart wouldn't let him stop. Kelley knew Kyriakides would pull away now, he could see second place, what seemed like his perpetual finish, looming. Nason could see it too.

After twenty-four miles of running, Kyriakides had picked up the pace to five-minute miles, almost a sprint, and his arms and legs moved like a machine while Kelley tried to keep up. But the crowd was in a rage of excitement and that carried Kyriakides. In the press car, a short distance ahead, Nason couldn't resist leaning out of the convertible and yelling back to Kyriakides. "Go Stelios! Kelley is broke," and he settled back to fashioning his lead for what he felt would be the inevitable victory. "The Greek's eyes, in their sunken sockets, blazed with an inner light as he whipped his weary frame in a frenzied rush to the finish line," after a furious twenty-four-mile struggle with Kelley. Kyriakides, he said, was fighting his way to the finish "with the scowling spectre of exhaustion shadowing every stride."

As he came into Kenmore Square, an odd intersection of slanting commingling streets facing hotels and stores and a trolley stop, Kyriakides heard new cries in his language: *Zito E Hellas*. It meant *"long live Greece!"* and long had been the rallying cry of Greek Independence Day marking the date more than 120 years before when Greek patriots had started the war of independence against the occupying Turks of the Ottoman Empire. His old shoes, tattered to begin with, were flopping and nearly falling apart, slapping the pavement as he ran. He felt lighter the closer he got to the finish line. He passed through Kenmore Square and turned onto Commonwealth Avenue, less than a mile from the end. Kelley was trying one last time to catch him, but Kyriakides was opening the gap and now it seemed it would not be close. Kyriakides kept charging and driving, his expression back to the deadpan black-eyed gaze of a warrior. His best time had been the 2:43 in the 1936 Olympics in Berlin where he'd also finished ahead of Kelley, but the Irish-American had a personal best of nearly ten minutes faster than Kyriakides, so the Greek persisted in running hard, even with a growing lead.

But Kelley would not catch Kyriakides this day.

One sportswriter said Kyriakides' countenance was "seemingly carved out of expressionless bronze," so detached was he from the field. The Greek, his slim chest barely heaving under the shirt that bore the name of his country and his purpose, propelled himself forward in the odd gait of a racehorse whose front legs stepped in front of his body in an extreme angle. He was carried by the roaring crowd down Commonwealth Avenue and then made the last right turn onto Exeter Street, three blocks from the end. The crowd was delirious with joy now, their shouts an anthem bouncing off the walls of brick buildings in the narrow canyon leading to the finish. Then, in the closing yards, Kyriakides saw the throngs of officials and politicians and celebrities, and the bounding joy of George Demeter on his left, at the red twine of the finish line, holding aloft in his right hand the laurel wreath from Greece that Kyriakides had carried himself to Boston. Kyriakides reached into his pocket and pulled out the crumpled piece of paper with Demeter's words on it, the admonition of *e tan e epi tas*, and looked at the back side.

Demeter's note said, *nenikikamen*, the phrase supposedly shouted by Pheidippides who most historians believed had run from Marathon to Athens to carry the news of the Greek victory over the Persians. It meant "we are victorious," and over the centuries had come to be shortened to a single word, the name of the goddess which meant victory.

Nike.

Greek-Americans in the crowd, many dressed in suits and ties, danced with joy and the rest of the crowd exulted too at seeing the steely face of Kyriakides coming up to the finish line, carrying the mantle of Loues, who'd won the Olympic marathon fifty years before in Greece. Kyriakides tried not to show the joy releasing inside him. There was no smile on his face—unlike the unfettered beam of Demeter, who could barely keep himself from running onto the course as Kyriakides approached, looking down at his left arm, clicking off the time on his watch, as people closed in on him, wanting to carry him up in victory.

As he came down the last few hundred yards of Exeter Street to the finish by the Hotel Lenox, Kyriakides could hear the jubilant cheers of the aroused crowd ringing in his ears. The ovation sounded like a wall of noise, but he didn't change his countenance from the stern mask of determination that had carried him more than twenty-six miles and more than twenty-five hundred years. Mounted Boston police led the glorious charge home, their steeds galloping, nostrils snorting in excitement with the ceaseless beat of the crowd, their cheers a crescendo of glory. The public-address announcer couldn't contain himself either and he was giddy with excitement as he saw who was going to cross the finish line. He shouted breathlessly through the PA system to let those in the crowd who could not see know what was happening. They knew he wasn't running for glory or for himself because the newspapers had been filled with the words of his plea. Kyriakides could hear the words too, as he whipped himself to the end. "Ladies and gentlemen! He came from the country of the three-hundred Spartans and Leonidas, from the country of 1940 that said 'No' to the Axis powers and many in the world thought this country could not stand up to Hitler!"

The crowd was pushing to converge on Kyriakides, but the mounted police and two on motorcycles flanked him to the end. He wasn't smiling yet, but Kyriakides, filled with strength and charging hard, released, at last, the emotion he'd carried for six years, through war and his own near-execution, past the years of hunger and horror and he saw the faces of his dead Olympic teammates and friends who'd died in the streets of Greece, and still were falling while he was running.

As he cut through the red twine of the finish, he raised his hands aloft and cried, triumphantly, a phrase heard five-thousand miles away: "For Greece!"

8

The Altar of the Great Victor

Filothei, Athens, Greece, Easter Morning, April 21, 1946

It had been a long night for Iphigenia Kyriakides, waiting for news of her husband's run in the Boston Marathon. The race had ended hours before, in the middle of the Greek night when there were no BBC broadcasts available and she didn't know how he had finished. She had not slept well, tossing and wondering about her husband. *Was he okay? Oh God, had he survived even?* She was a short, compact woman and her face showed the eternal weight of worry and love for her husband. All she could do in their tiny house was wonder and worry and wait. She had prayed hard the night before on Easter eve, as she readied for the midnight service, but now this morning she would have to set off on the holiest day without him. She thought of their young children, Eleni and Dimitri, and of her husband so far away. She had worried for his health, and even his survival, running with so little training and after so much deprivation. She was a small and quiet woman, believing in God and family and prayer, but she didn't think Stylianos would be able to win in Boston. He was too frail, too weak from years of hunger and had not been training, but she hoped God would think of him in the long run. Now it was in the early morning hours of Easter and she had turned on the brown, German-made radio, listening to the BBC, hoping for news and wondering if the name of her husband would be mentioned. She was sitting in a chair in the dining room, holding Dimitri in her arms,

193

feeding him. Then she heard it. It was the somber-toned voice of a BBC announcer, who had been talking for several minutes about world news that did not interest her.

"Now I'm going to give you a heartening bit of news," the British newscaster said dryly. "The Hellene, Stelios Kyriakides, came in first in the Boston Marathon," he said, in the dispassionate, matter-of-fact sound the BBC preferred in its broadcasters, imparting objectivity and distance.

She got dizzy and thought she was in a dream, and dropped her young son. She was dazed, almost ready to topple over herself. *This is a dream.* She couldn't hear or see or think, until she heard Dimitri crying, and looked down at him, tears in his eyes and started to cry herself. She scooped him into her arms and ran to her parents' home, upstairs to see them. They looked at her, wondering what was wrong. "I heard that Stelios won in Boston," she said, trying to hide the joy in her voice and eyes.

"Are you sure?" they asked in disbelief. "Or are you saying what you wished you wanted to hear?"

"That's what I heard," she insisted.

She didn't know whether to feel joy or relief. She couldn't come to grips with what she was thinking. Then there was more noise at the door and banging. It was neighbors who had heard the radio. "Did you hear the news on the radio?" they asked, gasping themselves. Soon there was another, and another, and it seemed the whole neighborhood that had known Stylianos Kyriakides as a bill collector for a utility company had converged on the house, sharing in the excitement. She called Simitsek, Kyriakides' coach, who came bounding by, rejoicing with the news. Lazarides and Kemp came running in, seeing a room of laughing, thankful people. There were peals of laughter in the air from neighbors and friends. The Easter morning air became giddy with joy, and Iphigenia felt gladness in her heart. She made the sign of the cross.

The news burst outside the house and into the streets of Athens. Men, some of them in their fifties and sixties, who had stoically survived the hardship of war and starvation and the loss of loved ones, erupted into tears, the happiness surging forth.

Know thyself

—inscription on the Oracle of Delphi

Ten hours before his wife heard the news, Kyriakides was still looking down at his left wrist when he crossed the finish line to win the Boston Marathon, checking his time. It was 2:29:47, nearly fourteen minutes faster than his time in Berlin ten years before. It was the fastest time in the world for 1946. Still, Kyriakides' expression had not changed from a hard, bronzed mask of determination, even though just a few feet to his left a joyous George Demeter was raising aloft the laurel wreath Kyriakides had brought himself from Greece. Demeter would have to compete with zealous race officials who wanted to throw a blanket over Kyriakides' shoulder, which the new champion refused. Police officers on horseback held them at salute as he ran past the finish line, chased by motorcycle police and official cars and a suddenly swarming crowd of delirious watchers, many of them Greeks and Greek-Americans who exulted in joy that a Greek had once again won the race that started in their country eons before.

The six years of war and sacrifice, and the past few months of training and hope and sweat caught up with the resolute Kyriakides. He put down his arms and started to cry, tears of relief and unfettered joy at what he had accomplished. He was looking back at the course, looking for Kelley, his vanquished friend who would again not win his hometown race, this time because of Kyriakides. *Boston Sunday Post* sports columnist Arthur Duffey was nearly overcome with emotion himself and started to scribble his thoughts for the next day's story, while other sportswriters quickly converged, jumping from their press cars and scrambling after the winner, as the finish line crowd brought a roar that veteran observers said was the most joyous they had ever heard. The radio announcer, Saunders, was as surprised as everyone at the victory. "The guy they said was going to die in the streets just won," he laughed out loud.

The happiest was Demeter, who couldn't restrain himself anymore. Dressed in a topcoat and suit and tie and fedora, he ran out onto Exeter

Street to embrace his countryman, already aware that this was not an ordinary race, even for the fiftieth anniversary of the Boston Marathon. Demeter knew what Kyriakides' victory would mean to thousands of Greeks hungry for food and good news after years of war and starvation and fear that their nation, the cradle of democracy, would not survive. When Kyriakides saw the sublime happiness on Demeter's face, the Greek's hard look finally gave way to a bright smile too as he realized what he had done. Demeter laughed as he dashed onto the course to put the laurel wreath on the sweating head of Kyriakides, just over his black, curly hair as motorcycle police officers and BAA officials in suits gathered to surround the victor. Kyriakides, spent, almost went under from the weight of the wreath and what he had accomplished. Harry Demeter, George's nephew, started to cry too, from his vantage point at the finish. He couldn't speak and was shaking with emotion, mirroring so many others standing by.

Kyriakides was quickly taken onto a stand for the crowd to see the wreath, the sweat breaking through the cotton shirt that bore the name of GREECE on his chest. Kyriakides was weary now, and was ushered into a waiting room, but before he left, he looked back again on the course for his friend Kelley. He didn't see him. Stride-for-stride down the homestretch, Kyriakides had broken away with a heart-bursting pace that left Kelley far behind. The diminutive Irishman, the race's champion a year before, would finish exactly two minutes later. His time would be the world's second best that year. It was his seventh second-place finish in the Boston Marathon.

A weary, sweating Kelley came into a room at the BAA headquarters at the finish line and saw his friend surrounded by reporters and photographers, flashbulbs an aurora around him. An excited crowd of reporters gathered, including Nason. Kyriakides put on a blue sweat suit that stated ΕΛΛΑΣ, the Greek name for Greece, and was taken to a seat to talk to reporters. But as he sat, he looked up and saw the smiling face of Kelley, bringing him a glass of water and embracing him with a gap-toothed grin. The photographers asked them to repeat their embrace, but Kyriakides took it further, suddenly bussing his startled friend with a

Kyriakides and Kelley, the two running friends, embraced after the race where Kyriakides managed to plant a kiss on his rival. Courtesy of the *Boston Globe*.

kiss on the cheek. It was a genuine display of emotion, and Kelley graciously returned it, along with his words.

"It's great you won, Stanley," Kelley said, calling Kyriakides by the English version of his name. "It's great for your country." He got kissed again. The kiss was repeated a number of times for photographers. Kelley said, "What could be better than having a Greek win the golden anniversary race?"

He said, "Me? I'm satisfied. The odds are against repeating and as long as I had to be beaten, I'm glad he's the one who did it. How can you beat a man who's running for his country?" He was smiling earnestly now, and he turned to Kyriakides. "You won for more than yourself—your country. Me? You just about killed me—but I can honestly say I love it this time." Kyriakides smiled brighter and the two embraced again.

Kyriakides came over to his friend Nason, and sat with him to talk about the victory. The Greek's stoicism hadn't broken yet, but he was still plastered with sweat and nearly overcome with relief and joy, his features trembling a bit, but no smile showing. He was remembering what had brought him to Boston. Nason looked at him, pen in hand.

"The poor little children," Kyriakides said softly. "They have no eggs or milk," he said, his voice trailing off. Kelley was listening nearby and he couldn't take it anymore either. The two had just run twenty-six hard miles, finishing in a tête-à-tête duel of wills and strength. Kelley burst out crying now, surprising Nason, who looked at him sympathetically. Poor Kelley had finished second again, but this time it was for a real reason, he thought. Then Demeter came by and talked about how selfless Kelley was in giving advice to Kyriakides before the race and he praised the former champion's grace. "Kelley is the embodiment of American sportsmanship. He doesn't get half enough credit for his unselfish sprit," Demeter said.

Kyriakides chimed in quickly in approbation. "He's a good boy. I like him very much. I should not feel sorry if he beat me. I think he will do well in the 1948 Olympic marathon," scheduled for London, Kyriakides said.

As the previous champion, Kelley had worn number 1. Later, when Kyriakides mused that with more food he might have broken the marathon record of 2:26:51, Kelley said, "You certainly would, Stan, you certainly would."

"Stanley," Kelley said, calling his friend by his pet name, "nobody deserved to win today more than you," as he slipped his arm over Kyriakides' shoulder at the end and they cried together, as a crowd swarmed around. Kyriakides embraced Kelley and said, through his tears, "Johnny. You fine boy."

BAA president Walter Brown gave Kyriakides a medal bearing the year, an American flag on either side of a ribbon attached to a gold medallion that bore the crest of the BAA and a diamond stud signifying the fiftieth anniversary, and a wreath symbol. Like the other officials, for whom this was almost a formal affair, Brown was well dressed, in a double-breasted suit and fedora. Kyriakides held the wreath aloft for all to see. "This wreath," he said, "this I give to my little kid." It was a fairy-tale mythological finish.

"All the time, like I tell you at the start, I have the feeling I am going to win. Once I think of my wife, and the two keedies, you don't believe it, but many times they have only peas, just a few peas to eat!" he told the reporters. Tears came now, which had been held back by his grim running countenance of pure determination. Kyriakides said, "I did my best for Greece. And my best today was far better than I had ever hoped to do."

"The race is over now, but now comes my real work. I'm going to tour the country seeking donations of food and clothing for my friends in Greece, the folks who paid to send me here on this mission. I'm going to try to do as much as I can. I'm also going to try to get some track equipment because we have none left in Greece. Absolutely none." Kyriakides took off the sweatshirt top that said *Ellas* and put it down for a moment. He would never see it again. Someone picked it up for a souvenir and Kyriakides, sweating and wearing the laurel wreath, began talking with the reporters, who sensed the enormity of the story. "What does this mean to you?" a reporter shouted as flashbulbs popped and the room became crowded. Kyriakides paused only a moment and his face began to brighten slowly, like a light on a dimmer gradually being turned up.

"My victory belongs to America and to Greece," he said. "What about the note, Stylianos?" another said, asking what was written on the piece of paper he had been seen carrying. Kyriakides reached into the sweat-drenched pocket and pulled it out, his hands weary, showing it.

Kyriakides wore his laurel wreath when he was escorted around Boston after his 1946 win by adoring Greek-American fans, including George Demeter (to the left of Kyriakides). Courtesy of Peter (Cougialis) Andrews.

"It said *e tan e epi tas*. It means 'with your shield or on it,'" Kyriakides said, explaining the Spartan tradition and meaning of the phrase as reporters scribbled furiously, their hats cocked back, already figuring the angle on the story. But as they did, Kyriakides, holding back his emotions, offered another answer. "I will save this note forever," he said, his words a jumble of gravelly tones and fatigue, along with exultant joy. "What it really means is 'win or die,'" he said.

Kelley was being interviewed too, toweling off and thinking about his second-place finish, disappointed because he had run so well down to the last two miles. But, he shrugged, it was destiny. "How can you beat a guy like that? He wasn't running for himself. He was running for his country," he said. Reporters said Kyriakides saved his best for last, tearing away at the twenty-five-mile mark on a torrid pace that showed he would not be denied. From Lake Street to Coolidge Corner, Kelley had gained a thirty-five-yard lead after a battle on "heartbreak hill," when the two had been side-by-side and alone from the pack before Kyriakides' frenzied finish.

In 1945, Kelley had sung "Sweet Adeline," with Boston politicians John F. "HoneyFitz" Fitzgerald, a former mayor, and Gov. Maurice Tobin, and had been the toast of his hometown. This time, he knew, belonged to Kyriakides, and he stepped aside to watch his friend garner kudos for the victory. Kyriakides again held aloft the laurel wreath, about the time that the man he feared most, Cote, finished third and immediately left for his hotel to shower and change. Kyriakides continued to talk about the victory with reporters eager for everything they could learn about the man few of them knew. Except Nason.

Kyriakides said he wasn't sure what would happen in Greece. "Maybe there will be a national holiday," he smiled, kidding. Kelley was telling other reporters that while he wanted to win, Kyriakides' victory probably meant more to the race and the world. "It's the greatest thing that's ever happened to marathoning," he said. "It will do more to boom the game than all the fancy writing in the world." He talked glowingly of Kyriakides. "He's a great boy and a fine sportsman and I wouldn't ever mind losing to him." Despite his easy insouciance, Kelley had a ferocious desire to win.

Kyriakides said he had noticed during the race that some of the runners, such as Robbins and Cote, had poured water on their legs to cool them, a tactic with which he disagreed. "The muscles are too hot and the water is too cold. It makes your legs tight," he said. Then he said he would like to invite some of his rivals to Greece, for a marathon there. "I don't think any of them could finish a Greek marathon because it is too hot in Greece, even in the fall," he said. "The weather is so hot it melts the asphalt on the road and it would be much too torrid for them because they would not be used to it." He said although the Newton hills were a test, they were no match for where he had trained in Greece. "The Greek mountains would make the Newton hills look flat," he said.

He sat on a training table and showed off his bare feet to prove there were no blisters this time. "See," he smiled proudly. "Not a blister. Not anything." Kyriakides was weary, and wondering what news was reaching Greece, where it was midevening, a few hours before Easter Sunday would begin. Kyriakides' victory would save thousands of lives in

Greece, but also bring international attention to the Boston Marathon and make it an even more prestigious event, on its fiftieth anniversary, starting a modern era of running.

It took a while for Kyriakides to answer all the questions with which he was bombarded now. Nason was looking on, satisfied to watch for once. Kyriakides was getting edgy because he was anxious to get some news to his family and friends. Finally, with Demeter's help, he was ushered to the Minerva, only a few hundred yards from the Hotel Lenox where the race had ended. Before he could, though, a smiling Cote came back, all showered and slicked up and looking for the Greek who had run him into the ground. There was an easy-to-like quality about Cote, for all his charming arrogance and self-confidence. He was anxious to greet and tweak Kyriakides, and the doctors who thought the Greek shouldn't run.

Cote laughed and said, "Where's the Greek? Dying someplace?" Kyriakides was cheered by the staff and Contanis, the chef who had fed him, but asked that a telegram be sent to his home in Athens, to his wife, addressed to "Kyriakidou," at Kefkia 9, Filothei. It said: OUR CHILDREN'S LUCK GAVE ME THE VICTORY TWO HOURS TWENTY NINE MINUTES. KALO PASCHA [HAPPY EASTER] KISSES TO ALL. It cost the large sum of $6.07.

Kyriakides sent a telegram to Lazarides at the utility company, putting his success succinctly: FIRST KYRIAKIDES TWO HOURS TWENTY NINE TWENTY SEVEN SECONDS KELLEY AMERICA TWO THIRTY-ONE TWENTY-SEVEN THIRD COTE CANADA TWO THIRTY-SIX THIRTY-FOUR HARD RACE HAPPY AT VICTORY. Then he sent a telegram to Leslie Kemp, his boss, because he had made it possible for Kyriakides to get to Boston, and another to officials of SEGAS, which had helped him.

It was late afternoon now and an exhausted Kyriakides knew he would not be resting this night, Easter eve. He talked with Demeter about what must be happening in Greece, where it was past 10:00 P.M. and where he knew his wife was readying for a midnight service without knowing what had happened to him, because the radio announcements from the BBC wouldn't come until the morning. He wanted to go to the nearby Boston Cathedral, the largest Greek church in the area, where the somber midnight service would be held, breaking for many a long fast and ushering in the most prominent religious holiday for Greek Orthodox observers.

The cathedral, with its huge dome and ornate exterior, loomed over nearby Huntington Avenue and the world-famous Museum of Fine Arts, and several thousand packed the interior and spilled onto the street that night. When Kyriakides arrived by car and stepped out, a buzz started to spread through the crowd like fire following fuel, although this was a holy observation and people tried to remain respectful. Kyriakides didn't want to cause a stir either, but he was instantly recognized with his wavy, black hair and good looks. It was midnight now—7:00 A.M. in Greece where Iphigenia Kyriakides and her family and friends and the neighbors of Stylianos Kyriakides were hearing the news and beginning a celebration at the same time they were trying to observe a holy holiday.

He was brought by George and Harry Demeter and an uproar began as the crowd of three thousand realized Kyriakides was entering. There he was received by Rev. James A. Coucouzes, the dean and already a rising star in the Greek church hierarchy. It is a custom that churchgoers have their Easter candle lit by a candle from the altar's eternal light. Rev. Coucouzes, holding a candle, went to Kyriakides, who was holding a cream-colored candle with a gold cross in the middle and a blue stripe around the bottom, standing uneasily near the altar while the entire church watched in silence.

Reverend Coucouzes said, "This time we shall light our candles from the candle of the great victor." Each churchgoer filed up to light from Kyriakides' candle, as he stood reverently, while some of those who came up tried not to smile too broadly. The sweet smell of incense filled the air and the heavy religious atmosphere of the ornate interior, the Byzantine sounds of a choir and the somber attitude contrasted sharply with the buoyant happiness in Kyriakides' heart and those of his countrymen, who were praising God and greeting one another with the refrain "Christ Has Risen." Church bells rang loudly as the crowds spilled out onto the stairs, the incense wafting out to reach them. Everyone was watching the man who had saved a nation.

The day had started many long hours ago for Kyriakides and now carried over past midnight, and would last several more hours because, after the service, so many people wanted to talk with him and the Demeters found more waiting when they got him back to the Minerva. The little man who had made himself the champion runner of the Balkans and survived World War II had suddenly been thrust into a hero's role, especially in Greece, where the news was rapidly spreading.

Kyriakides' shy nature made him feel oddly more introverted now and he was very tired, but he knew his role had changed from runner to ambassador and he was good naturedly trying to carry the message of his country and greet so many people who wanted just to be near him. After church, he went to the home of influential businessman and Greek War Relief leader Tom Pappas and they ate the traditional soup known as *margaritsa,* which contained lamb intestines, kidney, and liver with a tomato sauce and an anise herb. It was 4:30 A.M. when he finally got to bed, about three hours before he was due in the nearby city of Salem to talk about his race and his life and his country. He fell asleep right away, the champion of the Boston Marathon. And all of Greece.

> Excellence much labored for by the race of men
>
> —Aristotle

Kyriakides got up for the start of his real mission in America: to alert people about the conditions in Greece and try to raise money and bring back food and medical supplies and other goods, even maybe athletic equipment. It would be as grueling as training for and running a marathon, he knew, and he was especially weary, less than eighteen hours after crossing the finish line. He had sent a letter to his wife the night before.

> I did the best I could for my country. It was a race of victory or death. I would have even given my life. While I was running, I had in my vision the image of the Greek flag. With the speed that I ran, I don't know if I really could have finished, if I hadn't also put on the five

pounds in the 15 days I was in Boston before the race. I knew I had to win this marathon to show the plight of our poor nation. Even now, tears come to my eyes when I think of the run and our flag in front of me, and I kept trying to reach it. When I got close to Kenmore Square, that's when I really woke up, from the loud clapping and the roaring of the crowd. They were cheering for me and for Greece.

He went to Salem where he spoke on a radio show that Easter morning and later lunched with the Demeter family, going to Ruggles Street for a barbeque of a whole lamb on a spit in an oil pit in a garage owned by A. Stathakakis, a native of Crete. There were many Irish-Americans as well, gathering around the roasting lamb, the oregano smell making everyone's mouth water. Kyriakides' victory had transcended race and cultures for them. His admiration for their own running hero, Johnny Kelley, was well known. The headlines of his triumph filled the Boston papers.

VICTORY BELONGS TO TWO NATIONS, the *Boston Sunday Post* roared, and a story by Arthur Duffey had Kyriakides talking about the weight of the win and what it meant to Greece and the United States. "My victory belongs to America and to Greece," Kyriakides said. He was so underweight and undernourished when he came to Boston, he explained, he was worried not only for his ability to run, or win, but to survive. "I won. I would have died had I not," he said. In a moving piece, Duffey wrote about the tears of Kyriakides at the finish line, which came after twenty-six miles, 385 yards of running, and nearly $2^{1}/_{2}$ hours of stoic, steadfast determination that kept his face hard and tight. "I have seen many athletes weep before in victory and defeat. Some were wonderful actors. This noble Athenian shed real tears, tears right from his strong Grecian heart. A heart that didn't weaken for more than 26 miles, but which nearly burst at this point amid a mixture of pride and sorrow at the recollection of years of hardship his country has just recently endured," Duffey wrote.

In the *Boston Sunday Advertiser*, Kyriakides said, "I did my best for Greece but it was a victory for America as well as for my homeland. If it hadn't been for those American steaks, I probably would never have held up to the finish." Perhaps the most telling story was in the *Sunday Advertiser,* which showed Kyriakides crossing the line and clicking off his watch while Demeter held aloft the laurel wreath and motorcycle police and the crowd converged. A double headline over him shouted I DID IT FOR MY COUNTRY, and IT WAS WIN OR DIE SAYS GREEK MARATHONER.

The *Boston Traveler* trumpeted GREEK WINS MARATHON and proclaimed that Kyriakides had come into the race as the champion of Greece, Egypt, Turkey, and the Balkans for the previous decade, including the war years when there were not any races, and said his time was only three minutes off the record. Bill Cunningham of the *Boston Herald* wrote that no runner had ever overcome such odds. Under a story headlined KYRI WILLING TO OFFER LIFE, he wrote that Kyriakides meant it. "He said after the race that he had been determined to win or die, that he would have given his life for victory, if necessary, for he would have felt that he was giving his life for his people." Cunningham went even further: "There's seldom been more drama behind any single human being's athletic effort and none probably felt himself so truly obligated to give better than his best in an attempt to do something for others."

The *New York Times,* on page one, bannered KYRIAKIDES OF GREECE BEATS KELLEY IN BOSTON MARATHON, and the lead paragraph gushed in tones unlike the staid paper of record. "A true son of Pheidippides, Grecian immortal who ran the first marathon almost 2500 years ago, courageous Stylianos Kyriakides from war-ravaged Athens, today won the Boston AA 50th anniversary race of 26 miles, 385 yards in one of the most capable fields in its long history." The *Boston Post's* Joe McKenney, in some golden, if overwrought prose himself, likened Kyriakides' victory to that of mythic proportions. "In classic Greek tones, this noble descendant of Pheidippides brought the Gods tumbling down from Olympus and the Spartan warriors to life once again," noting the marathon "sprang from the soil of Greece more than 2000 years ago." There was so much exuberance with Kyriakides' win, he said, that "once more the torches of victory burned on the Acropolis and Homeric song spread through his historic land by Athena and by Zeus." Kyriakides' victory had created a philhellene euphoria in Boston and throughout the land.

Dave Egan wrote in the *Boston Advertiser*, "There must be a feeling of satisfaction throughout ancient Greece this Easter morn, for today they know in the hills of Athens that the human spirit is imperishable," as he lauded Kyriakides' victory. He scored the most popular upset in the history of the race, Egan added. "He looked like a refugee. There was not a pinch of meat on his lean little body, nor the hint of a smile on his swarthy face," in contrast to the jolly Englishman Kenneth Bailey. Kyriakides looked like a bare survivor of those he'd left behind, where one-eighth of the population had been lost to war and starvation. He said he carried in his mind a picture of the Greek flag and refused to quit when Kelley had a fifteen-yard lead with two miles to go before catching Kelley. Egan described the Greek as running "with desperate nervous energy."

In New Bedford, a city with a long seafaring tradition on the southern coast of Massachusetts, and where many immigrants were living, the sports editor of the *New Bedford Standard-Times*, George Patzer, like many other sportswriters, was given to hyperbole and could not resist likening the victory to a triumph equal to the glories of the Greek gods. "The story of Stylianos Kyriakides is a tremendous one which neither the spoken nor written word ever will record with justice. His performance was as great and noble as his purpose," he wrote.

It was left to Nason to summarize the historic place of the race he said was perhaps the most important ever run. "It was, without doubt, the most significant Boston Marathon of them all . . . His story, that of a hungry, impoverished Greek who journied thousands of miles to run a 26-mile errand of mercy, will be retold a century from now in Greece."

A Greek newspaper said, "No matter what we offered to the world, in the ancient world as well as Byzantium, in both world wars . . . in the face of Kyriakides, we saw the life of our race. We Greeks have never given in to any difficult obstacle."

Another headline in Greece told the drama of the story for the Greeks. It was declarative and descriptive: IT WAS A CONTEST OF WIN OR

DIE. The subhead told what had driven him: It was Kyriakides stating, "I Saw Continuously in Front of Me the Vision of Our Flag," and it made Greeks delirious with joy and pride, especially after the struggle of the Resistance against the Nazis and the continuing hurt of the civil war that had split the nation. Despite those political differences, Kyriakides had united the nation in his triumph.

9

The Fruits of Victory

Boston, April–May 1946

It was an uneasy time in Greece where the civil war that had abated was restarting and Greeks, weary of war, were bearing arms again and feeling there was no end to the turmoil and little to cheer about. Kyriakides too thought that while he was well and eating and triumphing, people in Athens and throughout Greece were still starving, and he longed to get back to them and his family.

The war had ended, the world was changing, and Kyriakides was an important fulcrum. In America, readying for a postwar boom, Kyriakides saw the chance to bring help to Greece. Americans were in the embryonic stages of a burgeoning renaissance. This Easter Sunday brought other news, and a headline that read LOW COST HOME PLAN ORDERED, a program setting housing at $50 a month rent and $7,500 for a new home.

The first exhausting day behind him, a weary Kyriakides went to bed about 8:30 P.M. because he had a big day on Monday, with visits to Governor Tobin and Mayor James Michael Curley and then to his first formal reception and first plea, a reception at the Ritz Carlton. At the reception, he said the demands for his time were growing rapidly, wearying the deeply fatigued runner who said he would not turn down any appearance that would help Greece. Thanks to the Demeters and the food at the Minerva, he had gained some weight, but still looked tired.

George Demeter said the reception had been planned beforehand. "It wasn't a case of overconfidence. We just wanted to be prepared, just in case," he laughed.

But against this backdrop of glory and triumph and celebration, another story—the reason for which Kyriakides ran—continued to unfold across the globe. On this Easter morning in 1946, the American government released a list of suggestions for "helping the world's hungry millions" and came up with this list for housewives:

1. Never throw a piece of bread or a teaspoon of fat away.
2. Make sure that the garbage consists only of bones, eggshells and the inedible parts of fruits and vegetables.
3. Don't overeat.
4. Never over-serve a guest.
5. Don't fry meats, poultry, fish. Bake, broil or stew them.
6. Serve home-made salad dressing, vinegar or lemon juice, not rich salad dressing.
7. Use meat drippings to flavor vegetables, dressings, sauces.
8. Store bread in moisture-proof wrapping in refrigerator. This retards mold.
9. Use dry, leftover bread in toast, puddings, and stuffings.
10. Give each person only one small slice of bread at a meal.
11. AND, IF YOU'RE A MAN:
a. Eat all they serve you at a restaurant.
b. Stay away from pastries. Order fruit instead.
c. Be a one-man information bureau. Spread the word around that the world food situation is critical and will remain that way for at least three months.
d. Plant a vegetable garden.

At the same time, the news of Kyriakides' triumph was overtaking Greece. There was shock and disbelief and joy and the win was bringing together people divided by civil war. The news of the victory was causing a sensation in Greece, dominating headlines in every paper with the recounting of the win and of the glory it had brought to that impoverished country. One headline said: THE VICTORY OF KYRIAKIDES.

On Monday, two days after the race, Kyriakides was busy making appearances in greater Boston and told reporters his goal was to raise $250,000 in food, medical supplies, and other goods for Greece, but he was humble about it. "I am only an athlete. I wait for my countrymen here to ask me to speak. I tell them how bad it is in Greece. I say to have a tin of milk is a treasure. I just wait. I do not want to make myself heard," he said, not fully explaining that he meant he did not want to be overly eager to seek help. The meeting was at the Minerva, where reporters and admirers were coming to visit the reticent Kyriakides, uncomfortable in his newfound celebrity, although he knew he had to seize the triumph to help Greece. After the race, a lot of people wanted to buy him drinks, but he demurred, saying he did not prefer alcohol. "Maybe a little lemon or orange squash," he said.

He said he couldn't stop thinking about the people back home, though. "I win the race," he said in a good, but flavorful English. "That is only the start. Now I wait for Greeks in America and other Americans, maybe, to contribute to funds so I can help my people to get something to eat and some medicine when they are sick. It is hard to believe when you go to bed with the sickness today in Greece, you die. The doctor comes but he is not able to do anything. There isn't the food and there isn't the medicine, although UNRRA [United Nations Relief organization] is doing a good job." He talked again about how some of his Olympic and national champion friends had died during the war. "All die. No food, no medicine," he said sadly. "The Germans took everything from my country, our grain, our food, our seeds, our most prized possessions. They left us nothing but despair. America has given us food and clothing and hope. But it is not yet enough. My people are still dying."

That same day, April 22, he wrote a letter to his wife, and was photographed doing so, sitting in front of a typewriter in his room, with the laurel wreath and his first place medal visible to satisfy the increasingly insatiable appetite of the news media. It accompanied a story that said he was set to start off his aid tour for Greece. It would be the start of a busy day. He got a telegram from the Greek government, from Prime Minister Tsaldaris, stating PLEASE TRANSMIT STYLIANOS KYRIAKIDES.

WARMEST CONGRATULATIONS. WE ARE ALL PROUD OF HIM AND EARNESTLY HOPE THAT HIS BRILLIANT SUCCESS WILL OPEN THE WAY FOR MANY OTHER GREEK VICTORIES. The parade of telegrams was under way, nearly overwhelming Western Union. Another came from his union of Greek electrical workers, *Syllogos Ipalillon Apeco,* praising him for a "mega victory."

The Athenian mayor, Aristides Sklirous, was almost overwrought with his telegram. It said, WE ASK OF YOU TO BECOME THE AMBASSADOR OF LOVE FROM THE ATHENIAN PEOPLE TO THE AMERICAN ATHLETES AND TO AMERICA'S CITIZENS WITH WHOM WE HAVE AN EXCELLENT FRIENDSHIP AND SHARE THE SAME LAWS AND GOVERNMENT. Another was from Kemp, his boss in Athens, and stated simply, OVERJOYED AND PROUD OF YOUR FINE VICTORY. COMPANY ADMINISTRATION AND STAFF JOIN WITH GREEK PEOPLE IN SENDING CONGRATULATIONS.

The next day, Kyriakides sent a letter to Lazarides about all the invitations he received to speak, and of the good will it was bringing. "What is being said about Greece is hardly imaginable and many are the gifts of food and clothing. I have asked a committee to undertake all that and shall hold myself at the disposal of AHEPA and the Greek War Relief." He said, "I'll do nothing without the approval of the Greek government, and of our company." A Greek newspaper printed a poem comparing him with Spiridon Loues, the marathon champion of the 1896 Olympics and Greece's greatest running hero. Now there were two. "The rebirth of immortal Greece is once again born. And now, after 50 years, one Kyriakides ran again to a victory. It is his victory which once again makes Greece immortal," the article said.

That same day came some heartening news in a letter from SEGAS official Apostolos Nikolaides, who told him of what was happening in his homeland.

A thousand times congratulations. The deed you did was bigger than you can imagine. You have given a colossal service to Greek athletics and to Greece. People who have no idea of what athletics is were crying when they heard of your victory. Your name is in every newspaper and on the tip of every tongue. You understand all of this is putting a huge burden on your shoulders. That's why I believe it is my duty to write to you about some things you must listen to me about with attention. Mr. Kemp has spoken very highly of your victory because much of the credit of your victory should go to him and I'm sure your victory insured your position at the Piraeus lighting company.

I advise you to not take any type of invitation to any type of running event there. And the best thing you can do is thank them and not compete. They may even tell you to run a shorter distance but you have the great excuse of telling them that you must rest to get ready to compete in the European championships in Oslo, Norway. Many Greek American groups will want you to visit them but do not compete in any races and work closely with the Greek American athletic association in New York. Just like Paavo Nurmi became Finland's good ambassador to the United States, you now have the opportunity as well to become Greece's great ambassador to America. With humble courtesy "which are your natural characteristics" and the story of how everything and all our athletic facilities are non-existent and the poverty that we have been hit with. This should be your mission for today. With your own discipline and judgment and your humble and courteous way you will do the greatest good for Greece and all of our diplomatic ambassadors to America.

Kyriakides took some time to tell reporters he would stay in the United States a month hoping to gather food and clothes and medicine, bring attention to Greece's problems, and help the active Greek War Relief effort in America. The relief effort had started November 8, 1940, and was founded "to collect money and expend the same for the relief and the suffering of the Greek people." It was operated with the aegis of the President's War Relief Control Board, and shipments were distributed under supervision of an overseas staff. Membership was not limited to Greek-Americans, but to other philhellenes as well and 964 chapters were quickly set up for the daunting task.

Kyriakides said his run and his efforts weren't only for his suffering or that of his family. "I have seen men die . . . I will speak wherever I can.

Day or night, it does not matter. I will not sleep, if I can do more good,"
he said from the Minerva, where he was going over public-relations appearance schedules and plans. Even more than winning, he said, he
wanted to bring home a boatload full of food and milk and medicine,
and some athletic equipment for the youth. Some supplies were already
being sent to the Greek Cathedral on Ruggles Street. Sportswriter Joe
McKenney wrote that "this Kyriakides is far more than today's greatest
marathoner in the world. He is a patriot of the highest type with all the
selfish love of country that any great patriot would possess . . . he is a
Greek and he is begging help for Greece."

"I have seen athletes die for want of proper food and medicine," Kyriakides tried to explain as McKenney rapidly tried to keep notes and listen at the same time. The story spilled out about how Skiadas, the
hurdler; Travlos, the pole vaulter; Petropoulos, the hammer thrower
had died. They were my teammates on the national Olympic team of
Greece," he said sadly. "If athletes like these can die so easily, what
chance have women or a little child to live? What chance has Greece to
survive?"

Bostonian J. B. Connolly, who won the first Olympic gold medal in
Greece fifty years before in the 1896 Olympics, said, "Anyone who
knew what wonderful hosts the Greeks were to us in '96 in Athens
would be happy to help them now." In other cities in Massachusetts,
many groups, mostly led by Greek-Americans, were raising money and
collecting canned goods and clothing. It didn't take long for Kyriakides'
pleas to bring in money and goods. One respondent, W. J. Buchanan of
nearby Milton, sent a package and a letter and stated, "With this note
I've enclosed some track shoes and a shirt. I wore them three years ago
when I ran in school. They are not much good but perhaps they may be
of some use yet. Good luck to you and to your country, Greece!"

Kyriakides threw himself into an arduous schedule of appearances
that had him going steadily from about 9 A.M. to 11 P.M. most days,
speeches, interviews, photo opportunities, and meetings, repeating the
story endlessly about the need in Greece. "I don't belong to myself anymore. I belong to Greece now," he said earnestly, and he said he would
stay in the United States as long as possible, and try to meet influential

Greek-Americans especially. "I want to see and meet as many Greeks as I possibly can," he said.

In an interview for *Life of Greece* magazine, where he was featured on the cover, he met with editors and pounded his fist on the table in an unusual display of raw emotion, as he talked about what was happening in Greece. "There is nothing there! Nothing!" he said. When he was training, he said, he had water only three times a week, and there was virtually no food, clothing, or transportation facilities. The Greek War Relief was helping, he said, but there were too many needy people, and no roads and many homes had been destroyed. Distribution of goods could take months with donkeys and mules often the only means of transportation. "My people know that everything I do I do for Greece," he said. "They love me very much and during the war when I wanted to buy vegetables or cloth they would say, 'What can I take from you?' and would very often give them to me at little or no cost. When I decided to come to America, I was going to sell all my possessions to raise the necessary funds, but the Athens-Piraeus Electric Company wanted to sponsor my trip for me."

Kyriakides said Greece was his home and there he would stay. "You can't compare Greece with any other country. The climate, sea and sky are the best in the world," he said proudly. "I was happy for Greece. I believed I would win from the beginning—but after the first mile of the race, I knew I would win."

George Demeter loved holding court at the Minerva for all the reporters who were coming by now too, especially Nason, who had taken such an interest in the Greek runner, and who liked Demeter, who often hosted him. Nason wrote to him, "Just a note to express my enjoyment at having been your guest at dinner the other evening. I think I shall always treasure the memory of this boy . . . his refreshing character, wholesome attitude and tremendous sincerity. I cannot think of him, ever, as merely a great athlete—but always as a friend, much admired."

Still, Kyriakides yearned for news of Greece and his family and friends. On April 23, he received a telegram from his old running club on Cyprus: YOUR GYMNASTIC FATHER CELEBRATES YOUR BRILLIANT VIC-

TORY. Then he got one of his most satisfying answers the next day. It was from Simitsek.

You gave Greece its best gift, as well as the Greek people. Happy holiday, Christ is risen. My warmest congratulations on my behalf and everyone at the public utility company here. I hope your victory will give Greek athletics the boost it needs, just like Loues' run in 1896 did. The enthusiasm of your victory has been felt by the whole country, all the newspapers, both left and right are writing of the victory. But I'm a little amazed where they found all those photographs of you, both leftist and rightist newspapers. You are winding up on page one.

They have discovered that we do have athletics and for the moment they have forgotten about politics. From there you can understand what type of meaning your victory has taken. Without seeming like trying to build your ego, the victory has great worth. But not only the victory, but the results. It is very rewarding to me that all the time and effort we put in together finally bore the fruits of the crop.

I want you to understand that this Sunday of Easter was one of the best days of my life. Your wife called me early, early in the morning. I was one of the first to find out about your accomplishments. I know you have your head on straight. Be careful your enthusiasm does not lead you to give in to temptation. There will probably be people who will want to benefit by your victory and fame. Don't make any harsh, rash decisions. Study and think before you act. If you can't make a decision on your own, ask Frank Vassilopoulos, in whom I have great confidence.

If they ask you to run in any other marathons, let me tell you, they will pit their best athletes against you. They will try to beat you and after running in the marathon like you did, your legs are tired and they are not fresh and you will not have the foot speed to win again. You must rest very well. I don't know how you are going to rest, only you know. Try to put on some weight and run very lightly on your feet. I would not really train until the European championships. Do not run again in a difficult marathon. You have in front of you the European championships and you are not going to the championship of England but you will go to London for the 1948 Olympics. If they want you to run again in America, let them send you an invitation for next year for the Boston Marathon, or for the national title of America.

I am only writing you for the good of your own future and I only care about your progress as always. On your first opportunity, please send me all the articles from the newspapers. I also would like to know what you did the first 10 miles. I can imagine how the Americans felt when you beat them. You brought your blood back. Do not speak badly of anyone and say that your competitors will run better next time.

Please write to me what your intentions are. You must have learned that Mr. Kemp and Mr. Lazarides went to your home after the victory and both were very happy. Everyone in your home is fine. Your wife is very happy and I'm sure she will forgive you because you lead the life of an athlete. I am finishing my letter. I wish you a good rest and I hope you are the same person you were before you became famous.

He needn't have worried. The victory made Kyriakides only more humble, and thankful for what was happening in the aftermath of his win. The day after Simitsek's letter arrived at the Minerva, Kyriakides and Kelley made a trip together to a veterans hospital at Fort Devens in Ayer, about forty miles north of Boston, driving in an old Jeep. Then, they were surprised to find more than twenty-five hundred patients waiting for them at Lovell General Hospital. Kelley and Kyriakides came in just as they had run, shoulder-to-shoulder, both veterans too, and were moved by the sight of hurt and disabled men looking up to them.

Kyriakides talked about his running experiences, and said the Greeks had asked him to thank the Americans, especially the soldiers, for their part in the liberation of his country. Then he went on Armed Services Radio to deliver the same message. He was so well received that a letter was sent to his boss in Athens, Kemp, telling him that "he not only succeeded in arousing our patients interest in the marathon, but also achieved a more sympathetic understanding of the hardships now prevailing in Greece." As soon as he got back to Boston that night, Kyriakides went to see Gov. Maurice Tobin and sold him a $25 ticket for a fund-raiser for a hospital in Greece supported by the AHEPA scheduled for the Statler Hotel a week later.

The night before, at his desk in the Minerva, a weary Kyriakides sat down and carefully, with some lines written over and repeated, wrote how overcome he had been at completing his task, and the glad clamor that followed, and just how he would express his gratitude and pleading for his country at the dinner. It emptied his heart, as the race had made him empty his spirit with his ending dash.

> The God of Greece willed that I should win your famous American B.A.A. Marathon run in Boston, in 1946, so that I might specially plead the cause of my needy people in pitiful Greece before the generous people of your plentiful America—just as he willed that the Greeks would be victorious at Marathon, in 490 b.c., nearly 2500 years ago.
>
> My country, Greece, was the champion of human life then and your country, America, is the champion of human welfare today. Countless thousands of my people in Greece died from starvation, but there are millions of starving, clothless and sick Greeks needing immediate assistance today. But for your prompt and cheerful aid, they would not be alive today and Greece might be extinct. It is to you, the people of America, we owe our life.
>
> I pray, do not let us down now. Help us to recover, complete your mission. Give my people in Greece some food, clothing and hospitals to which to heal and resurrect. My people are determined to live. You alone can make this possible. Support fullheartedly the noble AHEPA hospital drive. It is a sacred cause—it is a means of resurrecting dying Greeks.
>
> To come to this noble country of yours, to try to win your hearts for people, I shared my babies milk and ate my . . . ounce of rationed meat. God was with me and I was victorious. I obeyed the millions command handed me at the starting line, H TAN E EPI TAS.
>
> I did my duty. I carried out God's will. Through this drive, of the AHEPAS . . . you are called upon to do a little bit more. May the God of your country always protect us and you do just that little bit more for human welfare.

From there, he went to the Boston Common where he was photographed accepting the gift of two cows and a bull from Congressman John McCormack. He admitted he was getting worn out by the duty he happily did. "If I had run three marathons I would feel better than I do now," he lamented briefly at one point. "But I feel I have an obligation, a duty, to tell the American public about the situation in Greece and not to lose an opportunity, especially with all the mayors of the surrounding city are giving me." That night, there was another dinner in his honor, and George Demeter talked about the oddity of Kyriakides and Kelley, who worked for Boston Edison, an electric company, being employed by utilities.

"Did you realize what a strange coincidence it is that an electrical worker from South Boston and an electrical worker from South Athens should struggle so desperately for the race?" Demeter said. A Back Bay admirer gave Kyriakides a dozen pair of nylons to give his wife, a gift that delighted Kyriakides because they were so hard to get in Greece. Kyriakides wrote a letter to Lazarides talking about the Fort Devens invitation, which had come from the War Department, and how he had spoken on shortwave radio to armed forces around the world. He said he hoped he was doing some good with his lobbying.

"I believe it is my duty to tell the people of America of the economic situation of Greece and I feel that I should not miss the opportunities offered me by the mayors of all the towns here. Clubs, churches, colleges, hospitals, companies and all manner of organizations here want to hear something about Greece from me," he wrote. Kyriakides was especially happy with a letter he received from his friend Athanasios Ragazos, the marathoner who had beaten him in their last race, in 1940, at the Balkan championships in Constantinople. Ragazos was a formidable runner and an equally good friend to Kyriakides. "Your victory is my victory, and Greece's victory. And as an athlete I understand what sacrifice and sweat you put into it. You should be proud of your accomplishment," Ragazos said.

Shortly thereafter, the president of SEGAS wrote Kemp how thankful he was for the company's role in helping the Greek win. The five million-drachma donation had gotten Kyriakides to Boston. The note said the victory meant "a success which will be of such moral help to our country and to Greek athletics generally." That night, Kyriakides went to another reception for the Greek War Relief effort and made an appearance before the Veterans of Foreign Wars there, with George Demeter being installed as commander of the unit. Kyriakides was busy with his typewriter that day and also wrote to a Boston-area teacher whose elementary school class had donated food for Greece: "I had a divine inspiration to win your great Marathon—for my country which is poverty-stricken. You wonderful American people have helped us so much. The food you plan sending will help my people."

He was asked to speak at many area cities and towns where there were sizable Greek-American populations, including Lynn, the hometown of a high school athlete named Harry Agganis, who was gaining a reputation as a great athlete, especially in football and baseball.

Kyriakides wrote a letter to the *Boston Globe* in which he stated, "The eloquent and generous plea for the relief of my country, Greece, which our able sportswriters have conveyed to your readers, is bearing fruit. Mayors of numerous Massachusetts cities and towns, including those of my own people, have made offers of immediate support of my special plea for Greece. The people of Greece are everlastingly grateful to the people of your magnanimous country."

He took some time to head back to New York to make a plea there too. He got there the same day in enough time to talk with editor Solon Vlastou again, and was pictured wearing his BAA medal for winning the Boston Marathon. "The Germans, Bulgarians and Italians picked Greece clean during the occupation. They took everything, the wheat, the grain, the animals, the trains. There is nothing left. We need not only shipments of food and clothing right now but we need also seeds of all sorts that we can produce our own food supplies." He was there too to find out about the shipment of fifty-five hundred pairs of shoes, a thousand cases of canned sweet milk, a hundred suits, and refrigeration units ordered by his company and to plan appearances before groups, predominantly Greek-Americans. He couldn't stay long though. He had to be back in Boston the next day for an AHEPA hospital banquet at the Statler Hotel.

The letters and telegrams were pouring in from throughout the United States, and especially from Greece, where his name was already being mentioned with the great heroes of the past. But although he lived now in Athens, Kyriakides never forgot his first home, Cyprus, and they remembered him too. There was pride on that island. Kyriakides got telegrams from Cypriot officials, including the Archbishop there congratulating him. TO THE GREEK ATHLETIC HERO, STYLIANOS KYRIAKIDES. A BRIGHT VICTORY OF THE MARATHON . . . WITH ALL OUR SOUL, YOU HAVE ACHIEVED EXCELLENCE. The little, frail boy of Cyprus, who had run with pebbles in his hand so many years ago to keep track of how far he had gone, had come again.

> Better to do a little well than a great deal badly
>
> —Socrates

Kyriakides remained close to Kelley and they made more appearances together. Kyriakides said he hoped to try to raise some extra money to try to bring Kelley to Athens to run in the marathon and unite the two in another match race. "Ah. Johnny and myself will have a fine race and the people of Greece will cheer him like he never before has been cheered. The Marathon in Greece is a tremendous event and they will throw flowers from the windows when we reach the city streets. Thousands and thousands of people will watch. We will get a marvelous reception in Greece. Over three mountains, on rough roads, we will run and Johnee will find it very hot, much hotter than we race in Boston," because it is run in August in Greece. He said he would bring Kelley to his house and would show him all of Athens.

On May 6, Kyriakides sent another letter to Kemp. "God and the wishes of the Greeks, it seems, were on my side and after a close run up to the 24th mile, I started sprinting and so finished first and was awarded the diamond studded medal of America," he said. On May 8, he received a telegram from the mayor of Athens, Aristides Sklirous.

IN ATHENS, WHERE THE FIRST MARATHON BELONGED, WE ARE VICTORIOUS WITH PRIDE WE RECEIVE YOUR JOYOUS MESSAGE OF YOUR VICTORY IN THE MARATHON OF BOSTON STOP WITH OUR WARMEST CONGRATULATIONS, YOU WILL BECOME THE AMBASSADOR OF LOVE OF THE ATHENIAN PEOPLE TOWARD AMERICAN ATHLETES AND THE AMERICAN CITIZENS

WITH WHOM WE HAVE SO MUCH IN COMMON, FRIENDSHIP AND WITH
WHOM WE SHARE OUR GOVERNMENT AND LAWS.

The next day, he got a letter from Michael Vrotsos, chairman of the
AHEPA Hospital for Greece, with appreciation for the $1,000 Kyri-
akides helped raise. It would be used to purchase a room for the hospital
in Greece, Vrotsos said, thanks to Kyriakides. On May 13, he went back
to New York for fund-raising and had lunch at the Rockefeller. At the
time scrambled eggs with shrimp went for $1.45 and a baked turkey loaf
with giblet gravy and cranberry sauce cost only $1.75 and wine was 40
cents a glass, small money for some Americans, but a lot for starving
Greeks, he thought.

He had a marathon of stops to make now, including in nearby
Peabody, a city with many Greek immigrants, where he met with more
than two-thousand students and was cheered by many of his former
countrymen, who had active Greek Orthodox churches and associations linking them to their home villages in Greece. At an Arcadian
dance on May 1, he was hailed like an Olympic champion, and he was
mostly pleased to see that money was being raised to be sent to Greece,
along with clothing and food. Meanwhile, at other Greek Orthodox
churches—which were many in greater Boston—clothes and canned
goods were dropped off in big crates to be sent back to Greece as well.

Kyriakides was taken to meet Boston mayor James Michael Curley.
Harry and George Demeter were there too, and all were dressed formally, in deep wool suits, and Kyriakides signed the mayor's guest register to show he had been there. Curley gave him his card and a
representation of the insignia of the state as a souvenir. Typically, Kyriakides thanked him and talked about the help he was getting from so
many Bostonians and residents, including money and donations of
clothing and offers of medical equipment and necessities, and even of
sporting equipment and other goods. Kyriakides went to the State
House too to meet Gov. Maurice Tobin and talk to the House and Sen-
ate. Tobin also gave him a personal insignia and state flag and said, "I
was amazed at your breakaway speed," in the last stages of the duel with
Kelley. "I never saw anyone with such speed down the stretch." A com-

bined session of the legislature gave him a standing ovation as he talked about the significance of the marathon in Athens and Boston's special place there, especially because many immigrants had settled in the area in places such as Peabody, Ipswich, and Lowell.

He went to Washington, D.C., where he met with Sen. Claude Pepper, whom he told about the anguish in Greece. "Continue what you're doing for your small and heroic country," Pepper told him. "The world owes Greece a big debt," he said, remembering how the Greeks had driven out the Italian army and stood stalwart against the overwhelming odds of the German divisions, then continued resistance efforts that bottled up German armies who were needed elsewhere in Europe. On May 21, only a few days before he was scheduled to leave, Kyriakides received an offer of $20,000 from some promoters to become a professional runner and stay in the United States. He rejected it. "I want to represent Greece in the Olympic Games," in London the following year, he said.

He visited New Bedford, a seaport in southeastern Massachusetts, going to the high school there, and arranged for students to have pen pals in Greece. The school band played for him and the students arranged to send pencils, paper, fourteen small crates of food and school utensils to Greece.

"These gifts will help a great deal. Students are going barefoot for the lack of shoes in Greece, and they are undernourished because of the lack of food," he said. The students formed a Kyriakides Club at the school. He left the school and walked among local stores, where he was greeted like a conqueror, recognized for his sudden fame, his handsome, chiseled face standing out, crowds attentive as he made his appeal for their help. One of the places he stopped was Lampos Groceries, owned by a Greek-American named John Lampos, who beamed. Lampos was a tall man, a veteran of the Balkan wars, but he was as delighted as a schoolboy at the sight of Kyriakides, and he reached into his cash register to make a donation, grabbing Kyriakides' hand to stuff it with money. Kyriakides was packing now too, and his luggage going back would include the nylons for his wife, along with soap, canned fruits, coffee, canned meats, cocoa, tea, spices, cotton fabrics, and worsted wool. Then a letter came from Vassilopoulos in New York, where he would go to depart from the United States in a couple of days, with the bounty of his win for his people:

> I want to tell you that it gave me great pleasure to be of some little service to you during your stay here, and I hope you feel that the service which I was able to render you did, in some measure, contribute toward your victory in the Boston marathon . . . I assure you that your visit here and your success in the marathon followed by the excellent work you did on your visits to various Greek communities has helped tremendously in stimulating Greek Americans to try and emulate you and I feel confident as a result many young Greek Americans will come out for track and field and long distance running in the United States.

Kyriakides sent a telegram to Governor Tobin too, in which he stated:

> YOUR EXCELLENCY, BEFORE LEAVING YOUR GREAT COUNTRY, I WISH TO THANK YOU AND THE OTHER CITIZENS OF YOUR FINE STATE FOR THEIR HELP AND UNDERSTANDING. MY STAY HERE WILL NEVER BE FORGOT-TEN—AND ALL OF GREECE SHALL KNOW OF MASSACHUSETTS AND ITS COURTESIES. — STYLIANOS KYRIAKIDES, MARATHON RUNNER.

Kyriakides' fame was spreading, and he got a letter from the editor of *Life* magazine and a complimentary copy of the May 27 issue about his win and subsequent efforts to help the Greeks. He was ready to go home. On May 22, a month after he had won the Boston Marathon, Kyriakides left on a train for New York to fly back to Athens. Kyriakides said he would probably return to run the Boston Marathon in 1947, and said, "If I come, I bring with me another Greek runner—a good one. He probably will win your ten-mile cathedral race easily." It was Ragazos.

He took the train to New York and helped oversee the shipment of goods being loaded aboard Greek-owned liners, carrying food, medicine, clothing, and other goods for his home country. It was a moving moment: this was the reason for which he had come to Boston, where other ships were also loading goods. He prepared to leave for Greece on May 23, on an 8:20 A.M. flight. He gave a last news conference to gathered reporters. "I feel myself a very fortunate man because despite everything I went through during the war and all the obstacles I faced getting to Boston, I was still able to represent Greece and win the marathon," he said at his departure. "But a portion of my victory I offer to the great American people of Boston and the Greek community who gave me moral support," because he said he could hear along the route the cheers of "Bravo Ellina," cheers for Greece.

10

The Ancient Drama Begins Again

Athens, May 23, 1946

Kyriakides had told the American reporters that he was almost afraid that he would be regarded heroically for his win, although he felt uncomfortable with the idea, especially because he had seen so many heroes die during the war. He had run as his duty to his country, he said, but he wasn't exactly sure what to expect when he arrived back in Athens.

Besides the food and medical supplies coming over by ship, he brought a few personal items: a gypsum mechanical doll for his daughter, a toy that opened and closed its eyes and said "mommy" and "daddy," and some nylons for his wife, whom he hadn't seen in a month now. He was nervous, apprehensive even, not so much for what he thought might be a welcoming, but for Iphigenia. Hers was the first face he wanted to see.

The American plane *Acropolis* was now flying over the mythical Mediterranean where Theseus, Aegeus, Jason, and Odysseus had sailed. Iphigenia and their children, $2^1/_2$-year-old Eleni and $1^1/_2$-year old Dimitri were waiting, eager with excitement to see their father. In a country where newspapers had political affiliations, where an on-again, off-again civil war and tension were ripping apart the country, there was unanimity this day: Kyriakides was returning a hero who had conquered. The headlines seemed the same. One stated: GREECE WILL HONOR ITS RETURNING VICTOR.

226

A nation of seven million people ravaged by war was waiting, hungry for hope. One headline put it simply: KYRIAKIDES OUR ONE AND ONLY SOURCE OF GOOD NEWS. In Athens, hundreds of thousands had already started lining the streets waiting for him. There were starved, homeless, poor, elderly, soldiers, and school children waiting for a glimpse, not of a king or powerful politician, but a simple Greek man. He was, like them, a working-class bill collector, an average man who symbolized "always excellence." His arrival schedule and his stops in all the Athenian suburbs were publicized nationally. His return had galvanized a whole country. A huge throng waited at the airport, edgy and shifting position and waiting.

As the plane approached Hasani airport, in the Athenian suburb of Elliniko, it cast a shadow over the sea, a winged shadow of the mythical flying horse Pegasus. Kyriakides looked out the window, not knowing the next sea he saw would be a human wave. The plane landed at 1:15 P.M. on a beautiful sunny Wednesday. Waiting for him to disembark were his family, members of SEGAS, officials from Athens and Elliniko, and the people he most wanted to see: his wife and children; Kemp, his boss and benefactor, who had brought him to America; and his coach, Simitsek. Newspaper reporters and photographers were jockeying for position as the passengers disembarked to tumultuous roars from the crowd anticipating the new hero who had elevated himself into a pantheon with Spiridon Loues and the immortal ancient heroes.

When the plane landed and the door opened, Kyriakides was as stunned as he'd been coming to the finish line in Boston a month before. A swirling, screaming crowd was outside, chanting his name and rushing toward him. Iphigenia was patiently waiting on the tarmac holding a bouquet of flowers. Suddenly her light green eyes locked on to a man who was the last passenger coming out. For a moment, the ancient love epic of Penelope and Odysseus was being replayed. She thought, "This man looks handsome, well fed, and his face has a glow like a shining star." She didn't recognize him for a moment.

She felt a rage of emotions—love, joy, pride, desire, anxiety—when she realized the man coming down the outside stairwell was her husband and she rushed to him before anyone else could reach him, hold-

He hadn't seen his wife, Iphigenia, for more than six weeks, so Kyriakides was happy to greet her with a kiss when he returned to the Athens airport in May of 1946. Courtesy of the Kyriakides family.

ing the bouquet before her, and he stopped, smiling but hesitating, unsure for a moment whether to embrace her or remain dignified. She spoke first.

"My Stelios, your wish of returning victorious has been fulfilled," she said, holding forth the flowers and waiting. Then both burst into smiles and, oblivious to everyone, they embraced in joy, ignoring the converging crowds anxious to touch the man who had saved Greece. Kyriakides and his wife were kissing and crying at the same time while the swirling roar of the crowd enveloped them. Kyriakides embraced his wife in an Odyssean hug and held her for eternity. He put the bouquet in his right hand and placed his left hand around her shoulders romantically. He looked into her eyes and kissed her again, softer this time, more grateful and happy than anxious. He immediately picked up his daughter. Eleni was crying and he kissed away her tears, his own replacing them. He cradled her in his left arm, Iphigenia standing beside them, beaming. He leaned down and picked up his son, kissed him, and put him in his right arm, as flashbulbs blinded them. Kyriakides could not stop crying or kissing, and began to embrace his other friends and family and officials.

Suddenly, around him, members of the Greek Air Force could not restrain themselves and were caught up in the delirium and joy. They rushed to him as he put his children down and lifted him onto their shoulders while the crowd waved and screamed and shook the blue-and-white Greek flags they were carrying, unfurling them frantically while they yelled. He was given a banner with the Greek colors and the symbol of the air force squadron that had embraced him.

The crowd was chanting in unison as if they were at a soccer match: "Long live Kyriakides, who honored Greece!" As Kyriakides was put down, smiling, he walked toward a microphone and the noise got louder. Finally, he lifted both of his hands to silence the crowd, and, remarkably, they complied, a few joyous screams lingering as he waited for his own tears to subside. He put down his arms and said, softly, in Greek, "Thank you." The roar started again and he tried to speak.

"The race itself was very big, one of America's greatest marathons," Kyriakides said, trying to stave off a new flow of tears, pausing to regain his composure.

At the halfway mark there were five of us left. Afterwards, one by one, three were left behind and Kelley and I were in full drive. We were nine miles before the finish line. From that point on I made ten at-

tempts to leave the American, but I was unsuccessful. Then one enthusiastic Greek, while trying to hand me an orange which I needed because my lips were dry, somehow got his legs tangled with mine. Kelley
gained forty yards. I caught up to him with a lot of effort. We ran side by
side and I could not believe the roaring words in my ears. The crowds
were cheering "Kelly!" and "Hellas!" as it was on my shirt, sometimes
in Greek and sometimes in English. I couldn't believe what I was hearing, that Americans were giving me encouragement over their own
patriot.

The crowd exploded with pride and joy, the sound rising like a tor-
nado, the vortex soaring over their heads and settling back down again,
the euphoria covering everyone, the fervor building with the applause
and yelling and dancing, Kyriakides surveying the scene, his wife holding their children's hands tightly. Kyriakides waited for the noise to subside and told them he had made many public appearances at city halls,
schools, hospitals, churches, and at the State House to increase the
awareness of Greece's plight. Then he held up a *Life* magazine in which
he appeared to let the people realize the kind of publicity he received.
The magazine had a circulation then of twelve million and a profound
influence, and Kyriakides told the Greeks of his experience in Boston
and the United States.

Over in America the people have a real Greek mania and they love
our land. When I reached the finish line the crowd was going wild, the
word *ELLAS* [Greece] was reverberating for hours and hours through
the air, the uproar was reaching the sky. Americans and fellow Greeks
of America gave me a message. We must agree with one another, to
unite, and to work together to love Greece as they love it and in return
they will help us with all their souls. America, where we all love to visit,
is a big country, where the people work intensively. Work for them is
everything. And I worked very hard and achieved the ability to share
with you my victory. All Greeks should unite and rebuild the ruins of
our bloodstained country! Thank you, my people. We must become one
again. Forget the past. Turn and embrace each other for we are each of

us Greeks! Let us fight no more, communists or not. America wants to help us if we will help ourselves and this we must do.

His eyes once again got misty and so did many in the crowd. These were the same people who lived through the horrors of war. They also were victims of the bloody civil war that saw brother against brother fighting over ideals and beliefs. The crowd was silent for a moment with the same emotion he felt, and then officials hurried him to a waiting convertible where he would make a grand tour all the way to Athens, along streets that were lined with throngs of people who wanted to see him.

Kyriakides would get a king's welcome, from the airport to the main center of Athens, Syntagma Square, where the government offices were kept and which little more than a year before had been the scene of bedlam with the liberation from the Nazis. It would be almost the same scene again, this time heralding the return of a man whose singular efforts had saved the lives of so many people, his victory bringing the fruits of survival. He got into a Rolls-Royce convertible, sent by the king. At first, he sat in the back with Iphigenia, while the rest of his family rode in a car behind them, but as the car pulled out, flowers began being hurled at him and were quickly filling the back seat, so he sat up on the top of the back seat and began waving his arms slightly, just a bit embarrassed at the attention but glad to see the relief on the faces of so many.

He was again overcome with emotion, seeing hundreds of thousands of people on what had become a parade route to Athens: schoolchildren screaming, men and women waving, throwing kisses, exulting in unfettered happiness at the glory and the meaning of his win. His words had been warmly received by the crowd, which kept cheering as the cars of the motorcade pulled away from the airport. There were white helmeted motorcycle police on both sides of the vehicles and leading the procession through streets that were packed with so many people that the cars were at a crawl. The people kept clapping all along the long route and yelled congratulatory remarks.

When he returned to Athens in May of 1946, a month after winning the Boston Marathon, nearly a million people turned out for a parade and almost mobbed the convertible in which he sat. Courtesy of the Kyriakides family.

"*Axios!*" they yelled, which meant "worthy," and "*Yia Sou Palikari*," which was "To your health, brave young warrior!" Police and soldiers tried to hold back the spectators who surged forward as the car crawled along and Kyriakides sat up high, trying to recognize everyone who had come out. Many were on rooftops and verandas trying to get a better view, straining and craning their heads to see him pass. The motorcade was still in the Athenian suburb of Elliniko, ninety minutes after the landing, when it made its first brief stop at the home of the president of the community, who had prepared tables filled with traditional Greek food and some refreshments. He promised all the reporters they could continue their interviews in his backyard area. When Kyriakides finally got near the food, reporters kept bombarding him with questions. He put down his plate and stood to answer.

"I'm used to standing up from eating meals in America because I really don't eat that much. The mayors of different cities in America always had a specialty meat at some of the receptions which often I didn't acquire a taste for. Whatever I could tell you about the wonderful American hospitality and our own expatriates I received would not be enough. I became an honorary member of the American Hellenic Educational Progressive Association (AHEPA)," he said, and he told of how one man had donated a bull that was valued at a minimum of $5,000, and two cows for him to give to a poor farmer.

Kyriakides continued addressing the multitude of reporters and photographers. He said, "Well, guys, I got tired always having to smile for photographers in America. America has taken all my smiles because Americans cannot bear to see anyone without a smile on their face." One of the reporters thought he still looked thin.

"Why do you look so thin despite having eaten so well in America?" Kyriakides paused and said, " When I arrived in Boston I had a prodigious appetite and put on five pounds and after the race lost four pounds. After the highly competitive race, I ran at least two more marathons running from place to place to speak about our Greece. I wanted the people of America to learn about the peas we ate without olive oil during the occupation, and I talked of the starvation, lack of clothing, medicine, and the sacrifices of our nation every public opportunity I received."

Iphigenia observed how happy everyone was after having lived through so many years of sadness. Just as they were going to depart, Athanasios Ragazos, his good friend and the athlete who won the Balkan championship in 1940, Kyriakides' last race before Boston, entered the yard. The two good friends immediately embraced for the longest time. They knew the struggle of being an athlete representing a poor nation, and the curse of a war that had taken the lives of so many teammates and best friends. The reporters paused and then one asked, "If Ragazos was with you in Boston, what would have happened?" Kyriakides said, "What can I say, for me it would have been good, as well as for him and Greece. I intend to definitely bring him with me to Boston next year, perhaps for a double triumph." He smiled and they looked at each other cognizantly. Ragazos would be in Boston, Kyriakides knew.

Kyriakides was escorted to his car and the motorcade started toward downtown Athens. It would be a long, slow drive because there were so many ceremonial stops planned. They reached the center of the suburb of Elliniko where the whole community was waiting outside the courtyard of the Holy Trinity Church. Kyriakides was stunned to look up and see someone he didn't expect. It was Nadina Tsaldaris, the wife of the prime minister. "I was so touched by your victory I could not wait for you to get to Parliament," she said, rushing to his side. It was almost overwhelming for Kyriakides. There were also hundreds of school-age children waiting to greet him, along with many dignitaries. "Thank you," Kyriakides said, choked with emotion.

They were all led into the church filled to capacity for a liturgy. The priest met them at the portico, holding a cross in his hand. Kyriakides blessed himself by putting his right thumb, right index finger, and middle finger together to symbolize the holy trinity. He then made the sign of the cross and kissed the gold cross the priest was holding, and the group entered the church. When the liturgy concluded, Kyriakides was taken to the entrance way on the top steps, where the community's president said, "From within our ruined homes which were once considered a beautiful suburb prior to the war, we have gathered a few leaves of laurel to give you to show our thankfulness for your great victory." Students from the local elementary school had formed two lines to his car, a couple holding the flag, when one, a little girl in a Greek ethnic costume walked toward him, holding up the roses.

"On behalf of all the students," she said shyly, "I am proud to present you these roses." Kyriakides could not hold back the tears. It was the starving children of this impoverished nation that he ran for. He knew the face of hunger and death. He looked at the girl with tears flowing down the side of his face.

"I want to thank you, and the children of America are going to send a lot to the Greek students," he said, wiping away the tears with his left hand. The procession started to walk down the church steps. When they reached the walkway the students were all holding rose petals, which they began sprinkling, throwing some at him as he walked to the open convertible. The car continued to fill with bouquets of flowers and the crowd was cascading its cheers over him as people surged past police and soldiers to crowd the car as it passed slowly along streets swelling with observers, men and women throwing kisses and exulting with joy, waving and screaming and throwing their arms toward the sky in blessings.

The motorcade was now being led by military motorcycled police into the suburb of Palio Faliro, which was especially fond of athletics. As the Kyriakides car was pulling into the square, the pandemonium increased, with other car horns blaring and people shouting, "Long live the victor!" The applause and cheers never stopped along Syngrou Avenue heading toward other Athenian suburbs. It seemed the whole population of Greece had turned out. Kyriakides arrived in the suburb of New Smyrna to a boisterous crowd waving handkerchiefs. Local students had lined the street holding flags. The athletes of the Panion Athletic Club greeted him and the mayor presented him to the throng before a schoolgirl came forward with a gift. Kyriakides said, "I am proud to be a Hellene. As a representative of this glorious country, in America I received honors that no other victor had received," and the crowd responded with a loud applause. Kyriakides started to walk to his car when several excited admirers hoisted him up on their shoulders like an ancient Olympic victor being carried to his chariot before he was carried to his car.

As they approached Athens, the crowds were getting deeper and larger. They were the same people who saw relatives hanged by the Nazis, villages burned, children starved, and their women raped. Many still didn't know what the Fates had in store for them in this post war world. In the ancient Olympics it was often the practice to make a breach in the walls of a city through which the victorious athlete would return. There was no city wall for Kyriakides. Instead, his breach was the streets of Athens. Flags were flying from buildings all along the route, and many people were on their verandas waving miniflags. At exactly 5:00 P.M. he entered Athens, named for Athena, goddess of wisdom and civilization. The motorcade stopped in front of Hadrian's Arch, which was built by the Roman emperor Hadrian in A.D. 132 and measured eighteen meters high, but it almost seemed too low now.

So I will praise you, and always sing of your power
—Cleanthes, Hymn to Zeus

Waiting to greet him were hundreds of thousands of people. The military was having a difficult time holding back the rabid crowds, who ignored attempts to quiet them until Kyriakides raised his hands to motion for silence.

Behind them, on the Acropolis, the Temple of Athena Nike and the Parthenon were shining in the sunlight. The Philharmonic Band of Athens immediately started playing the Hellenic national anthem and Kyriakides joined the crowd singing the stanzas, the same words sung in defiance by many Greeks while facing German execution squads. When the band hit the last note of freedom, the crowd let out a thunderclap that sounded as if Zeus himself was throwing lightning bolts. Kyriakides was hustled to his car and stood up again in the back seat. The crowd was in a frenzy and once again there were vociferous yells of "Zito E Hellas," for "Long live Greece," and "Kyriakides, may you live a thousand years!"

The motorcade came to a full stop several times en route to Syntagma [Constitution] Square, which housed government offices and was the location of the Tomb of the Unknown Soldier. People continued to throw flowers, and soldiers were throwing their hats in the air. Children were on their parents' shoulders trying to get a view; some even tossed gold coins at him and others simply wept. The tumult was getting beyond measure and Kyriakides, weary and a little stunned, tried to keep his composure on the back of the convertible, disbelieving that a simple man, a runner, a poor boy from Cyprus was suddenly the hero of a nation, of people hungry for hope and good news almost as much as food.

Kyriakides sat back in the convertible, his arms often upraised in stoic acceptance of the deafening roar of what seemed to be a million people crowding into the huge square where the Evzones, the feared and fabled warriors who wore the traditional *fustanella,* the skirtlike outfit that belied the ferocity of the wearer, stood guard at the gates of Parliament and over the cradle of democracy. There were so many people and the cars of the cavalcade moved so slowly to let the worship wash over Kyriakides that it had taken nearly six hours for him to get to the center of Athens, the celebration and passion pulsating like tidal sound waves over Kyriakides who was dressed in a suit on a spring day, sitting up high on the back seat so everyone could see him

There were cars in a row, but mostly it was the scene of all those people spilling onto the streets and out over the national gardens and pouring off the sidewalks that seemed supernatural to Kyriakides, a crowd twice that which had watched him run in Boston, but that had been over a twenty-six-mile course, not smooshed into a central place where it seemed everyone wanted to see and touch the new modern hero of Greece. There were schoolchildren, the elderly, the army; it seemed the whole nation had turned out and there was a tangible enthusiasm and massive passion that seemed alive.

The swell of the sound enveloped him and Iphigenia and his family and it seemed there was no place in the square that wasn't filled by a human being. Everyone was waiting for Kyriakides to arrive, and then to go to the sacred place, the Tomb of the Unknown Soldier. The scores of thousands raised their voices in an anthem, a grand Greek chorus not far from the ancient theaters of the Acropolis where their ancestors had seen Greek tragedies depicted. Then there was silence as a somber Kyriakides, who remembered too well the sacrifices of his colleagues and countrymen, stepped out of the car and into the only space that wasn't occupied, the area in front of the tomb. He walked out slowly, surveying the scores of thousands of people, all of whom had their eyes on him. Kyriakides then removed the large wreath from his neck and held it in his hands, Iphigenia watching proudly as he separated from the dignitaries.

He strode softly now, respectfully, toward the tomb. The wreath seemed heavier now, the heat of the concrete beneath him, the warmth of the crowd melting into the square. Kyriakides reverently walked up to the tomb and then knelt, placing the wreath and pausing in silent prayer, with the thousands of others who had seen the same horrors only a few years before when Nazis in black jackboots had killed indiscriminately and blood ran in the same streets where now people stood in reverence with Kyriakides. Kyriakides and a host of government officials in suits and ties started their walk to the Tomb of the Unknown Soldier as the crowd applauded and cheered. Photographers had positioned them-selves on both sides of the tomb. The crowd grew eerily quiet, scores of thousands of people silent, watching. Kyriakides walked by many on-lookers who were holding flags and banners representing various soci-eties and regions of Greece. There was a sudden tranquility as he walked closer. Military personnel from all branches of the service stood at at-tention, including mustachioed veterans of the Balkan wars.

Above the tomb engraved in the marble wall was an ancient hel-meted warrior lying flat on his back. Along the wall were carved names of the heroes and famous battles dating from ancient times. Kyriakides walked slowly, proudly carrying the wreath. Kyriakides reached the sa-cred tomb, stopped and leaned forward on his right leg. Holding the wreath with both hands, he stretched and placed it gently on the tomb. He stepped back two feet and dropped down on his knees in reverence. He seemed as if he were in a trance staring at the marble tomb. Kyri-akides slowly rose to his feet and walked to a microphone to address the thousands who were silent. As he knelt, Kyriakides said loud enough for many to hear, "I am very proud that I won for Greece." He was as famous now as anyone who had lived in Greece, and the crowd let him know it.

With a laconic articulation, he said, "Eternal memory to these chil-dren of Hellas who sacrificed their lives at this altar for their country, so we may live today in freedom." The Philharmonic Band immediately started playing the national anthem again, the words bringing tears to many who were singing sentimentally and proudly, the end bringing re-newed cheers for Greece and Kyriakides. The clapping and chanting went on echoing throughout Athens.

A weary Iphigenia and the children were escorted home to Filothei by motorcycled police. Kyriakides, though, wasn't done. He was escorted to the government's political offices, which were within walking dis-tance and was greeted by Prime Minister Tsaldaris, who shook his hand firmly and congratulated him. "I wish you to continue your patriotic deeds, just as you have up until today." The minister of education said,

On behalf of the Hellenic Government and all its Ministers we greet the chosen Hellenic victor of the athletic contest of Boston, our latest marathoner. Your great victory, honors Hellenic athletics and glorifies your birthplace, Cyprus, and our glorious country Hellas. It's the prerogative of Hellenes to be victorious. Victory in war and in peace time. Two thousand four hundred and thirty six years ago, another Hellene, the first marathoner, reached this city as a soldier fully armed from the battle of Marathon and while falling to his death the final words from his lips were "We are victorious."

Kyriakides said,

> When I left for America I had a secret hope and the holy belief that I would be victorious and continue the deeds of our ancestors. The God of Hellas and the good wishes of the American people who admire our country, and the Greek-Americans gave me so much courage that I did the last two miles at an exceptional pace, gratefully I beat by 700 yards the marathon favorite Kelly . . . the unimaginable honors which took place in America did not take place for Kyriakides, but were for Hellas.

He thanked everyone and was then escorted to an open convertible. Tens of thousands lined the sidewalks and streets for his final destination, Athens City Hall. As flags flew above store awnings, people had climbed street poles, children were clapping. Widowed women, dressed entirely in black for years, who hadn't smiled or laughed, applauded with them and their faces were light.

The police could barely contain the crowd. At city hall, he was presented with the gold medal of Athens and a certificate of achievement. The next speaker was the Cypriot representative, Mr. Lanitis, who talked of the politics of Cyprus, which wanted its independence from Britain.

> Stelios Kyriakides. Listen now to the voice of your country. As a proud fellow-countryman I come to greet one Hellenic-Cypriot victor of the world's marathon. I come as a child of the same athletic tracks that gave you birth. As a Cypriot you had the vision of your athletic triumph. . . . Stelios, your performance at the world's marathon in Boston enabled you to present your country with the Hellenic flag. The

Cypriot organizations of Athens emotionally touched, greet you and wish along with the whole Hellenic nation that the sacred and holy flag I am presenting you is the symbol of Pan Hellenic unification. Raise it proudly and gloriously may it wave wherever justice, the desire of freedom loving people, ethical and honorable politics is demanded. Ζητω η Ευωοις [long live unification].

Kyriakides was touched. "Hellas is Cyprus and Cyprus is Hellas," he said, drawing a boisterous applause even as the chants from thousands outside the city hall echoed inside.

City officials quickly set up a microphone on a veranda that overlooked the exhilarated thousands of admirers. When Kyriakides appeared, the crowd cheered tumultuously. He walked up to the microphone and after several minutes silenced the crowd with his hand gestures.

> From America I do not only bring you the beautiful victory of the marathon. I also bring you a message: If you want the admirers of Hellas, the Americans, to help us more we must join hands tightly and unite. The Hellenes in America and the American Philhellenes only through hard work have reached their point of success. Everywhere I went they told me the same thing to love one another, to put our hands together, grow as a nation through hard work and sweat. They will appreciate us more and they will help strengthen the healing of our deep wounds of war and occupation, so we may see one day the reality of our dreams a Greater Hellas.

The people went hysterical clapping and their encouraging cheers came from their hearts. Stelios thanked the people, but they just kept on cheering. He was then taken to a waiting car to be brought to his home in the Athenian suburb of Filothei.

In Filothei, in other neighborhoods such as Kifissia, Marousi, Paradisos, and Halandri—where he had narrowly escaped execution by the Nazis—people were still waiting for him, holding flowers and anxious to see him. When his car came to the house he shared with his mother and father-in-law, where he had left more than a month before without any send-off, his family and friends had formed a friendly gantlet, slapping his back and handing him flowers as he walked through them toward the front door. "Bravo!" they yelled as a tired and still shocked Kyriakides looked around, trying to acknowledge every face, every hand on his back, trying to smile and thank them, tears again showing where he thought none were left. He was being sprinkled with flowers and wreaths.

His relatives, friends, and neighbors were all waiting and cheering. After the warm welcome he received at his home, he finally was alone with his family. Stelios and Iphigenia hugged their children and each other as tears of love and joy ran down their faces. That evening the Acropolis was lit up for the first time after the war. The gods took their places on the Parthenon, looking down into the ancient theater of Herod Atticus. It was where the Greeks had come for eons, waiting, as the poet George Seferis wrote in *Myth of Our History*, "that the . . . ancient drama might begin again."

> Man is the measure
>
> —Protagoras

The next day, the parade resumed in the nearby suburb of Piraeus, the seaport entry for Athens, where a weary but happy Kyriakides was again escorted in a convertible through a growing sea of people, all resounding with his name. He had received a plaque from the mayor, a gold-leafed wreath, which he carried in his lap in the car. The narrow streets of the city clogged quickly and the crowds converged on the car, people reaching in to touch Kyriakides' hand as he sat up on top of the back seat, women throwing kisses and grabbing his hand, a still shocked Kyriakides smiling but bewildered at the adulation. But Kyriakides hadn't run for personal glory. Soon thereafter, ships began arriving in Athens carrying the bounty he had won for Greece: clothes, food, medicine, and other equipment. He wanted to make sure it went to the people for whom he had run. With the first shipment, Kyriakides was there with Tsaldaris's wife and they escorted trucks carrying the goods to neighborhoods and to Piraeus High School, where the clothes were put on tables and Kyriakides and Mrs. Tsaldaris stood together, passing out pants and shirts and shoes to the poor, to students, to the bedraggled, who reached out tentatively, their eyes wide with hope.

The war, and the race in Boston, seemed finally over.

11

Shadows in the Wind

Boston, April 1947

It was a different Kyriakides who came to Boston in 1947, a year after his great triumph. He had accomplished his goal in 1946 and many people's lives had been spared. He was not a driven man now, his soul at peace, and he was a mellower, happy man for whom running was not the same kind of quest. Promoted to assistant treasurer in his company, Kyriakides would forever carry the mantle of a hero and was one of the most famous people in Greece—then and in all its glorious history.

It had been a difficult time in one way for him because he was still essentially a shy and somewhat retiring man who preferred the privacy and joy of his family to the public adulation that had been bestowed upon him and forever would. He was thirty-seven now and already thinking of ending his running career, but he wanted to come back to Boston one final time as a gesture of thanks, and to bring with him a runner who had defeated him in Greece and in the Balkan Games—his great friend, Ragazos. Slim and intense, Ragazos was a fiery competitor, more given to emotion than the reserved Kyriakides. He had been unable to come to Boston in 1946, but Kyriakides felt Ragazos had even more natural ability than he and thought he would be a strong contender to win the 1947 race. What Kyriakides didn't know at first was that his success the year before would create such a strong field that it would be difficult for even a world-class runner to run away from the field.

243

Boston would also give him a chance to be reunited with another friend, 1936 Olympic champion Kee Chung Sohn of Korea, who would be running under his real name now that Americans had driven the Japanese army out of Korea at the end of World War II. Sohn had avoided the Japanese army during the war and managed to stay in shape, but this was eleven years after his Olympic victory and both he and Kyriakides were nearing the time when they could not be as competitive as in their twenties. American occupation soldiers in Korea were so impressed with the running ability of Sohn and some of his colleagues, however, that they raised the money to send three of them to Boston to compete. Because there were no Olympics in 1940 and 1944, Sohn had the unlikely title of being the reigning Olympic champion too.

Thanks to Kyriakides, the real international era of the Boston Marathon had begun. His victory had so electrified the running world and reverberated through so many countries where long-distance running was becoming a burgeoning sport that the Boston field in 1947 would include two Finns, a Turk, the two Greeks, three Guatemalans, many Canadians, and the three Koreans, Sohn, Seung Yong Nam, and twenty-four-year-old Yun Bok Suh, who was seen as the heir apparent in Korea to Sohn. Suh was only 5'1" and weighed only 115 pounds, little weight to carry over 26 miles, 385 yards, and he was as driven as Kyriakides had been the year before. He had something else in common with Kyriakides: one of his idols was Johnny Kelley.

Sohn thought Suh would win and so he did something to help him. He withdrew from the race, in deference to the younger man. The pre-race time and Sohn's withdrawal gave him and Kyriakides time to talk again, about 1936 and the Olympic Spartan helmet that was meant for Sohn but had been stolen by the Nazis, and was still missing. This time, a panel of writers picked Kyriakides to finish second behind Kelley, because, despite their sentimental selection of Kyriakides, the sportswriters knew he was not back with the same zeal or training. Kyriakides was reunited too with Nason and his Boston media friends and he was still as beloved as the year before. This time, Kyriakides talked of a rebuilding Greece and of his appreciation of the people in Boston and New England who had helped him and his people. He said people had danced in the streets at the news President Truman was seeking congressional approval of a $400 million-aid package to fight communism in Greece and Turkey.

Truman had given his speech at midnight and Kyriakides said more radios were tuned to Truman than had been to the results of the Boston Marathon the year before when the runner was trying for the title. "Everybody had their radios on and there were loudspeakers in the streets," he said. "They want to rebuild the country and have something to eat."

Kyriakides and Ragazos arrived in Boston early because they were going to the celebration of Greek Independence Day, which is March 25. When Boston reporters asked about his chances, Kyriakides smiled and said he was heavier now, thanks to all those American steaks from 1946 and better food distribution in Greece, and he talked about his friend. "Before the war, Ragazos ran me into the ground twice and he's capable of doing it again," he said. Kyriakides was no longer the singular exciting story of the Boston Marathon and the pace of the world was picking up now with more attention turned to other runners, although he proudly retold his 1946 story and what it had meant to Greece. Europe was beginning to rebuild too and there was a feeling that the Boston Marathon had already begun to outstrip its first fifty years.

He did have a mission, though, in 1947. Instead of food and critical medical supplies and other equipment, Kyriakides said he was trying to help raise $50,000 for the 1948 Greek Olympic team, which had virtually no equipment and was short-funded. There was talk that Greece, founder of the ancient and modern games and the first team to always enter an Olympic stadium, would not compete in London in 1948, a favorite city of Kyriakides', because he had run the marathon there too. "This would be the first time Greece would not compete. We need track shoes, rubber soled shoes, pants and shirts. We have no discus to throw for practice and no javelins," he said, two of the most ancient events. He was mostly afraid Greece would not send a team. "I would be very much ashamed if this happened—the first time in history no Greeks competed in an Olympiad."

Unlike the year before when he had obsessively concentrated on the race and allowed no other distractions, Kyriakides felt freer this time to spend prerace time talking about his win and what it meant to Greece, and to continue his ambassadorial duties. But there was still a race to run and he wanted to show respectably, because his pride would not allow him to merely go through the motions. Ragazos was more focused, he knew, and would be a formidable threat to win. It was a cool April day when the runners took off from Hopkinton. In the early going Kyriakides strayed from his usual strategy of laying back by running comfortably in fourth place in a large, competitive field. His own competitiveness made him push again. Suh was eleventh.

But there would be no catching Suh, who continued to move away and finished with a course and world record of 2:25:39, almost four minutes ahead of Heitanen. Gerard Cote, almost a forgotten man this year, was fourth in 2:32:11 while Ragazos closed hard to come in sixth. A new era had indeed begun because Kyriakides came in tenth at 2:39:13, almost ten minutes slower than his possessed run the year before, and Kelley dropped to thirteenth at 2:40:55. Kyriakides was happy, though, because there was no pressure this year, only the fun of running to compete for the joy of the event. When he returned home, it was for another victory ceremony of sorts, though, still commemorating his win in 1946.

Near his house in Filothei, he received a plot of land from the National Bank of Greece, where his father-in-law worked. Kyriakides would have a house built there and, as the foundation was poured, he put an American gold coin in each corner for luck. The beginning of the new home was blessed by a priest and then a rooster was killed, given to a worker who laid the first stone. Life was good for Kyriakides, but more was coming for Greece and the cause for which he had run.

On June 5, Secretary of State George Marshall attended the commencement at Harvard University and stepped up to deliver a twelve-minute address that would change the face of a devastated Europe. "I need not tell you the situation in Europe is very serious," the low-keyed Marshall said in an uninspired tone. "It is logical that the United States should do whatever it is able to do to assist in the return of normal economic health to the world, without which there can be no political stability and no assured peace." The Marshall Plan, officially called the

European Recovery Plan, would be presented by Truman to Congress on April 3, 1948, and Truman would come to sign the act that would authorize grants and loans of $17 billion to rebuild Europe. At the end of 1947, a huge package of goods arrived from America. It was from New Bedford High School in Massachusetts, where Kyriakides had spoken after his win in 1946. It included 18 coats, 15 suits, 100 skirts, 70 pair of shoes, 30 white shirts, blouses, and 160 cans of milk, which were given out at a ceremony at a high school in Halandri, a meeting attended by officials and 750 students. The troupe went to another nearby high school where more clothing and milk was distributed. Also included were the pencils and papers the students vowed to send. The promises had been kept.

Also in 1948 Kyriakides and Kelley would have one final chance to race together, and represent their countries. It was at the 1948 Olympics in London, a race that would be Kyriakides' last competitive event twelve years after he'd met Kelley. Both finished back in the pack, but a face from Kyriakides' past appeared. It was his friend Agoustious Alexiou, with whom he left Statos as a young man many years before. Alexiou was living in London now and had seen on the news that Kyriakides would be running. It was an emotional reunion. Kyriakides was interviewed after the race on the BBC, which had carried the news of his victory to his wife and family in 1946 on an early Easter morning, and he gave greetings to the American athletes and was also honored again by SEGAS.

After London, Kyriakides came home to his family, which now included another daughter, Maria, born on August 26. His running was over. He was thirty-eight now and the hundreds of races and the weariness of World War II had worn him out, mentally and physically. He still had an unbuoyed optimism about life but wanted to retreat more now into his family and to help the next generation of Greek runners. He became an official at track and field events and organized Athletics for Youths in his neighborhood of Filothei, working with youth groups. The running that had propelled him to fame, had brought him out of the poverty of his village in Cyprus to a man as acclaimed in Greece as the ancient heroes, was put aside.

In 1952, Kyriakides decided to return to Cyprus so his children could attend the British-run school systems and be part of the Greek-English culture under which he had been raised. But, after a year, he brought his family back to Athens, and for the next few years, Kyriakides kept an unusually ordinary life, working for his company and tending to his home and garden and family. But he would invariably be recognized in public, and well-wishers frequently interrupted his walks with his children and many came over just to shake his hand.

In 1956, a decade after his dramatic run, a forty-six-year-old Kyriakides decided to build an athletic complex in his neighborhood, and worked with a Boy Scouts group there because his son, Dimitri, was a member. The two worked side-by-side building the track and facility and Dimitri would throw shingles onto the roof where his father was working, and helped pack down the track, which they made with crushed coal, built for softer spikes. Inside was a photo showing Kyriakides winning the Boston Marathon. The athletic building would eventually take his name.

He never owned a car, but Kyriakides loved a bicycle he used to take around his neighborhood where the Boston Marathon champion was a familiar and well-loved figure. He could be seen pedaling everywhere, head down to avoid possible eye contact with well-meaning people who would want him to stop. Those who didn't see the middle-aged man on the bicycle, or the young, didn't know there was a treasure trove of running trophies, medals, certificates, cups, and awards in his house. The most prized was the fiftieth anniversary medal from the Boston Marathon. Some, especially those who weren't alive during World War II, could not appreciate what his victory had meant to their families. Kyriakides had bought the bicycle in 1947 while in Sweden. He bicycled everywhere in Filothei, when he wasn't walking, as he liked to do. He had a basket on the back of the bike and another in front. He would put Eleni and Dimitri in the front basket, and pedal around to the constant greetings of neighbors and those who recognized him, even as his hair slowly grayed and his face wizened and he no longer resembled the slender world-class runner who had brought Greece glory. Kyriakides loved this part of his life, casually pedaling around and waving back, smiling and laughing and remembering.

As leaves on the trees, such is the life of man

—Homer

Kyriakides, who survived World War II and his running travails, almost didn't survive a freak sports accident. He had been elected to SEGAS, and as part of his duties, he was judging a four-hundred-meter run in a stadium, the finish near the end of a javelin throw competition nearby on the field. A javelin thrower uncorked a long toss in the narrow oval-shaped stadium in Athens and it was heading for Kyriakides, who had his back to the event. Dimitri saw it coming, but not in time to warn his father and was horror-struck, fearing he would be killed. But another judge saw the javelin coming and leaped over to knock Kyriakides aside. "Watch out, Stelios!" he shouted as he jumped, bringing Kyriakides to the ground as the javelin landed inches away.

In 1969, Kyriakides came back to Boston after a twenty-two-year absence, bringing with him one of the promising young Greek runners who had been inspired by his legacy, Dimitrious Vouros. But Kyriakides' mind was not on running, but his friends in Boston. "Where is Johnny Kelley? I want to see Johnny Kelley," he said as soon as he got to Boston, and, of course, Nason, the sportswriter whose works had helped immortalize the Greek runner. KYRIAKIDES KNOWS ONLY KELLEY, read a headline in the *Globe*, under a story written by his old friend Jerry Nason. Kyriakides had retired a month before from his utility company and was amazed at how different Boston looked, from the new high rise buildings to the changed ending of the finish line of the marathon, no longer in front of the Hotel Lenox where he had triumphed, his arms aloft. One day, he just went out and watched as bulldozers plowed under part of the city's topography.

Nason was delighted to see his old friend again, but couldn't believe twenty-three years had passed since the greatest race in Boston's marathon history. "He is a grayly handsome man," he wrote of the

Greek champion, even as his own hair had whitened and his love for the long-distance run had grown with the importance of the event. Kyriakides couldn't wait, either, to see Kelley, and was amazed that he still ran the marathon every year. "Johnny Kelley is the same. He still runs," Kyriakides sighed. Nason wrote that "the Kyriakides vs. Kel confrontation of 1946 provided one of the great stories of the Marathon—the emaciated, starving Greek against the cherubic hometown favorite." Kyriakides reflected on 1946 and told Nason, "This is long ago. But in my mind it is often merely yesterday. I can still count the steps I took up Exeter Street to the finish." Vouros finished fourteenth in a strong field where the winning time was under 2:14, more than fifteen minutes faster than Kyriakides' astonishingly fast time in 1946, the best in the world at that time, and showing how far the running craze had taken record times.

Something else had been bothering Kyriakides for years. It was the disappearance of the helmet he had brought to Berlin in 1936 to be given to the marathon winner, an award he had hoped to win himself before his strategy of laying off the lead proved faulty. In the early 1970s, a German team came to Greece and Kyriakides told the story of the helmet to the new sport officials, wondering if they could help find it. "I brought the helmet for the winner of the race," he said. That was his old friend Sohn, the Korean who'd had to run under a Japanese name. Kyriakides described it, but doubted it would be found. A few years later he had his answer. It was a postcard from Sohn and a photograph showing him holding the helmet. It had been found, and he had promptly donated it to a Korean museum. For years thereafter, Sohn would send Christmas cards to Kyriakides and keep their friendship alive.

Although Kyriakides wanted to remain a private man, driven there by his reserved nature, he was still being constantly sought after by the government and groups. He had the quiet charisma of a dedicated man who believed in himself and his life and exuded a quiet confidence. He had a soft-spoken but engaging passion and genuine sensibility that enthralled his audiences when he was asked to speak, because there was a passion in him. He went everywhere he was asked—churches, social events, functions—and audiences invariably were quiet and rapt when he talked, because he meant so much to Greece. The honors began to pile up quickly, especially in those first few months after his return in 1946, and, again, after his retirement from running in 1948.

In 1960, Kyriakides' homeland of Cyprus was granted independence by Britain, but part of the island was kept for strategic military bases. In 1976, *Runners World* carried an article about Kyriakides, written by Jack Galub, who was in Athens for an interview and wrote the story entitled "Marathon to Athens and Beyond." Even so many years after his triumph, he was being written about, in newspapers, magazines, and in books such as *The Boston Marathon,* and in his homeland in Cyprus, where he was ranked as one of the greatest athletes. He was listed in *Who's Who in Europe,* and in the Greek version, as much for the influence of his victory as for the running. He was in *Guinness Book of the Marathon* because of the Boston victory, which set a European record, and for holding the Greek national record for more than thirty-three years. He was highlighted in another history of the Boston Marathon, under the headline STARVING GREEKS.

His old friend Johnny Kelley dedicated a chapter in his autobiography *Young At Heart,* where he spoke fondly of their rivalry and friendship. The story of the 1946 race was entitled, "I'm Glad You Won, Stanley." A photograph of their duel showed Kyriakides carrying the famed "win or die" note. Kyriakides' fame followed him for decades. In 1979, he received a plaque from the city of Limassol on Cyprus, where he started running so many years before, honoring him for his athletic deeds and for the attention he brought to the island. That was put in his collection, including the medal he received for participating in the 1936 Olympics in Berlin, his cups and medals from his Balkan victories and from many municipalities and associations, all stored in glass cases in his home.

In 1981, a prominent Greek television show host, Freddy Germanos, featured Kyriakides on a special that gained widespread attention on the thirty-fifth anniversary of Kyriakides' win in Boston. Germanos said, "This show is not about his athletic victory. It is a victory of mankind through Stelios' fate and the fate of a country." There was a shot of Kyriakides, a lot stiffer and grayer now, going out for a run

His Boston victory was many years before when Kyriakides and Iphigenia posed for this photograph near their home in the early 1980s for their friend Jordan. Courtesy of Payton Jordan.

with his grandchildren, and he choked up again in an interview, remembering the words from the crowd in Boston, telling him he had to win for Greece and his country. Kyriakides also went to his birthplace of Cyprus, where he was featured on television there.

In 1983, George Demeter, the Boston lawmaker-businessman who had befriended Kyriakides and provided him with a home in Boston, a place to stay and eat and nurture himself, died at age ninety, the day after his birthday. He had been suffering from circulatory problems and a series of strokes and was a patient at a home for veterans. To this day, *Demeter's Rules of Parliamentary Procedure* is a standard in many legislatures. Kyriakides continued to ride his bicycle through Filothei, until it was stolen in 1985. He was heartsick at losing the bike, and that someone would steal it. He had used it to carry his grandchildren in the same baskets where he had carried his own children.

In 1986, at the Rotary International Symposium entitled "Olympic

Spirit," Kyriakides was honored by the International Olympic Academy with a certificate and recognition from ancient Olympia as one of Greece's greatest athletes and ambassadors.

> No evil can happen to a good man, either in life or in death
> —Socrates

Stylianos Kyriakides could barely believe he was seventy-six now, his champion running career long behind him, but he was glad too that he could come here, to Pyrgos, to the summer home of his son, Dimitri, a mountainside retreat with a view of the ocean near Corinth, look out at Delphi in the distance, and be surrounded by cherry and apple and apricot and plum trees, with an abundance of olives and currants and grapes, smell the lotuses and flowers of the spring that permeated the sweet air around him. *There was so much food, so much abundance,* not like when he was a boy and there weren't even shoes. Kyriakides kneeled in the garden and planted tomatoes, tilling the earth, his back a bit stiff now and the thin legs that had carried him to so many running championships feeling the ache of age and not having been used for so many years. Around him his grandchildren played and the peal of laughter was as sweet to him as the smell of the food and flowers and the joy of a whole family intact. He stopped a moment and creakily put his arms to his legs just above his knees, arching his back in several stiff movements, smelling the dirt too on his clothing and hands and looked around him. *This is where I will be buried someday.* He liked it here, overlooking the sea and a valley and the mountains, only a small village nearby. It was quiet, almost isolated compared with the home in Athens where he and his family had lived for so many years, through World War II and the rapid growth that had changed his neighborhood so much, so much noise and so many cars and pollution and noise. This was different, this was like his tiny village in Cyprus where he had grown up, the mountains and the quiet and the earth and its goodness. He got back up and walked to a chair where he could sit and think and look at the land and out at the ocean, remembering where his life had taken him. Iphigenia and his children would be there often, and the grandchildren who delighted him but did not know he had been a great runner for his country.

Late in 1987, Kyriakides became ill. He had not run for years, of course, except for a few photo opportunities where he would be pictured stiff-legged, jogging with his grandchildren. He had grown heavier since his lean days of World War II and his road-running fame, and his black hair had turned white. But he still retained the genteel manner that endeared him to rivals and writers and those who met him.

He went to a doctor for a checkup. For ten days, doctors conducted tests and tried to figure out what was wrong. Then came the worst news of his life: he was diagnosed with myeloma, a bone cancer. On October 26, St. Demetrios Day, the name day of his son, Kyriakides was admitted to an Athens hospital.

He had pneumonia now as well and he was becoming thinner and weaker. His blood was changed, his lungs filled with water, and his condition was worsening. He was finding it difficult now even to speak, as his wife and children and family huddled by his bedside, day after day. He tried to make hand signals, the motion wavy. He was trying to tell them, without words, that his end was near, but Iphigenia did not leave his side. She stayed morning to night, comforting him, talking with him of their life and love. His family was overwhelmed with the cost of his care. But a hospital medical board made a ruling. "He will pay nothing," they said. What Kyriakides had done for Greece forty years before had not been forgotten.

His condition worsened quickly now. Outside, in the Mediterranean sun, a modern Athens, its ancient history and architecture being overwhelmed by gray concrete apartments, busy smog-filled streets and a ceaseless cacophony of traffic and tourists, residents remembered the man who had run for Greece more than forty years before. Newscasts kept them in touch and many worried. Kyriakides, it was said, was dying. A television reporter came in for an interview. Kyriakides was in great pain, his hair thin and white and patchy, his once-athletic body wizened with age and disease. Breaths came in sad brief gasps, far from the finely tuned aerobic lungs that made him a marathon champion.

A pained Kyriakides, struggling to be heard through a weak voice grown raspy, looked directly at the camera and delivered a message. "There are many marathoners today in Greece . . . but many of them go out to dance and drink . . . they dance and drink and nothing can happen that way," he said, struggling between labored breaths that made his eyes bounce with hurt. He felt that those who hadn't known war and the famine couldn't understand the sacrifices he and so many Greeks had made.

Then he softened a bit and said he wanted especially the young of Greece to be happy but to work and never forget what had happened before they were born. "To all the youth of Greece, whatever I did . . . Mandikas, Frangules," he said, remembering his teammates, "they should try to follow in our footsteps." He reached his hand to his chest hard, almost as if trying to excise his soul and said to the young, "I give them my soul as a last blessing," pulling his fist away from his chest and opening it to let his spirit spill toward them. His open hand reached out to them.

On December 10, 1987, the birthday of his son, Dimitrios, Stylianos Kyriakides died from a bone disease. He was seventy-seven—the same number he wore on his shirt in Boston so many years before, the number he wore for luck. News of his death quickly swept the small nation. There were tears from those old enough to remember his triumph in Boston and who watched the procession that greeted him in Athens, like Alexander the Great returning from another conquest.

A Cypriot-born sprinter Kyriakides admired from his days in the thirties at the Balkan Games, Dominitsa Lanitou, who had married and taken the last name of Kavounidou, spoke about Kyriakides' influence on continuing generations of athletes and his beginnings in Cyprus. "Cyprus today bids farewell to a great athlete, an athlete who glorified both countries. They both salute you." At the funeral, wreaths covered the church and citations came from the country's leaders and government officials, including Prime Minister Andreas Papandreou and the president, Christos Sartzetakis, from the religious and government leaders of Cyprus, including the president, Spirou Kyprianou, who sent a huge wreath as well. Papandreou said, "Stylianos Kyriakides will always be a living example of ethos and competitiveness." Sartzetakis said,

"Kyriakides, through his great victories, once again glorified Greece. He was truly an athlete and a wonderful man. Stelios Kyriakides taught by example and his ethos. Not only do our athletes honor his passing, but the whole Greek race."

His friend and running rival Athanasios Ragazos said, "We had a friendship of 55 years." He talked about Kyriakides' great resolve. "He stood out from the rest of us because of his obstinance, his hard work, and a disciplined life. We may have been rivals in the marathon, but we were friends . . . and he was, above all, a good family man. We will always miss Stelios."

Kyriakides was buried in Athens's original cemetery, where only dignitaries now were laid to rest. His coffin was covered with the Greek flag, whose vision had inspired him to overtake Johnny Kelley in 1946. Three years later, the remains were unearthed and kept for a time in a tomb, where his wife would come to light a candle and pray. But she wanted him brought to where his happiest last days were spent and she had the remains taken to a burial plot in Pyrgos, Corinth, near the vacation home where he gardened and played with his grandchildren. There, she stood near the grave and smiled. Now both their souls were at rest and she was happy.

Six months later, Kyriakides' was memorialized with the start of races called *Kyriakithia*, cross-country events held throughout Greece. The first was in Pyrgos, near the place he loved so much, followed by others in Filothei and Crete, each with hundreds of participants. The winners received silver-colored medals with blue-and-white ribbons.

In 1988, the Olympic Games were held in Seoul, South Korea, and that country's flag bearer was Sohn, the winner of the 1936 games in Berlin where he had outraced Kyriakides and the rest of the field, and become friends with the slender Greek who never forgot him.

In 1993, a bust of Kyriakides was unveiled in a park in the neighborhood of Filothei, near the track facility named for him. His family stood beside the likeness, glad at the memory, sad to miss him. Underneath the bust, it reads: Stylianos Kyriakides, marathoner, Boston 1946. Some of his former Balkan Games and Olympic teammates, those who, like him, had survived the war, stood there to look at their friend again, athletes sobbing softly at the loss as the Greek flag was unfurled slowly, falling away to reveal his face. In 1994, a new running club was established in Limassol, Cyprus. It was named for Stelios Kyriakides.

In 1996, on the one hundredth anniversary of the Boston Marathon, a special *Boston Globe* edition on the event reiterated Nason's contention that Kyriakides' victory over Kelley in 1946 was "the most significant Boston Marathon of them all." On the walls of Kyriakides' home still hang the reminders and mementoes of his life, plaques with insignia from Massachusetts officials, a card from former Gov. Maurice Tobin; a photograph of a farewell banquet in Boston in 1946; a picture of a balding man with the inscription: For my good friend and marathon champion. It was from his former boss and mentor, Leslie Kemp. There is a large photograph of a victorious Kyriakides after his Boston win from the cover of a magazine, a beaming man with a smile of triumph, wearing a laurel wreath over his sweat-soaked shirt bearing the name of Greece and the number seventy-seven. The shirt hangs there too, along with the silver watch he wore while running, along with the gold diamond-encrusted medal he received.

All that's missing is the note he carried in Boston, urging him to "win or die." That, as the sweatshirt bearing the name of his country, has disappeared.

Athens, 1996

The man was nearing eighty years old now, but he didn't walk stiff-legged or with any of the infirmities of age. Instead, there was a sprightliness in his step and you could see this was an athlete, a great runner who had not let age overcome his talent or desire to continue to run. His hair was white, but his body was still lean and taut and his eyes were bright, and he was looking for someone.

Payton Jordan was back in Greece, twenty-one years after he last came and stayed with Stelios Kyriakides, and seventeen years since a brief stopover in 1969, when he was touring Europe and the Soviet Union with an American track team. He had missed Kyriakides' funeral in 1987, but there was a still lingering longing for the Greek sense of "philoxenia," the hospitality he

The 1936 Berlin Olympics credentials on the left were in his pocket the night Kyriakides was stopped by a German patrol in Athens in 1943, and saved his life. The 1948 credentials for the London Olympics ended his competition. Courtesy of the Kyriakides family.

had enjoyed when he stayed at Kyriakides' house. It was good to be back under the Greek sky, to help celebrate the one-hundredth anniversary of the modern Olympic Games. With him was Rafer Johnson, the 1960 gold medalist in the decathlon, and the two were embraced by the Greeks, who recognized athletic greatness.

 In 1969, Jordan had been a guest of honor at a banquet with Kyriakides and now he was still amazed at the honors still heaped upon his old friend, fifty-three years after his great marathon win in Boston. So much had happened since 1955 and the two took time to talk about it, to share once again the oneness of running and a friendship that had transcended continents. After the 1955 visit, Jordan returned to Occidental College in California as the track coach, but he didn't stay long. In 1957, Jordan had become the head track coach at Stanford and took his team to a second-place finish in the 1963 collegiate championships. In 1962, he organized the first cold war games be-

tween the United States and the Soviet Union, which drew more than 150,000 people over two days. In 1968, Jordan led the U.S. Olympic track team, considered the greatest ever. Jordan had continued to run too, setting world records in the master's division for the hundred-and-two-hundred meter races until his retirement in 1994.

In many ways, he and Kyriakides had been mirrors of each other's character and personality: soft-spoken, understated, disciplined men of character, whose achievements didn't distort their humility. Jordan was still competing in running and was the world champion in the sprints in his age group. Today, though, he was in Athens to hand out medals for a special Olympics competition and walked into the stadium where the games were being held when a man walked over to shake his hand as he crossed the field. Jordan didn't recognize him.

"You don't remember me," the man smiled. He waited a moment and said, "My father was Otto Simitsek," the coach of the Greek Olympic team who had been a mentor to Kyriakides and a friend to Jordan. "If he were alive, he would be so delighted to see you again," the man said. The son had been only nine in 1955, when Jordan had come over to help with the 1956 Greek Olympic team. Jordan wondered what had happened to those men he had helped train and asked Simitsek's son. "Are any of them here?"

Simitsek told an official, "Take Mr. Jordan to the finish line to see if any of his athletes are here." Halfway across the track, Jordan heard shouts of delight and saw a group of men in their sixties, running toward him with tears in their eyes. It was the Greeks he had met in 1955, athletes he had helped prepare for the Olympics. "Coach Jordan! You are back!" they screamed before surrounding him like a rugby huddle, a mass of men cradling and kissing and almost carrying him. Jordan began crying too, and the whole group jumped en masse, bounding and almost toppling over in their exuberance.

A few days later, Jordan went to the ancient stadium at Nemea, where there hadn't been a competition for twenty-three hundred years. In the ancient times, games were held at Nemea and Isthmia and Olympia. He was asked to run in games where he would again win the one-hundred- and two-hundred-meters in his age-group, a field of still accomplished elderly athletes he had dominated for years. Jordan never had the chance to even compete for Olympic gold, but that was a distant memory for him now and he said he still remembered the words of Kyriakides as they sat in the backyard of the Greek's home in 1955, the chilling story of how Kyriakides had almost been executed and the gripping horror of the occupation when Greeks didn't know every day when they awoke if they would be killed indiscriminately.

After Jordan won, he donned an ancient toga to commemorate the spirit of the ancient Olympics, which had begun in Greece a millennium before. But his thoughts were with Kyriakides, and the warmth of the night in the Athens backyard where they had talked, and of a warm, sunny day at Marathon where they had visited in 1955, where Kyriakides had kiddingly put on a laurel wreath, the kind he had brought to Boston in 1946 and wore when he won that race, and of the last time the Greek runner had put on his running clothes to again fly down the dirt road from the ancient site where the Greeks had won the day for their country nearly twenty-five hundred years before.

Jordan could still see the picture of a happy, healthy forty-five-year-old man, his friend, in the full bloom of joy, a bright blue sky above and the plains of the old battlefield behind him, a serene sight so exquisite it seemed to erase the horror and loss of the world war that had enveloped Greece little more than a decade before, a time that had given Kyriakides his destiny and real reason to run, the ghosts of those teammates who had not survived, and the men of Marathon, the fallen and the victors who, like Kyriakides, had saved their country.

Unlike Boston, where he wore a grim mask of determination, this time Kyriakides could muster a slight smile because Greece was recovering, the sun was shining, his son and friend were nearby, and it was good to run free. He jogged easily and gracefully, but could feel over his shoulder a slight wind that seemed to come from another runner, a zephyr that cooled his back as he could almost sense a presence next to him now, a wraith in the wind, a man dressed in an ancient warrior's uniform, only his helmet off, but stiff sandals carrying him with ease on a run he had been making for twenty-five hundred years; running, like Kyriakides, not for himself, but for Greece, running for the human race. It was the same shadow that would follow every marathon runner.

Kyriakides and the apparition known only to him continued into the distance, their feet kicking up small puffs of dust, their sights set on Athens, their missions the same and, finally, almost over.

Pindar

Olympian 14

Bless the land of beautiful horses, the pastures
close to the steady currents of Kephisos,
dwelling place of the Graces, Orkhemenos,
where deep furrows are turned into rich strophes.

Guardians of the Minyai's ancient race,
royal sisters, listen to my prayer.
Whatever we admire in the world is lost
without your gift. If someone is brilliant,
or lovely to look at, the center of attention,
your light is the source. Without the holy Graces
not even the Gods in heaven can conduct
their bright festivals and circle dances.

Triple thrones have been set on Mt. Olympus
where the glory of Zeus is praised to the skies
and the Graces sit next to golden Apollo.

The gleam of Aglaia, or a simple melody
from Euphrosyne is enough to warrant success,
daughters of divine power. And you, Thalia,
whose steps are always light, mark these dancers
who show their respect by keeping the line graceful.

Listen, I've come to celebrate Asopikos,
offspring of the Minyai, with songs of triumph
carefully measured in the Lydian way.

Go now, Echo, to Persephone's dark-walled house:
deliver the winning message to his father.
When you find Kleodamos, tell him his boy
was crowned at the foothills of Olympia.
Then watch the dark wall suddenly brighten.

—Pindar, fifth century B.C.
(*Translated by George Kalogeris*)

Bibliography

Index

Bibliography

"Athenian Wins Boston's Fiftieth Marathon Race." Associated Press, Apr. 20, 1946.

Boston Athletic Association. Programs, American Marathon Race. Apr. 19, 1938; Apr. 20, 1946.

Boston Marathon: 100 Years of Blood, Sweat, and Cheers. Chicago: Triumph Books, 1997.

"Boston Marathon Victor To Visit City Tomorrow." *New Bedford (Mass.) Standard-Times*, May 2, 1946.

"Builders of Life: The Age of Beauty." *Boston Globe*, Feb. 21, 1935.

Cloney, Will. "Kyriakides Beats Kelley in Sprint." *Boston Herald*, Apr. 21, 1946.

———. "Kyriakides Wins Marathon for Greece." *Boston Herald*, Apr. 21, 1946

———. "Taxi Fare, Dry Gullets Move B.A.A. Officials to Revise Plod For '39'" *Boston Herald*, Apr. 20, 1938.

Cunningham, Bill. "Kyri Willing to Offer Life." *Boston Herald*, Apr. 20, 1946.

"Cyprus, A Living Mosaic." *Greek American Monthly* 3, no. 2 (Feb. 1997).

Cyprus at the Crossroads of History. Nicosia: Cyprus Press and Information Office, 1997.

Cypriot Athletic Annual, 1979.

Daley, Frank. *Greece: Gallant, Glorious.* Haverhill, Mass: Record Publishing, 1941.

Decopoulos, John. *Acropolis of Athens.* Athens: John Decopoulos, 1987.

Derderian, Thomas. *Boston Marathon: The History of the World's Premier Running Event.* Champaign, Ill.: Human Kinetics Publishers, 1994

Drakou, Antoniou. *Cyprus Track.*

Duffey, Arthur. "Greek Champion Walks Course." *Boston Sunday Post,* Apr. 11, 1938.

———. "Greek Road King Trains Strictly." *Boston Sunday Post,* Apr. 10, 1938.

———. "Victory Belongs to Two Nations." *Boston Sunday Post,* Apr. 21, 1946.

Egan, Dave. "Greek Tops Kelley In Epic Race." *Boston Sunday Advertiser,* Apr. 21, 1946.

Falls, Joe. *The Boston Marathon.* New York: Macmillan, 1977.

Ferris, Daniel. Letter to Frank Vassilopoulos, May 18, 1946. Amateur Athletic Union Collection.

Fitzgerald, Tom. "Greek Star Wins Marathon." *Boston Sunday Globe,* Apr. 21, 1946.

———. "Kyriakides Enjoys Honors of Victory." *Boston Sunday Globe,* Apr. 22, 1946.

Foye, Fred. "Greek Wins Marathon." *Boston Traveler,* Apr. 21, 1946.

Gage, Nick. *Eleni.* New York: Random House, 1983.

Galub, Jack. "Marathon To Athens and Beyond." *Runner's World,* Apr. 1976.

"Gifts from America." *The News* (Athens). Dec. 15, 1947.

Gillooly, Mike. "I Did It for My Country." *Boston Sunday Advertiser,* Apr. 21, 1946.

"Golden Moments of Stylianos Kyriakides, The." *First Page.* ERT Television, Freddy Germanos, Athens, May 20, 1981.

"Greece Honors the Returning Victor." *Kathimerini* (Athens), May 19, 1946.

"Greek Flies from Athens to Win Distance Race." *Life,* May 27, 1946.

"Greek's Final Dash Enables Him to Capture Golden 'Marathon.'" *Boston Sunday Globe,* Apr. 21, 1946.

"Greek Tops Kelley in Epic Race." *Boston Globe,* Apr. 21, 1947.

"Greek Wins Marathon." *Boston Evening Globe,* Apr. 21, 1946.

Gynn, Roger, ed. *Guinness Book of the Marathon.*

Hamilton, Edith. *The Greek Way.* New York: W. W. Norton, 1930.

Hern, Gerry. "Greek Gets Tired and Takes a Bus." *Boston Post,* Apr. 20, 1938.

Herodotus. *The Histories.* London: Penguin, 1996.

Higdon, Hal. *Boston: A Century of Running.* Emmaus, Pa.: Rodale Press, 1995.

"Hiroshima Runner, 19, Wins Marathon." *Boston Globe,* Apr. 20, 1951.

"How I Won." *Freedom* (Athens), May 24, 1946.

Hyland, Dick. *Hyland Fling.*

"I Bring One Message to Unite." *Kathimerini* (Athens), May 24, 1946.

"I Want To See Kyriakides. *The News* (Athens). Nov. 11, 1982.

"'I'll Finish in First Five,' Says Greek Plodder." *Boston Evening American*, Apr. 13, 1938.

"It Was a Race to Win or Die." *Acropolis*, May 24, 1946.

Kalellis, Peter M. *One More Spring*. New York: Crossroad Publishing, 1995.

Karanikola, George. *Unwise: Misfortunes of the Nation*. Athens: Thucydides Publishers, 1985.

Kelley, Johnny, and Dick Johnson. *Young at Heart*. Waco, Tex.: WRS Publishing, 1992.

"Kyriakides Arrived Yesterday, Thousands of People Addressed Him." *Embros*, May 24, 1946.

"Kyriakides Arrives Today." *The News*. Athens. May 23, 1946.

"'Kyriakides Beat Me,' Said Kelly, 'Because He Was Running for His Country.'" *The News* (Athens), May 2, 1946.

"Kyriakides Beats Kelley in Sprint." *Boston Globe*, Apr. 21, 1946.

"Kyriakides Departed Yesterday, Returning to Greece." *Atlantis*, May 22, 1946.

"Kyriakides of Greece Beats Kelley in Boston Marathon." *New York Times*, Apr. 21, 1946

"Kyriakides Rejects Pro Offer." Associated Press, May 21, 1946.

"Kyriakides Says Greeks Danced for Joy." *Boston Herald*, Mar. 30, 1947.

"Kyriakides Wins for Greece." *National Herald*, Apr. 28, 1946.

"Kyriakides Wins Marathon for Greece." *Boston Globe*, Apr. 21, 1946.

"Kyri Best Kisser in Kissing Parade." *Boston Globe*, Apr. 21, 1946.

Kyrris, Costas. *History of Cyprus*. Nicosia, Cyprus: Lampousa, Publications, 1996.

Legacy of Gold. Colorado Springs, Colo.: U.S. Olympic Committee, 1922.

"London Marathon, The." *Sporting News*, July 7, 1935.

"Loses Shirt at Finish." *Boston Sunday Advertiser*, Apr. 21, 1946.

McKenney, Joe. "Kyriakides Begs Aid for Greece." *Boston Post*, Apr. 29, 1946.

Magoulias, Harry J. "The Origins of the Olympic Games." *Hellenic Chronicle*, Aug. 1, 1996.

Mandell, Richard D. *The Nazi Olympics*. New York: Macmillan, 1971.

"Marathon, The." *Boston Post*, Apr. 19, 1936.

"Marathon of Eternity, The." *Freedom Press* (Athens), Dec. 12, 1987.

"Marathoner Kyriakides Visited the Old Olympic Victor Loues, The." *Athletic Voice*, Sept. 8, 1934.

"Marathoner Winner Kyriakides at the Office of Atlantis, The." *Atlantis*, May 2, 1946.

Mazower, Mark. *Inside Hitler's Greece*. New Haven, Conn.: Yale Univ. Press, 1993.

Nason, Jerry. Archives. Sports Museum of New England.

Nason, Jerry. "Athenian Boston-Bound to Run B.A.A. Marathon." *Boston Globe*, Mar. 30, 1938.

———. "Backers of Kyriakides, Greek Bearer of Marathon Laurel to B.A.A., Feel He May Take It Home." *Boston Globe*, Apr. 13, 1938.

———. "Departing Kyriakides Aims to Be American." *Boston Globe*, May 21, 1946.

———. "Greek Arrives for Marathon." *Boston Globe*, Apr. 3, 1938.

———. "Greek Marathoner Arrives, Sold Homes, Clothes to Live." *Boston Globe*, Apr. 9, 1946.

———. "Greek Runner Hopes Marathon Victory Helps Impoverished Countrymen." *Boston Globe*, Apr. 11, 1946.

———. "Greek Runner Wins Wreath and Nylons." *Boston Globe*, Apr. 21, 1946.

———. "Greek Won Marathon." *Boston Globe*, May 16, 1946.

———. "Kyriakides Is Best Plodder in Greece." *Boston Globe*, Apr. 14, 1938.

———. "A Modern Pheidippides Visits These Shores." *Boston Globe*, Apr. 5, 1938.

———. "Next Chapter of B.A.A. Marathon Duel May Be Written over in Athens." *Boston Globe*, Apr. 22, 1946.

———. "Wood of Newton Chalks Up First Win in Cathedral Run." *Boston Globe*, Apr. 16, 1946.

"Newly Released Top Secret WW2 Papers Reveal Full Story of Daring Kidnapping." *Greek American Monthly* 3, no. 7 (July–Aug. 1997).

Newsweek, Apr. 29, 1946.

"One Hour With the Triumphant Victor." *Proini*, Oct. 25, 1934.

"One of His Letters." *Embros*, May 5, 1946.

"Our Only Happy Event." *Free Greece*, May 24, 1946.

Perseus Project, Tufts Univ.

"People of Athens Receive the Godly Marathoner Kyriakides, The." *Battle*, May 24, 1946.

"Position of the Greek Military, The." *Athens Zappeion Megaron*, 1968.

Robbins, Charley. *Charley Robbins' Scrapbooks*. Cranston, R.I.: Modern Press, 1982.

Rosenthal, Harold. "Five Hundred Thousand Watch Pawson Take Marathon Race." *New York Herald Tribune*, Apr. 20, 1938.

"Runners Seek Glory in BAA Marathon Today." *Boston Globe*, Apr. 19, 1929.

SEGAS, Dec. 1987, No. 6.

Siegel, Arthur. "Greek Food Relief Rides on Marathon." *Boston Traveler*, Apr. 18, 1946.

Shirer, William, and Arthur Siegel. *The Rise and Fall of the Third Reich*. New York: Simon and Schuster, 1960.

"Spies and Sabotage During Occupation." *Nightly News* (Athens), Jan. 31, 1977.

Stassinopoulos, Arianna, and Rolof Berry. *The Gods of Greece*. New York: Harry N. Abrams, 1983.

Traiforos, Mimis. *Sophia Vembo*.

Truman, Margaret. *Harry S. Truman*. New York: William Morrow, 1973.

Turiello, Edmund. "Olympiad." *Hellenic Chronicle*, Aug. 1992.

"Two Letters from Kyriakides." *Freedom* (Athens), May 5, 1946.

"Victory in Marathon a Victory for Greece." *New Bedford (Mass.) Standard-Times*, Apr. 21, 1946.

Wallechinsky, David. *The Complete Book of the Olympics*. New York: Penguin Books, 1984.

Whitely, Don. "Greek Champ in Marathon: He's Protégé of Kyriakides." *Boston Globe*, Apr. 15, 1969.

"Who's Who in Europe," 1964–65. Edited by Edward A. deMeyer.

"World War II, from D-Day to V-J, 40 Years Later, June 6, 1984." *Boston Globe*, Aug. 16, 1985.

WWW.Columbia.edu/acis/bartleby/htn.

"Yesterday's Huge Welcoming of Stylianos Kyriakides." *Acropolis*, May 24, 1946.

Zur Erinnerung an die XI Olympiade Berlin, 1936, Der Reichssportsfuhrer. Berlin: Hans V. Tschammer und Osten, 1936.

Index